D1207892

American Television on British Screens

American Television on British Screens

A Story of Cultural Interaction

Paul Rixon

© Paul Rixon 2006

All rights reserved. No reproduction, copy or transmission of this publication may be made without written permission.

No paragraph of this publication may be reproduced, copied or transmitted save with written permission or in accordance with the provisions of the Copyright, Designs and Patents Act 1988, or under the terms of any licence permitting limited copying issued by the Copyright Licensing Agency, 90 Tottenham Court Road, London W1T 4LP.

Any person who does any unauthorised act in relation to this publication may be liable to criminal prosecution and civil claims for damages.

The author has asserted his right to be identified as the author of this work in accordance with the Copyright, Designs and Patents Act 1988.

First published 2006 by
PALGRAVE MACMILLAN
Houndmills, Basingstoke, Hampshire RG21 6XS and
175 Fifth Avenue, New York, N.Y. 10010
Companies and representatives throughout the world

PALGRAVE MACMILLAN is the global academic imprint of the Palgrave Macmillan division of St. Martin's Press, LLC and of Palgrave Macmillan Ltd. Macmillan® is a registered trademark in the United States, United Kingdom and other countries. Palgrave is a registered trademark in the European Union and other countries.

ISBN-13: 978–1–4039–4120–6 hardback
ISBN-10: 1–4039–4120–3 hardback

This book is printed on paper suitable for recycling and made from fully managed and sustained forest sources.

A catalogue record for this book is available from the British Library.

Library of Congress Cataloging-in-Publication Data
Rixon, Paul, 1963–
   American television on British screens : a story of cultural interaction / Paul Rixon.
      p.   cm.
   Includes bibliographical references and index.
   ISBN 1–4039–4120–3 (cloth)
   1. Television broadcasting—Great Britain. 2. Television programs—United States. 3. Foreign television programs—Great Britain. I. Title.
   PN1992.3.G7R59 2006
   384.55′0941—dc22   2005055273

10   9   8   7   6   5   4   3   2   1
15   14   13   12   11   10   09   08   07   06

Printed and bound in Great Britain by
Antony Rowe Ltd, Chippenham and Eastbourne

Contents

List of Tables

Acknowledgements

I would like to thank all those that have supported the development and writing of this work over the years. In particular, my father and mother, who have helped with their television reminiscences, and my sister, who directed (dominated) my viewing in my younger years; David and Maria for the regular discussions in the Red Lion; all those that came down to provide support and company in my sojourn down in Devon; to Sarah and Harvey with whom I've watched the last couple of series of *24*; and, lastly, to my colleagues and students, past and present, for their support over the years.

Introduction

Preamble: A personal view

Looking back over the years, American programmes have always been part of my television diet – from *Bonanza* and *The Virginian* in the 1960s, *Mission: Impossible*, *M*A*S*H*, *The Rockford Files*, *Star Trek* and *Starsky and Hutch* in the 1970s and, more recently, *Nip/Tuck*, *24*, *Frasier*, *Friends*, *Sex and the City*, *Homicide: Life on the Streets*, *The Wire*, *The Shield* and *Lost*. This does not mean I only watch American programmes but, when discussing my memories and experiences of watching television, these programmes are as likely to surface as British ones. Indeed, from my perspective, I see little difference between the two. American programmes have always, for me, been both part of British television while also appearing different; they were often faster paced and strangely colourful, while infused with different narrative rhythms. I particularly remember the Quinn Martin Productions with their prologues and epilogues, which no British programme seemed to use.

Many years later, while staying in a motel in America, much in the way that Raymond Williams had many years earlier, I saw some of the programmes I had watched in Britain as a child. They were obviously the same programmes – I recognised the characters, the setting, the formula of the series, even occasionally the actual episode – but they were not shown in the same way; the whole experience of watching such programmes was different. Indeed, I noticed that the rhythms of the programmes I had once found rather strange now made sense. For example, in *Star Trek*, when watched on the BBC, there were, every so often, strange fade-outs and fade-ins which seemed to happen for no reason, appearing as a kind of reiteration of parts of the narrative; they happened around important moments in the story. Now it made sense, they had been made to fade out, on a narrative high, to the commercials

1

and on our return we faded back in with a small recap of what was happening. Seemingly, programmes were changed when they were shown on different types of channels in different cultural contexts; in some way they were assimilated. It is this interest, in this idea of assimilation, which has led me to attempt this work, to explore the way American programmes are selected, used and assimilated into British television – to study the changing role of American programmes on British screens.

Constructing an approach

With the coming of the first American programmes on British television in the 1950s, many viewed them in a similar way as they had other forms of American culture over the past decades – American culture was crass, standardised and formulaic. American television programmes were commercial products imposing American values and outlooks upon British audiences; British culture had to be defended. Such a view held to a belief that the programme, a text of sorts, was imposing inbuilt meanings and values on a rather passive audience. However, over the years, this position has been countered by an active view of the reader, a reader who is able to understand text in a different way – that the text did not have one possible reading but many. It could, however, be argued that both positions need to take account of the other more than they do. On the one hand, America does dominate the global flow of many cultural goods, their cultural industries are the largest and strongest in the world and billions of people consume their culture; on the other, just because someone watches an American film it does not mean they will automatically become American. There is, therefore, a need for an approach that can accept both positions, that can offer an understanding of how cultures interact. Therefore, in this work, I wish to take a more dynamic view in which American and British television cultures are in an active dialogue with each – one which can focus on the interaction between imported programmes and the domestic television culture.

Therefore, in Chapter 1, after exploring past and existing discourses about American culture and work undertaken on American programmes and British television, I will – by building on work of Nancy Morris (2002), Jeffrey Miller (2000), Nick Browne (1984), Steemers (2004) and John Ellis (2002) – develop a multifaceted approach to study and explore the reasons for the trade in programmes, the way broadcasters act as national mediators between cultural systems, how programmes are actively assimilated into the national schedule, the public discourse that seeks to frame such imports and where this might be going with the development of new technologies.

Nancy Morris's model (2002) is a useful starting point in understanding how a predefined culture might adapt to new imported cultural elements. She suggests societies have shared cultural 'deep structures' that influence how culture is constructed, shaped, produced and consumed. Therefore, if an external culture, say a television programme, enters an existing cultural system, it will be shaped into an acceptable and understandable form, what she calls a 'surface structure'; this process will be guided by existing structures, for example by national broadcasters, who are informed by the wider shared cultural 'deep structure'. As the audience interprets and reacts to these surface structures, elements of the new external culture might enter and become part of the deep structure of that society, nation or community in question (Morris, 2002: 283).

In a similar way to Morris, Jeffrey Miller presents a dynamic view of how we can understand the way cultures interact with each other. He does this by using the work of Bakhtin to develop the concepts of dialogue, utterance and assimilation (Miller, 2000: 7–11). Miller talks about utterances as the smallest unit of intercourse, the speech act made concrete. However, these are not heard in isolation, they are part of a dialogue, a dialogue between a speaker and a respondent, both of whom are situated within a web of dialogues, meanings and discourses. Therefore the meanings of such utterances are not fixed and closed, they include past and current utterances, with 'every element of discourse . . . itself a response' (ibid.: 8). In this way, the idea of dialogue, if transposed to the interaction of television programmes and television systems, suggests a 'process through which a text created in one culture enters another for any number of reasons and is apprehended by any number of people for any other reasons' (ibid.: 9). Such a view moves away from the idea that text, such as programmes, have inbuilt ideological effects or meanings and are imposed on other cultures (Schiller, 1969), and suggests, instead, that a culture selects, reads and uses cultural imports in many different ways, often differently to how they were understood and used in the original context of its production.

Miller is not suggesting, however, that text have no meaning, or that no hegemonic processes are at work, either between nations or within a nation, but that forms of negotiation happened over meaning, and that possible alternatives can also be found within the text (ibid.: 10, 181). To help understand this process, he develops Baktin's concept of assimilation; he defines this not in terms of a 'dominant set of meanings grabbing and devouring meaning introduced from a foreign source', but one where 'both partners in the act of assimilation have something to say about the transaction' (ibid.: 10). The interaction, in this way, is dynamic; no one side imposes its views or values on the other, though equally neither is completely powerless.

In Chapter 2, to provide a context for this work, I will present a historical overview of the development of British broadcasting in which I will focus on its changing relationship with American television and the different roles played by American programmes. I begin by noting that much of the current historical work that covers American programmes on British screens is rather limited, and when covered, it often discusses them through particular cultural, social, political and economic discourses. However, by pulling together a number of these accounts I am able to present here a useful diachronic overview of the changing role of American programmes, one which can help situate the following chapters with their more synchronic focus, where they tend to dig down to explore various issues, processes and discourses in more depth. In Chapter 3, I will explore the economic rationale of why a trade in programmes exists, why broadcasters import and export programmes and why America has come to dominate the international trade of certain programme genre. I will therefore explore the different push (for exports) and pull (for imports) factors that operate in the British and American environments and the relationship that has developed between the two. The chapter ends by focusing on how a market discourse, which for so long had taken second place to cultural, social and political concerns, has recently become more dominant, playing an important part in the creation of more open competitive regimes around the globe which American firms are trying to take advantage of.

One important way of exploring and understanding the cultural interactions at work, at least in terms of broadcasting, is by focusing on the role of broadcasters as mediators (Steemers, 2004: 17–20). Therefore, in Chapter 4, I will explore, through a series of interviews, how British broadcasters perceive and experience the trade in programmes; how they professionally 'read' American programmes, judging their worth, their fit with the domestic sensibilities and the brand of the channel and what economic or cultural benefits they see them bringing; I will then explore their views of how American programmes are scheduled, edited, changed, marketed and promoted and indeed, how they become part of British television culture.

To explore some of the issues raised in Chapter 4 in more detail, I will, in Chapter 5, focus on how American programmes come to interact with and are altered by their use within British television. To do this, I will develop and utilise three concepts suggested by Nick Browne (1984) – text, supertext, megatext – to which I add another, that of context. While Gripsrud suggests that the programme proper can be stripped of the surrounding elements, my approach will hold to the idea that there is no finished text; they are constantly being adapted, changed and assimilated depending on the context in which it is screened and consumed (1995: 131–2). A programme, as it enters a new environment, or megatext, with its own history and conventions, can be altered, can be edited, the sound track can be changed and, if a series, it can be shown in a new order; it will be shown within a schedule of programmes, a different supertext for which it was originally produced, with which it will interact, dynamically, creating new associations and meanings; it will be framed within a larger cultural discourse, or context, one that will again change and create new understandings. Programmes, as such, have to be understood in how they work within the particular supertext, megatext and context in which they are shown and watched.

In Chapter 6, I will explore the different types of television criticism and reviewing that have appeared over the last fifty years and how these have covered and represented American programmes. Though this discourse is not all-important in how programmes are watched, or what is popular, it is indicative of wider debates about American culture. While earlier forms of criticism aligned themselves with a widely held derogatory view of American culture, other forms have appeared over time that, while not threatening the dominant cultural hierarchy, do present more popular, alternative and, sometimes, subversive readings of American programmes. As American programmes have changed, as they have been shaped to target more upmarket audiences, much of the earlier attacks on its formulaic and standardised form have been replaced by critical acclaim; increasingly, American programmes are now offering a cultural distinctiveness sought by critics and the affluent niche audiences.

I will end, in Chapter 7, by exploring the current and future developments affecting the role and use of American programmes on British television. I will initially explore how both the British and the American markets are changing, changes that are affecting the relationship between the two: on the one hand American firms, as they face competition at home, have gone through a series of mergers as they shore up their American businesses (Holt, 2003), which has led to the development of new strategies to tap into the international market; likewise, on the other hand, as more channels appear in the British market, the demand for and use made of American programmes is changing. I will then end by exploring the various technological developments which, for some, signal a move away from television as a form of broadcasting aimed at and serving a large national audience by use of schedules of programmes, perhaps towards a form of Me-TV; towards a form of television that will allow a viewer to select and buy programmes to watch whatever and whenever they want (Hoskins *et al.*, 1997: 133; Winston, 1998: 127). Changes that will affect how American programmes are watched and experienced by British viewers in the future.

Conclusion

This work has two main aims behind it: to re-evaluate the use of and roles taken by American programmes on British television while developing a suitable methodological approach. Rather than to conceive of such relationships as either an imposition of the culture of one nation on another, as those taking a cultural or media imperialism position often do, or, alternatively, to view the text with no inbuilt meaning, where the receiving nation subjugates and uses the cultural product from another nation as it wishes, I have tried to utilise a more dynamic approach – an approach that seeks to understand such processes in terms of a dynamic interplay between cultures. In this way American programmes, as they enter the British television environment, are mediated by broadcasters, who select what will fit best with their and the audience's needs, and who will alter and change American programmes as they are assimilated into the British schedules. Then, through their interaction with surrounding programmes, they become part of, while changing, British television. They are then framed and marketed to audiences in particular ways. So, even before the audience has viewed an American programme, what they will experience has already been selected, filtered, changed and shaped to their sensibilities.

This work is not, therefore, an attempt to textually analyse American programmes, or to explore how they are consumed or to highlight the number of programmes bought and sold, or even to look at the trade in formats or the development of co-productions, but to analyse the way American programmes, originally produced and shown in America, become part of British television, the way they are bought, used and framed within and for the British television environment. In such a book as this, there has been little space to explore every avenue fully, indeed as many questions are raised as answered, the point has more been to indicate something of the multifaceted approach that is required to understand, the 'process through which a text created in one culture enters another for any number of reasons and is apprehended by any number of people for any other reasons' (Miller, 2000: 9).

1
Theories of Cultural Assimilation

1.1 Introduction

In many ways it is hard to comprehend the way American programmes have been accepted, watched, talked about and assimilated into British (television) culture without, in the first instant, understanding the wider discourse concerning American culture; partly as it has been so influential in later discourse about the role and use of American television programmes within British schedules. I will therefore, in the first chapter, begin by surveying the wider cultural debates that have developed over the last couple of hundred years that have come to link the coming of the mass society and mass culture with American culture. I will undertake this by exploring the work of those writers often labelled as part of the cultural and civilisation tradition, those such as Matthew Arnold, F. R. Leavis and Q. D. Leavis, before turning my attention to similar debates of the left; here I will focus on the work of the Frankfurt School. Following this, I will turn to work by Richard Hoggart, a forerunner of the cultural studies approach, and his work *Uses of Literacy* (1957), in which he, while expressing worries about American culture and its affect on British working-class culture, begins to open up a space to discuss and analyse popular culture.

I will then turn my attention to more recent attempts to understand and confront the unequal flow of American culture; initially this will involve exploring the debates that have arisen since the 1960s around issues relating to forms of media or cultural imperialism. While such approaches focused, in the first place, on the continuing relationship of the core and peripheral countries, the First and Third World, these were later extended to understand the developing media and cultural relationship between America and developed countries. Much of this work accepted, without much detailed research, the presumed effect of the media and cultural flows and relationships between countries; flows which are often asymmetrical, with one nation and its media and culture being in a position of dominance over another. After this I will move on to look at later work that has, by exploring the way texts are actually consumed, refuted these unsubstantiated views of media and cultural effects (for example, Katz and Liebes, 1986).

I will end the first section of this chapter by looking at some of the few works that have come to focus on the way American programmes have been acquired and used by British broadcasting organisations, for example Segrave (1998) and Lealand (1984), and those that have looked at how programmes have been bought and sold, for example *Selling Television* by Jeanette Steemers (2004). However, as I argue, these are the exception rather than the rule; most work has focused on the micro level, on the text or its consumption, or at the macro level, on international flows of programmes and relationships between nations. In the second part of this chapter, utilising a number of existing concepts and ideas, I will develop a multifaceted approach to study the way an external culture is assimilated within and by a different culture; the way British television incorporates American programmes into its schedule and the way they interact; the way American programmes become part of British (television) culture.

1.2 Discourses on the mass media and Americanisation

1.2.1 Mass culture and mass society debates: Culture and civilisation tradition

Debates about and concern over the rise of a mass culture have been around for hundreds of years. Indeed, Strinati (2001) notes that Lowenthal (1957) suggested that such worries are found in the writings of Pascal and Montaigne dating back to the 16th and 17th centuries, respectively (ibid.: 2). In many ways, at least in the British context, such concerns start to appear as Britain went through huge changes from the 18th century onwards; as it moved from a feudal towards a mercantile and then a capitalist society; as it started to exploit global markets, develop an empire, employ new forms of technology in agriculture and industry and move towards an industrial form of production and contract employment. For some, as people moved off the land and into the cities, the agrarian communities of old broke down; as this happened, the feudal-based society, the old order, changed and the spectre of the masses raised its head. This was a primeval mass; a mass of people in which the rules of old, the old hierarchy, and the tensions kept in check by civilisation and its associated values were thrown off; where the individual was subsumed into the crowd, leading to a loss of individuality (LeMahieu, 1988: 108–9).

This was a 'mass' that, partly through the developing media, began to become aware of itself and the new ideas of democracy. Increasingly, this mass of people, encouraged by various writers and activists, pressured for political and social change (Thompson, 1982: 84–110). On all fronts the old order was under attack. The elites, in apprehension, saw the rise of a mass society leading to the spread of democratic ideals and forms of democracy. Many looked to America, some in apprehension, as one of the more open societies, politically and economically, as an example of what might happen to the old order (Tocqueville, 1961; Aron, 1983: 191–206, 219–32). This was not the emergence of a new egalitarian society in which everything would be fairer but, instead, the beginning of the tyranny of the masses: the rule of the mob. The traditional hierarchy, built as they saw it on the right of the best educated, cultured and bred to rule, was being undermined by an idea that suggested everyone's voice was as equal, that everyone's views were valid, that 'everyone's general cultural preferences are as valuable and as worthy of being respected and fulfilled as those of the traditional elites' (Strinati, 2001: 7–8).

Linked to the spread of ideas of democracy, of enfranchising the masses in societies around Europe, was the rise of the mass media. While for some the media, if used in the right way, offered a means of informing the citizens, a way of uplifting the populace culturally (for example, see the influence of Arnold's ideas on John Reith, 1949), for others it was viewed more negatively as creating a standardised form of a mass culture, one which did little to encourage thought or obedience in the masses (LeMahieu, 1988: 103–5). This was a culture of the masses, one pandering to the lowest common denominator. Critics, such as F. R. Leavis, Q. D. Leavis and T. S. Elliot, writing between the wars, were interested in preserving the status quo; they accepted the idea of a cultural hierarchy, with the elite culture being worth more than mass produced or simplified versions of culture. Standing at the top of the cultural pyramid was culture produced by the creative artist, the sole genius who attempts to understand man's place in the world, who creates art to stimulate thought. However, it required certain cultural capital to enjoy; a capital only they, the elites, had. This hierarchy had to be defended against the development of mass culture, against the rule of the masses, against democracy; standards had to be maintained. There was a need to combat '...the steady influence which operates silently in any mass society organised for profit, for the depression of standards of art and culture. The increasing organisation of advertisement and propaganda – or the influencing of masses of men by any means except through their intelligence' (Elliot, 1939: 39–40).

America was viewed as the nation at the forefront of the development of the mass media, of creating a cultural industry organised along factory-like lines, with Hollywood being an early proponent. As America started to successfully export its products abroad, especially its cultural products, the various fears about the development of a mass society, mass culture and democracy started to conflate. All three became linked to the idea of America and its cultural output (Strinati, 2003: 19–21). Its cultural industries were the most developed, the most driven by the profit motive and the one most likely to be dominant in an open market. As Leavis argues, 'American conditions are the conditions of modern civilization, even if the "drift" has gone further on the other side of the Atlantic than on this' (cited in Johnson, 1979: 96). It was producing a culture able to attract huge audiences rather than one that was made to educate, to stimulate or to create works of genius; it was a culture of the masses, not the culture of the elites or the working classes.

1.2.2   Frankfurt School

Another group, interested in the development of a mass culture, while holding different political views shared some of the concerns of the cultural and civilisation tradition, was the Frankfurt School. This was a group of leftwing German academics which escaped Nazi Germany in the 1930s eventually settling in America, where they stayed until after the Second World War (Brookeman, 1984: 77–88; Strinati, 2001: 53–6). Much of their work, for example *The Authoritarian Personality* (1950), was focused on understanding how fascism had developed in Germany and whether such processes were also at work in America. They saw the capitalist system with its factory-like cultural industry eroding a more organic culture that had grown out of the endeavours of artists and craftsmen over hundreds of years. This 'new' culture was formulaic, standardised and could easily be consumed with little active thought. Such a culture produced a passive, malleable and controllable mass. For John Carey, the Frankfurt theorists (except Benjamin) shared the view that mass culture and the mass media, as developed under capitalism, had degraded civilisation in the twentieth century: 'they regarded the masses as dupes, seduced by capitalism's equivalent of Prolefeed. Happily gobbling down the products of the commercialised "culture industry", the masses had developed a "false consciousness", so that they no longer saw things as the Frankfurt theorists wished' (1992: 43).

However, unlike those cultural critics like Matthew Arnold and F. R. and Q. D. Leavis, those associated with the Frankfurt School were not worried about the onset of cultural anarchy – anarchy resulting from the end of the cultural hierarchy and the standards it promoted – but, instead, saw such developments leading to the manipulation and control of the masses (Storey, 2003: 27–9). They saw the capitalist system, most highly developed in America, creating a cultural industry that produced a culture that helped stupefy, to control, the masses, thus allowing or helping in the rise of authoritarian-fascist states. They did, however, agree with the conservative cultural critics that the finest culture, that which had a life beyond the now, 'that kept alive the human desire for a better world beyond the confines of the present' (Storey, 2001: 86), was that of the elites – the avant-garde, classical music, opera and painting – culture that had been produced by the lone artist or groups of craftsmen outside of the cultural industry and appreciated by a privileged elite (Adorno, 2002: 29–60).

For those of both the culture and civilisation tradition and the Frankfurt School, mass culture, often conflated with the term 'popular culture', required little detailed study. Its effects could be read off from its conditions of production and consumption. American culture, produced by a culture industry, in a factory-like system, was viewed as formulaic and standardised; it was viewed pessimistically as it eroded the existing authentic or organic culture, leading to a controlled mass or a form of cultural anarchy.

1.2.3   The cultural turn: Richard Hoggart

From the 1950s, Richard Hoggart, writing alongside such contemporaries as Raymond Williams and E. P. Thompson, studied the culture of the working classes. In many ways he was one of the founders of modern cultural studies in Britain, a field of study that sought to redeem popular culture for study (Turner, 1996: 12). Employing existing forms of textual and historical studies, Richard Hoggart analysed the changes occurring in working-class culture, leading to the publication of his seminal work, *The Uses of Literacy*, in 1957. Unlike the earlier cultural critics, and the Frankfurt School, he was not completely pessimistic about the developments that were occurring:

It was in the latter half of the last century and the opening years of this century that the effects of these changes first came home forcefully to the bosoms of working-class people, in the extension of the franchise, the possibilities of much greater material comforts than had been known before, the effect of the Education Acts, and in much else. (Hoggart, 1957: 171)

The Uses of Literacy is divided into two parts. The first section explores what is left of the traditional working-class culture, through textual readings of popular cultural texts such as magazines, books, newspapers and films, as well as analysis of his experiences, conversations, interviews and forms of textual analysis and observations. Through such work he explores how the development of working-class culture had, traditionally, been linked to working-class needs; it was not imposed from outside. It was a culture they made their own, whether as a means of surviving the daily grind or for making sense of the world around them. Indeed, to understand this process, to comprehend the way culture was made their own, Hoggart suggests, requires not just an understanding of the text but the context within which it gained meaning (Dyer, 1973: 40).

The second part of *The Uses of Literacy* concentrates on how the working-class culture was being whittled away by the rise of a mass media, indeed, how it was, at certain moments, becoming Americanised. Such a reading has similarities to those of Leavis and Elliot in that mass culture and Americanisation are viewed as having an eroding influence on what was there already, of an alien culture imposed from above by capitalist concerns:

This kind of shiny barbarism is having some success here... [s]urrounded by a great quantity of material goods designed to serve and amuse and yearly increasing in number and ingenuity, but with little sense that these are the end-products, and in many cases the more trivial products, of centuries of slowly-acquired knowledge and skill. (Hoggart, 1957: 193)

This was a culture that provides no substitute for 'a popular culture experientially connected to the social conditions of those who produce and consume it' (Turner, 1996: 45). Hoggart, however, is not completely dismissive of all these developments; he accepts that some of this new mass culture, for example crime novels, for some working-class readers was closer to their experiences and lives than that produced by British writers (Strinati, 2001: 28–9). He also, throughout his work, tries to understand how this imported culture is assimilated and consumed by the working classes: How 'much that is new and may seem, at first glance, merely injurious, is assimilated and adapted' (ibid.: 323). Such formulations, in some ways, seem to pre-date much of the later work on active audiences undertaken in the name of Cultural or Media Studies.

Hoggart is important for this discussion in the way he helps open up a discursive space in which popular culture could be studied, he is not just interested in elite culture. He does not dismiss popular culture out of hand as being completely imposed on the consumer by cultural industries. While worried about American culture, he is prepared to understand what it means to people, to the working classes in particular. Through his work he provides a more active view of the media user than many before him – they are not passive dupes, they actively use and make this culture their own. Though Hoggart's analysis asks new questions of popular culture, his approach is limited by the continuing strength of the existing critical traditions and the need for more complex conceptual tools. By the 1960s and 1970s we start to see the development of other new ways of understanding and approaching the study of American media and cultural exports, namely around the idea of media or cultural imperialism.

1.2.4   Media and cultural imperialism

Another influential input into the discourse around American culture and its impact on British culture developed in the 1960s and 1970s in relation to America's growing worldwide hegemony. Many saw America's worldwide influence not just in terms of its military or economic power but also as the result of its growing dominance of international media and cultural markets (Schiller, 1969). Rather than being a set theory, this approach should be thought of more as an area of conflicting discourses, focused on aspects of media or cultural imperialism (Tomlinson, 1991: 8–11). Those advocating such ideas argued that even with the end of the colonial epoch western nations continued to exercise power over ex-colonial nations; the imperial relationship continued but in another form. While this discourse was first developed in relation to the Third World, it was soon expanded to investigate and explain the apparent dominance, and possible effects, of the American capitalist system upon other developed societies (Boyd-Barrett, 1979). Many of the early approaches found under this umbrella have tended to study such developments at the level of the international, elevating supposed structural relationships between nations (cultural, economic, technological and ideological), seeking to explain a power position: 'imperialism' (Tomlinson, 1991: 34–41).

Those holding such positions view broadcasting, along with other media and cultural activities, as replicating and reinforcing this structural relationship, helping the dominance of one nation state, culture or system over another – for good (with moves down the road towards socialism for traditional Marxists) or ill (underdevelopment/dependency and hence stagnation for neo-Marxists) (Schiller, 1969). Such a position can, however, be divided differently: into the still ideologically loaded conspiratorial or intentional version and a more pluralist/liberal or economic-dominated version (Pool, 1977; Hoskins and Mirus, 1988). Both see forms of domination but the former takes a more traditional Marxist position, seeing it connected to a greater ideological battle, and the latter sees it merely as the inevitable result of the economics of television, which can therefore change over time (Lee, 1979: 41–2; Tomlinson, 1991: 21–3).

Those interested in exploring such ideas in relation to television often studied the international televisual relationship by way of a number of different 'visible' or quantifiable elements: the numbers of programmes bought and sold, the foreign ownership of production and broadcasting companies and the degree of control over advertising (Nordenstreng and Varis, 1974; Varis, 1985). This is usually expressed by the direction and size of the 'flow', whether programmes, ideas or investment, which is indicative of the strength of the relationship between the nations. Underpinning this, for those taking an ideological or conspiratorial position, is an assumption of the effects of such a 'flow' or relationship on the society in question (Tomlinson, 1991: 35–41).

Thus, for those working within this field, the concern has centred less on the actual effects of these international relations – whether and how such flows and contacts affect the national system and audience in question – than on an assumption of its effect upon the 'nation' in question (Schlesinger, 1991: 148–9). So that if imbalances exist so, it is assumed, does a situation of dominance and all that that implies. While this has led to criticism of such an approach being more a methodology for supporting a particular ideological position lacking a coherent theory or framework – being ideologically loaded – it still remains 'an elaborate and sophisticated approach with its reformists and revolutionaries' (Kivikuru, 1988: 9–34).

Preben Sepstrup (1990) has attempted to take note of these various criticisms by extracting a methodological approach from the ideological positions noted earlier, presenting a more firmly grounded framework.

To do this he has divided the study of the internationalisation of television into two: the first being the international flow or relationships (in his case, centred on programme flows), its associated effect being transnationalisation; the second level taking the transnationalisation as the independent variable with resulting effects being the substantial effects. The substantial effects are '... effects relevant from a cultural, economic, or consumer point of view, such as the formation of values, programme contents, conditions for national public-service broadcasting, or patterns of consumption' (ibid.: 11).

While Sepstrup's work concentrates upon the first level, the flows occurring between nations and their effects (transnationalisation), it does so within a framework that both accepts the need for further study on the resulting effects of the transnationalisation and that understands transnationalisation as related to 'a specific "area" such as a country, group of countries, or specific group of TV viewers', and that therefore is basically a national phenomenon (ibid.).

Thus, for Sepstrup, to understand how national television systems are interacting requires not just a look at the amount(s) and level(s) of flow between them, but also a look at how such flows and relationships are being mediated or assimilated into national services. For example, Lee (1979) shows, in his study of the influence of American television flows upon Taiwan and Canada, that the two broadcasting systems have reacted differently – American flows did not have inbuilt effects, and national conditions and factors were important in the reactions of broadcasters. Thus it can be suggested that what is needed is '... a rather more discrete, subtle and empirical approach ... to the socio-cultural experience of the flow of international television and therefore the notion of the likely dominance of US TV' (Tracey, 1988: 9). That is, an understanding of the national context is required to understand the effect of, and relationship with, the international sphere.

1.2.5   Active audiences

In the 1980s there was, what many have called, a turn towards the audience. Research was undertaken to explore how audiences actually read, understood and consumed text. Such work showed that television texts are polysemic; that they are 'open', allowing different interpretations or reading by different viewers – indeed, that the cultural and social context of reception plays an important role in the production of meaning. Some, going further, started to explore the use of the media within people's lives, moving further away from trying to understand how particular texts are read (Boyd-Barrett, 1995: 498–504).

For example, Liebes and Katz (1990) in their work exploring the way audiences understand *Dallas*, undertook a series of interviews with families from an array of backgrounds then living in Israel. One of the main conclusions of this work was that family groups, depending on their social backgrounds, understand *Dallas* in different ways. There-fore, the way an American text is understood in another national context needs to be approached not by providing an authoritative textual reading but by understanding how the audience(s) actually makes sense of it. Such work suggests that quantitative work, focusing on the international trade of programmes, could tell us little about the impact of such flows; indeed, if the text is polysemic and the context of reception is important in the understanding of such a text, then whether or not American programmes dominate the flow is of little concern (Fejes, 1981: 287; Liebes and Katz, 1990).

Generally, this audience work has focused on the reading experience of identifiable programmes – as noted above, *Dallas* and *Dynasty* are two American programmes that, because of their international popu-larity, have been the centre of much of the early work in the area (Ang, 1985; Liebes and Katz, 1990; Gripsrud, 1995). This is done, often, by extracting the programme from the schedule or programme 'flow' within which it is experienced. In this way, work on audience reception has tended to focus on particular programmes, or the context of consump-tion, with less thought or analysis of how programmes are selected and assimilated into the national television schedule. As Gripstrud notes, '[i]n Katz and Liebes's project the explanation for the "diffusion" of US television is only sought for in the interactive relationship between viewers and the text. They do not ask why the text is there to be inter-acted with in the first place' (1995: 26).

1.2.6 Global–local

Some, in the light of these debates and with further developments in the global economy, have presented a more complex dynamic view of media and cultural global interactions, one where there are many different flows, some dominated by America while others by leading regional nations or local cultural producers. Such approaches accept the power of the audience but, at the same time, still question what is being offered to the audience, and also highlight that some media firms domi-nate the ownership of channels, international flow of programmes and programme formats. For some there is therefore a need to revisit and update the cultural and media imperialism approaches (Lee, 1979; Boyd-Barrett, 1998; Chadha and Kavoori, 2000); such trade in programmes might be more complex, operating in different directions, but there are some nations that still dominate.

For others, such approaches are superseded by an interest in how the global media firms have taken account of the local (Sreberny-Moham-madi, 1996); how media-cultural firms have restructured their operations to operate on a world level but with an awareness of the regional and local needs; where such developments have led to a more flexible system of production, more post-Fordist, with different production and transmission operations spread around the globe, though controlled from the centre. This has led to a complex global system where cultural and media flows move in many different directions (usually from the centre to the periphery, but sometimes the other way or even between peripheral markets), where some programmes are sourced locally, where cultural workers and programme ideas move from market to market (sometimes from the periphery to the centre) and where homogenising tendencies of global firms are countered by local needs and demands – a tendency that Robertson has called 'glocalisation' (1995: 40). For some, these developments signal a move towards a New International Division of Cultural Labour (NICL), one where the 'emphasis on local taste markets is increasingly reflected in the organisational structure of some entertainment companies, especially the most global ones' (Miller and Yúdice, 2002: 82). However, while such approaches suggest a spreading out of power, of the creation of hybrid forms of culture, it does not invalidate the necessity to explore issues of how certain nations or firms dominate certain forms of programme production and programme flows, and the relationships that develop between national systems (Steemers, 2004: 10).

1.2.7   Existing studies of the buying and scheduling of American TV programmes

However, some work has been undertaken on the way programmes are sold by American distributors, and selected, bought and used by British broadcasters in British schedules; for example, in Geoffrey Lealand's working paper for the Broadcasting Research Unit *American Television Programmes on British Screens* (1984), he explores the wider British context within which American programmes are acquired, scheduled and watched. He starts by looking at the trade of programmes on a worldwide basis and, more particularly, on the trade between British and American broadcasting systems, before focusing on how American imports have been used on British television. For example, he notes that American programmes in the mid-1950s, while used in limited numbers by Independent Television (ITV), were often popular draws, but, he argues, were mostly scheduled in late afternoon/early evening slots and, in many ways, were used to support domestic productions; likewise the BBC, while using them less, used them in similar slots (ibid.: 13–14). However, much of the focus of this work, on the buying and use of American programmes, is limited in scope and detail; the majority of the working paper focuses on audience responses. Also, while raising some interesting points – for example, that American programmes are often popular and much appreciated, and that the British context is different to other nations – much of this work is now dated. For example, 'Because British viewers demand so much from their television entertainments numerous American sitcoms fail to attract a following or at best attract a 'cult' following. They do not measure up, for their approach, style and elements of entertainment are inappropriate for a British audience' (ibid.: 94). A view that seems out of place with the success of American comedies, such as *Friends, Frasier* and *Will and Grace*, since the time when the working paper was written.

In a similar way, but from a different perspective, Kerry Segrave (1998) has studied the way the American film and television industry has, over the last fifty years, sold programmes around the world. A number of sections in the work deal specifically with the way American distributors sell programmes to the British market. Unlike Lealand, this work touches little on the audience and its appreciation of programmes but more on the sales strategies taken by American distributors; it looks at strategies for encouraging sales, what is sold, their costs and, only briefly, their popularity. This work uses a number of sources – trade and industry journals and magazines, newspaper stories and interviews. In many ways this fits within Preban Sepstrup's first stage of studying internationalisation – that of the transnational flows (1990); it is a well-executed and detailed study of the attempts and practices by American distributors to sell and to dominate the trade of television programmes.

However, overall the British broadcasting market is given only limited coverage with much of the work relating to marketing and selling strategies of American companies; there is little analysis of the way British broadcasters view such programmes and how the programmes were eventually used in British schedules. As Segrave notes in his introduction, 'This book is the story of how ... U.S. producers have tried to dominate the world's television screens to the same extent that they dominate the world's cinemas' (1998: 2).

Jeanette Steemers (2004) in her work, *Selling Television*, is the reverse to Segrave's, as she has studied the way British broadcasters are selling their programmes, formats and co-productions into overseas markets. Through a large number of interviews with broadcasters, buyers and sellers, she explores their perceptions and experiences of the international programme market and the role and use of British production within this. Her work illustrates the complexity of the market, the different approaches taken by different producers and broadcasters, how such markets are affected by domestic changes and how programmes are used by different markets. However, her main focus is on British sales abroad, often through case studies, rather than on the British market and its use of American imports, and does not look in much detail into how the programmes are actually used and assimilated by the new television culture.

However, Lealand, Segrave and Steemers's work does open up a space of inquiry; they start to explore the relationships between American and British broadcasters and the flow of programmes both into and out of the British system and, in varying degrees of detail, the way imported programmes have been used in the schedules and watched by British audiences. Elsewhere little work has been published that specifically looks at the role and use of American programmes on British screens; the view they give of American culture, the way they interact with programmes around them and how they become part of the British television culture, though Ellis (2002), with his interest on scheduling, is an important exception. There has generally been little attempt to explore how American programmes have become a part of a site where the 'nation is constructed for its members' (Hartley, 1978: 124). Indeed, it could be argued that the question should not be one of an alien culture invading our screens, but how American programmes work as part of our television culture; how they merge, conflate and exist in the flow of programmes that make up the 'national' schedule; as Morely and Robins suggest, 'perhaps America is now within, now part of a European cultural repertoire, part of European identity' (1997: 57).

1.3   Cultural assimilation: An approach

1.3.1   Introduction

From the overview above it is evident that little work has been undertaken on the way American programmes are acquired and assimilated into, and the way they work within, the British national schedule (though Miller [2000] does attempt something along these lines in relation to British programmes on American television). Most work, on

American programmes in the British context, have tended to be from a micro or macro perspective, studying the text or its consumption by audiences or programme flows. Indeed, for Phillip Schlesinger, there is need for a greater understanding between the two; for those involved in more macro approaches, those involved in studying flow, to be more aware of audience work and the actual impact of programmes and, likewise, for those working at the micro level, the ethnographic, to understand what programmes are dominating television, what choice is actually provided (1991: 149).

I wish to argue that there is a need for more work able to bridge these two positions. Cunningham and Jacka suggest, in their work on the export of Australian television, a middle-range approach (1996: 22), which Steemers defines as lying between 'the "total" explanations of political-economy or institutional analysis and a narrow 'micro-situational' audience approach informed by ethnography' (2004: 18). I will use a similar concept, but refer to it as a meso perspective, and will locate it between those concepts which focus on the flow of programmes between national systems and those that study television's consumption; this is an approach that focuses on the way an external culture is assimilated into an existing culture; the way American programmes become part of British television. I will now develop a number of linked ideas, concepts and methods of analysis, with which to guide the approach taken within this book.

1.3.2 Mediating culture: A dynamic model of assimilation

One way to understand broadcasting and its relationship to the cultural and social worlds is by employing the concept of the circuit of culture (Johnson, 1996). Such a model helps to map out the relationships that exist between producers and consumers in the production of cultural meaning and identity within a specific society. Moving on from the early one-way communication models, such a circular model presents a more balanced understanding in which the media, working within a particular context, produces certain forms of cultural representation that are actively consumed by audiences within their lived experiences; this then feeds into the wider culture and, eventually, back into the context of production. This is a dynamic view in which producers and consumers are equally important in the production of meaning.

There is, however, a need to add on to such a concept of relationships with other systems of production, other national circuits of culture, from which programmes, television channels, personnel and practices flow or move from and to. Such a relationship must, however, be understood dynamically, it is not one of the programmes or ideas with fixed meanings or outcomes being imposed and impacting on an existing fixed culture, or one where such programmes are separate from and have no interaction with the culture in which they are consumed. It is more a question of active assimilation, where the resident culture(s), while remaining stable and important to those living in such a society, is able to adapt to and change these new elements. However, this active incorporation and understanding does not just operate in terms of audiences or viewers, as advocated by much audience work in the area; it is also a question of how broadcasters act as key mediators, choosing, adapting, changing and assimilating programmes and ideas from many sources (Steemers, 2004: 18–19). It is they that attempt to 'nationalise' the bought-in programmes, the external flows, and who attempt to frame and market them to the viewer.

One way of developing Johnson's model further is offered by the work of Nancy Morris (2002). In her work, she merges two existing models, Klaus Bruhn Jensen's generative model, in which a 'predefined structure gives shape to meaning elements' (ibid.: 282) and Staubhaar and Hammond's feedback model. Morris merges these to create a model which provides an understanding of how a predefined culture adapts to new elements. She suggests that every society has a cultural 'deep structure', which is shared by producers and consumers, that influences how culture is constructed, shaped, produced and consumed (prefiguration); similar to Johnson's idea of the circuit of culture. When an external culture enters such a system, for example a broadcaster acquires a television programme, it is shaped by the pre-existing structures generating 'surface structures'. These are then interpreted and consumed by the audience (configuration); the audience's reactions to these new external cultural elements might then enter and become part of the deep structure of that society (refiguration), nation or community in question (ibid.: 283).

Jeffrey Miller, in a similar way to Morris, develops a dynamic idea of how cultures interact with each other. This he does by utilising concepts of dialogue, utterance and assimilation as suggested by Bakhtin (2000: 7–11). Miller suggests that when two cultures interact, when a speaker interacts with a respondent through 'utterances', this constitutes a dialogue; a dialogue that is two-way and interactive. This dialogue is not, however, made up from a closed set of utterances, but from many past and present utterances, often of many different dialogues, such that 'every element of discourse... is itself a response' (ibid.: 8). If this idea of dialogue is transposed to the interaction of television programmes and television systems, it would suggest a 'process through which a text created in one culture enters another for any number of reasons and is apprehended by any number of people for any other reasons' (ibid.: 9); that is, a programme, while in a way, is an utterance, it is understood through the interaction of many other past and present utterances, within many dialogues. This suggests that the text has no in-built meaning and it is read differently depending on the culture in question. Miller, to maintain the idea of a two-way cultural interaction, introduces a similar concept to Morris of assimilation.

For Miller, assimilation is not a 'dominant set of meanings grabbing and devouring meaning introduced from a foreign source', where a text has little or no meaning or is affecting the indigenous culture, but one where 'both partners in the act of assimilation have something to say about the transaction' (ibid.: 10). Miller is suggesting that there is a form of interaction between the foreign and the domestic culture; between meanings within the text, and the way it is consumed and understood within the other culture, such that, while hegemonic forces might have encoded the text in one cultural situation, and similar forces are at work in another cultural context trying to impose a reading, forms of negotiation occur over meaning and possible alternatives can also be found within the text (ibid.: 10, 181).

However, Miller accepts that such a view, while dynamic, is rather hard to study. He suggests therefore that the complex interaction of cultures can be approached by way of the concept of 'reading formations' (Bennett and Woollacott, 1987). Such a concept allows a dynamic way of understanding the way a text and audience interact; indeed, it suggests that they are not separable. Meaning does not reside in the text or with the audience; it comes, however, from how these two work together within particular concrete historical contexts. Therefore, to approach the study of the way television programmes become part of another cultures television system requires an understanding of, 'part of a complex relationships between text and audience defined by specific and determinant elements of the histories and cultures' of the society in question (Miller, 2000: 12).

The models offered by Morris and Miller provide dynamic views of assimilation, of how existing cultures incorporate cultural imports, of how they select and assimilate them in an active way – they are not imposed. All cultures change, otherwise they become stale but, at the same time, they are not swept away by new imported cultures; deep structures are already present giving meaning to these new imports. These models allow a move away from crude views of cultural effects or domination, of the imposition of one culture on the other, while still accepting that change does happen. Likewise meaning is not just the result of how a text is read; some form of interaction is occurring between the cultural import and the pre-existing culture. As Morris notes, 'This feedback loop allows newly incorporated elements from external sources eventually to become part of established cultural traditions and thus part of the cultural "deep structure"' (2002: 282).

While the way audiences consume, make sense of and respond to programmes, whether indigenous or acquired, has been fairly well researched, the role of broadcasters has been less so (Ellis, 2002: 132–3). They stand at the point of entry and exit from the system, they mediate between systems, mixing and matching acquired and commissioned programmes to create a schedule; in a sense they assimilate the external programmes into the national television culture. They make 'decisions based on their understanding of domestic audiences, channel requirements, scheduling practices and the prevailing television environment' (Steemers, 2004: 18). Through marketing and promotion, they create a pre-image of the programme, of how they would like the critics and audiences to understand the programme. Broadcasters, sharing the deep cultural structure with the rest of society, come to create 'surface structures', which are then consumed by the audience(s); they change and adapt the imports into a form more apt for that cultural context. I will now look at how we can conceptualise the role of broadcasters as active assimilators.

1.3.3　Active assimilators

As noted above, it must be accepted that no cultural community is hermetically sealed; cultural products leave and enter all cultural systems. In relation to the television medium, personnel, investment, programmes, formats and ideas 'flow' in and out of the national system. Likewise, we must accept that programmes are not consumed in isolation; they are merged with the television output of the channels operating in that society, and as they do so they become part of the televisual culture of that particular nation. 'Industrial, institutional and cultural conditions peculiar to each territory and the way life is lived and how television is presented to the public therefore affect the circulation of overseas programmes even before issues of audience reception and how the audience is constituted can be considered' (Steemers, 2004: 18). When imported programmes are shown as part of the schedule they might become part of people's lives, they will become part of the deep cultural structures, as a form of reconfiguration occurs. For example, *Starsky and*

Hutch, with its success in the 1970s with millions viewing it each week, has now become part of British (television) culture. Most middle-aged people remember as children watching it on television.

Playing a key role in buying in programmes from other systems, and shaping them for the needs of the schedules and audiences, are the broadcasters; they buy, commission, select and schedule, market and promote programmes. In many ways they act as professional decoders and encoders. They are an audience, a professional audience, who watch or, if it is only a pitch or script, imagine the 'text' – the television programme; they, in a sense, decode them, culturally, economically and professionally, as they seek to understand their economic and cultural worth to the channel. They are able, as they share the cultural deep structures with the rest of society, to choose programmes that they know will probably be accepted and become popular. They are the point in the process where decisions are made about buying programmes.

Once a programme is purchased, the decision of how to actually use it arises. Broadcasters will, through their actions, come to encode these imports; this they might do by editing a programme and then by placing it within a particular place within a larger text, the supertext or schedule, they will also seek to market the programme in a particular way to a target audience, in this way any preferred meaning or narratives structure encoded within them at the time of initial production will be altered or reinforced. Broadcasters try, using their understanding of the shared deep cultural structures of that society, to shape the surface structures of such programmes so that they will be understood and assimilated by the wider audience. Perhaps, it would be more helpful to think of this process as a number of steps, one of ongoing adaptation and change directed by the needs of the medium and the social and cultural context. A text, in this way, while having certain characteristics or dispositions, a certain form, which have been structured into it in its initial production phase, can be altered or changed at other stages (Hall, 1996).

In this way, by understanding how British broadcasters and broadcasting assimilate non-indigenous programmes into the scheduler, we can begin to explore the dialogue that has existed between American and British television cultures for the last fifty years or so. Such an approach will help us understand the way the national schedule is constructed and how any 'imported show is inserted into this context of scheduling and its cultural identity is significantly altered as a result' (Ellis, 2000: 36). It allows an approach that can understand television both as a national and as an international activity, an activity that involves not discrete complete texts but texts that are unfinished, that are temporarily fixed and encoded for and by national broadcasters working in particular contexts.

1.3.4   The broadcasting text: Flows and schedules

While a concept of active mediators allows a way of conceptualising the role of broadcaster in a dialogue between different broadcasting systems, and different cultures, there is also a need to develop a more detailed understanding of how programmes and films work as part of the national schedule, how they become part of and interact with, what some have called, the television flow – the real output of broadcast television. One place we can start to consider this idea is with the work of those such as Williams (1979) and Ellis (1982, 2000, 2002). They suggest that broadcast television is not simply a sequence of discreet programmes but, instead, it is a temporal flow; one in which different types of narrative flows exist within and between programmes, trailers, adverts and channels.

Raymond Williams, in Chapter four of his intriguing book *Television: Technology and Cultural Form* mentions his, now infamous, experiences of watching television in a motel room in America (1979: 91–2). Through such an experience he reflects on the way the temporal flow of television is both constructed and experienced. In Britain, he suggests, at least for a time, television output was composed of discreet text, those with identifiable starts and finishes; indeed, this notion is maintained by the way programmes are listed in TV guides and by how many still refer to individual programmes. It is a useful organising device. However, in America he experienced a form of television where, on screen and in his mind, programmes were cut apart by trailers, advert breaks and announcements. Such that these different 'text' begin to merge to form a flow of narratives; a flow of images and sounds which do not sit easily with the notion of discreet text; indeed, while the programme guides and critics talk of specific programmes, there is another powerful organising process at work, one that shapes the programmes to the rhythms and needs of the schedule; 'it is a flow series of differently related units in which timing, though real, is undeclared, and in which the real internal organisation is something other than the declared organisation' (ibid.: 93). Indeed, many years later, one notable Italian film, *The Icicle Thief* (Dir. Maurizio Nichetti, 1989), uses this idea to great effect as it highlights the increasing commercialisation happening in Italian television in the 1980s; characters in the programmes and surrounding adverts find themselves, because of the new fast commercial rhythm of

Italian television, slipping out of their programmes and adverts and into those around them.

John Ellis, writing in his seminal work, *Visible Fictions*, takes up the concept of flow in a number of places (1982: 111–26, 127–44, 145–59). Ellis, while acknowledging Williams's contribution to the debate about flow, criticises him for holding to a notion of 'cinema-style texts which appear in a context that reduces their separation one from another' (ibid.: 118). He suggests that broadcast television is more complex than this. While at one level, the flow is made up of advertised text cut apart by adverts, trailers and interruptions, at another level other forms of organisation are at work: segmentation. Television works narratively in a different way to cinema. Television audiences do not elect to watch, to gaze at the screen, so much as glance at it; this is a medium of the everyday, not an event like cinema. Its mode of production, therefore, works to attract and re-attract the attention of the viewer, a viewer who might glance occasionally. It needs to create a form understandable for these glances. The main unit, therefore, of the television flow is not the programmes, but the segment. These segments make 'extensive use of standard-length, programme building blocks consisting of several shots but sustaining a focus on the same action and setting' (Corner, 1999: 65).

These segments, which could be adverts, scenes within a programme or even whole programmes, depending on the circumstances, are short 'coherent pieces of dramatic, instructional, exhortatory, fictional, or documentary material' (Ellis, 1982: 122). There is no necessary link between them. Television does not depend on the forward narrative movement that exists within film; it depends instead on repetition, on images and sound, on the detail, on the close-up – segments provide this. However, providing some coherence, at another level, are the programme forms of series and serials, '[t]he recognition of the series format tends to hold segments together and to provide them with an element of continuity and narrative progression from one to the next' (ibid.: 147).

Such work by Williams, Ellis and others has been criticised in an interesting chapter in John Corner's book *Critical Ideas in Television Studies* (1999). Corner's work explores a range of work by Williams (1979), Ellis (1982), Modleski (1983), Fiske (1987), Dienst (1994), Jensen (1995) Gripsrud (1997), Ridell (1996) and Heath (1990), who have used the concept of flow in disparate ways; as flows of programmes between nations, flows as experience, flows as disorientating or 'some kind of politically suspect meta-meaning' (Corner, 1999: 69) and flows of everyday domestic life. He suggests that this work, defining flow in different ways, undermines the concept's usefulness. Such that, in conclusion, he suggests that 'rich though the phenomena are which it has been used to explore, it would be best if its legacy of confusion were not allowed to cause any further problems for television theory...its rehabilitation would be a bold, perhaps imprudent, project' (ibid.). I would like to argue here that while confusion might exist around this concept, that it might have been used in variety of ways, it does not lessen the need for an approach that can focus on the way television programmes and schedules are constructed, how television exists in its broadcast form, how this has changed over time and how it is experienced. Only by doing this can we start to explore how programme texts from different national sources are assimilated into a national schedule.

For Corner, Williams's work has three main problems: an overall focus on the analysis of the internal aspects of the programmes rather than on that between programmes; too much concentration on news; and, finally, he 'does not exemplify just how "the flow of meaning and values of a specific culture" (1979: 118) is managed by television' (Corner, 1999: 64). These criticisms seem less to be a criticism of the concept of flow, or the need for an understanding of the way programmes work within a schedule or supertext, than the focus and detail provided by Williams. Because Williams does not analyse the flow proper, concentrating mostly on news, and does not explore the way television manages the 'flow of meaning and values of a specific culture' (1979: 118), does not mean that this could not be done. Ellis, in some ways, helps answer some of these problems. For example, he develops a way of exploring, in some depth, the nature of television as a constructed flow; unlike Williams he does not see an undifferentiated flow, with everything becoming like everything else, where all sorts of texts are mixed up together (Ellis, 1982), instead he suggests the idea of moments of coherency within the flow; he suggests that television produces its text in a particular way, using the segment as the main unit. However, for Corner, some of Ellis's criticisms of Williams, for example Ellis accuses Williams of 'working with a model of the "cinema-style" text', do not hold up with reference to Williams's work (Corner, 1999: 65).

Perhaps, more usefully, we should think of television as a mixture of different forms and processes working in a variety of ways at several levels, often in tension. So, for example, there will be moments when broadcasters, critics and audiences will view, engage with, experience and understand television in terms of identifiable text, being able to forget or ignore much of the material around them; there will be other moments when it will be experienced, watched, understood and organised in terms of a segmented flow, where there will be smaller moments of coherency, or, at other times, where television will act and be experienced more as a flow, with few moments of identifiable coherency at the level of the programme or segment.

Nick Browne offers a number of concepts that are useful in providing a clearer understanding of the different levels at work, as well as a method of approaching the study of the television output: the megatext, supertext and the text. While the megatext as a concept, might seem too wide, referring to 'everything that has appeared on television' (1984: 177), it can be more practically undertaken by the analysis of the 'history, logic and form' of the television schedule (Gripsrud, 1995: 131). This allows a way of understanding the way television develops and works in specific national contexts over time, and the changing conventions and relationships between different channels. The supertext refers to 'the particular program and all the introductory and interstitial material – chiefly announcements and ads – considered in its specific position in the schedule' (Browne, 1984: 176). The concept of the supertext allows an understanding of how the text is subsumed into the larger output of television for which it is produced and shaped; it allows a study of the way such programmes react horizontally with each other. For Browne, such an analysis of the supertext requires at least at first a distinction, however problematic, between the text and the surrounding material. The text is still a useful concept as it allows the study of how the produced programme is constructed, of identifying 'the traces of flow, segmentalization, and the cultural forum' (Waller, 1988: 60) of the original broadcasting context for which it was produced; it will allow the study of the 'relations that exist across television...the paradigmatic dimension of the text...as a particular instance of a television format' (ibid.: 61). While Browne notes the problems of doing this, when the text is 'apt to be broken at any moment by an ad or a turn of the dial' (p. 176), Gripsrud feels that '[t]his can clearly be done' (Gripsrud, 1995: 131). The text, in this way, can be, with the stripping away of the surrounding elements, identified; what is left is the program proper. However, a television text is only experienced within the supertext – if watched outside of this it is not part of the television medium, it is a DVD or a video text. Programmes, by their nature, are designed with the flow in mind. The flow, in turn, is constructed to make the most of the programme.

Therefore to understand the role of American programmes on British screens requires an approach that can take account of the interaction and relationships that occur between these three levels. In the first instance, British broadcasters might well change the American text, for example they might edit it. Likewise, the American programme will be shown within a British supertext, one with which it might interact dynamically creating different and new meanings and experiences. Also, the supertext or television schedule exists within a larger national context and history, which has its own practices, conventions, regulation and ways of working, which might affect the way an American programme is used and experienced. As Ellis notes:

> [T]he factors that make every nation's television specific are...not just to do with individual quirks...so much as with the architecture of the entire output. As such, they are not easily amenable to the traditional forms of content analysis which privilege the systems of particular texts. Instead, they are produced and reproduced within the dynamic process of scheduling. (2000: 36)

1.4　Conclusion

This chapter began with an exploration of the main discourses that have played an important role in how American culture, of which television programmes are one part, has been viewed within Britain. Much of this discourse has been fearful that this 'shinny' American culture would, over time, erode British culture. While more detailed and sociological work began to appear from the 1960s which sought to analyse the possible impact of American culture on indigenous cultures, there were still echoes of these earlier debates. One line of work, which developed at the macro level, measured the international flow of programmes. The results of these studies seemed to confirm the view that American programmes were dominating this international trade (Nordenstreng and Varis, 1974). For some this meant that a form of media or cultural imperialism was at work and that, therefore, American culture was eroding and subjugating other indigenous cultures (Schiller, 1969).

Another approach, developing in the 1980s, turned towards studying the way people actually watch, read and consume television programmes. This work suggested both that text were polysemic, with many different meanings, and that audiences are active in how they read them (Katz and Liebes, 1986). Therefore, if the audience is more active in how it reads and makes sense of a text, and if a text has many means, it would seem that the fears of the imposition of an American culture on another was misplaced. The question, therefore, was not what are the effects of American programmes on an audience, than, how does an audience read and understand such a text in that particular social situation?

However, some have argued that both views, by dismissing the concerns of the other, were weakened (Schlesinger, 1991: 149); that there was a need for those taking a macro view, of programme flows, to think more about how the programmes were actually used within the national schedule and watched by the audience; likewise those interested in audiences had to understand that while audiences were active, there was still a need to acknowledge that the programmes on offer might be dominated by the output of a certain nation; an output that might tend to present a certain set of values or views of the world. It would seem that there is a need for a more complex understanding of the trade in programmes, how and why particular programmes are selected, how they are changed as they are used in a new context and how they are framed for an audience.

Therefore, in the last section of this chapter, using work by those such as Morris (2002), Miller (2000) and Browne (1984), I outlined a possible approach for exploring this meso level, one situated between the macro studies of flows of programmes and the micro studies on the consumption of programmes by audiences. Drawing on such work I propose to use the broadcaster, a key actor in the dialogue between the American and the British television environments, to explore how and why programmes are bought and how they are used; these are actors that are able to shed light on the workings of this cultural industry, they are also active mediators who make important decisions. It is they that sit between the wider economic, cultural, political and social forces and the actual operations of broadcasting. By using concepts of text, supertext and megatext, we can then study, in detail, how such programmes have been used over time, across different channels and within the schedule itself; indeed, we can study how American programmes interact with and are changed by their insertion in the British supertext. As Morris and Miller both note, perhaps the way to conceptualise the way cultures interact is by way of active assimilation, such that when a programme enters another cultural context it is both changed by and impacts on that culture as it is assimilated; neither culture is completely powerless or dominant in such an interaction. Before I move on to study these processes in more detail I will, in the next chapter, begin by exploring the existing historical narratives about American programmes on British screens.

2
Re-evaluating British Television History: From *I Love Lucy* to *Desperate Housewives*

2.1 Introduction

Many histories of British broadcasting have been written over the years. Some have been scholarly works running in some cases to a number of volumes, for example the official history of the BBC by Asa Briggs (1961, 1965, 1970, 1979, 1995: Vols I–V), while others have been single volume affairs often focusing on the history of particular organisations, such as the BBC or ITV, or exploring specific periods or themes (for example, Scannell and Cardiff's *Social History of British Broadcasting*, 1991). More popular histories have also appeared, often written by those with direct experience of working in the industry, for example by Peter Black (1972, 1973). Such histories, while focused on British broadcasting also, by extension, touch on, in different ways, the role and use of American programmes on British screens. However, as I argue below, the coverage of American programmes has not been the main focus of the above-mentioned work, and therefore there has been little attempt to fully explore the complexity and detail of its changing use and role on British television.

If one looks through the various histories covering the area, it becomes clear that their main focus is on the workings of the indigenous British broadcasting system and its output; the moments it touches on the role of American imports, or on contacts or comparisons between different national systems, are infrequent. While there are moments when such accounts do highlight the role and importance of American imports, they are usually through particular discourses, for example fears around Americanisation, social concerns about violent or sexual content or the wish to protect British jobs. For Michele Hilmes, part of the reason for this lies with broadcasting, in nations like Britain, historically being engaged in 'the task of national unification, definition and dissemination of a national culture and defence against the inroads of other nations...' (2003a: 1). This focus is duplicated in the main histories of British television. It would seem that the dominant way of understanding and evaluating television as a form of cultural production is in terms of the importance of domestic programme production and its role in the creation and sustenance of the national culture. The more industrial and business parts of broadcasting, including buying programmes and constructing schedules, of creating national schedules of programmes from a number of sources, including America, have tended to be downplayed.

This is not, however, to suggest that no detailed work has appeared. For example, while not broadcasting histories in the pure sense, in Segrave's (1998) *American Television Abroad: Hollywood's Attempt to Dominate World Television*, there are a number of chapters which focus on the way Hollywood has since the 1950s sold its television programmes to British broadcasters; Geoffrey Lealand's work (1984), has studied the way American programmes became part of the television output of British broadcasts and how they were consumed by British audiences; and Steemers's (2004) *Selling Television*, where she looks at the way British programmes are sold overseas. There are also a number of more theoretical works that have, increasingly, looked at American programmes from a more British perspective; for example, Osgerby and Gough-Yates (2001), Janet Thumin (2002), and Davis and Dickinson (2004). However, these works often focus on a particular text or genre and their consumption by audiences, with less interest in how or why they are scheduled by British broadcasters.

In this chapter, by collating and drawing on disparate references in existing histories, and other secondary work and primary resources, I will re-evaluate the role of American programmes on British television. Such a diachronic overview will provide some form of context for some of the following chapters with their more synchronic focus. Throughout, I will remember the way all histories, including the one presented here, are constructed through narratives. As Michele Hilmes notes, '[w]e cannot get at the past except through narratives or accounts of some sort, and even the historians who construct these histories must rely on some kind of preserved traces of the past, themselves usually constructed or written in some way' (2003a: vii). Therefore, throughout this chapter, I will highlight the various ways that such histories have written about American programmes; the way such narratives tend to highlight certain themes, developments, fears, relationships and values, while omitting others – narratives that tell us something about the concerns of the time written about as well as those of the time when the histories were written.

2.2   Historical coverage of American programmes and television

When one surveys the major and minor historical works focusing on British television, it is evident that there are many different types which focus on an array of different aspects and themes – including the political, technological, economic, social, institutional, cultural and creative aspects of broadcasting. It is also apparent, as noted above, that there are few that focus primarily on the role of American programmes on British screens. With that point taken, I would also like to argue that, within the plethora of published historical works, there is a paucity of references to or analysis of American programmes and their uses within British broadcasting. This can be illuminated by, in a not very scientific approach I admit, looking through the index pages of the official histories of the BBC and ITV written, respectively, by Asa Briggs (1961, 1965, 1970, 1979, 1995: Vols I–V) (soon to be continued by Jean Seaton) and Bernard Sendall (1982, 1983: Vols 1–2) (and, in later volumes, Jeremy Potter [1989, 1990: Vols 3–4], Paul Bonner and Lesely Aston [1998, 2003: Vols 5–6]). For example, in Volume V of Asa Briggs' work on the BBC (1995), there are some four thousand terms referenced in the index, whereas only a hundred of these could be associated in some way with American television or its programmes. If one looks at the number of American programmes mentioned, one notices, first, the absence of some prominent programmes and, secondly, that when they are noted in the index, the lack of multiple references. For example, *M*A*S*H, Star Trek* and *Perry Mason*, which were popular long-running shows in Britain, have only one reference each, often limited to one page only. This compares with British shows, such as *Dr Who, Z Cars, Steptoe and Son* and *It's a Square World*, which have multiple references to a number of pages (ibid.: 416–37).

If one actually looks at the coverage American programmes do receive in the text, they often appear only as name checks, as part of a programme list and, occasionally, for the more well-known works such as *I Love Lucy*, with small descriptions or anecdotes. For example, in Briggs (1995), where he refers to the popular American show *I Love Lucy*, it is just to mention that it was to have, as he puts it, 'as prosperous a British future as it already had an American past' (ibid.: 21). In a similar way, Sendall, in Volume 1 of his history of ITV, makes only three minor references to *I Love Lucy* whose star, Lucille Ball, was to become 'a fixture on...ITV or BBC for many years to come' (1982: 322). Where they do touch on such imports, in more detail, it is mostly when dealing with debates about quotas or their presumed societal effects (Sendall, 1983: 98–102). For example, in Volume IV of Briggs's history of the BBC, many of the references to American broadcasters are framed within debates about Americanisation (1979: 430–1, 472, 719) or commercial broadcasting (ibid.: 35, 37, 48, 52, 430, 893–4).

Beyond the official histories, many others have also presented historical accounts and analyses of British broadcasting over the years; for example, work by Ralph Negrine (1994), Kevin Williams (1998), Andrew Crisell (1997), James Curran and Jean Seaton (1997) and Colin Seymour-Ure (1993). If one looks in detail at these works, it is evident that American programmes are not the main focus. Within Crisell's (1997) work, an overview of the development of British broadcasting from radio to television, there are forty or so references out of thousand that could be construed as relating to American television or its programmes. References to specific American programmes appear rarely, six in terms of named television programmes. American programmes that often topped the ratings, that were often the leading draws of their time, that stayed on the screens for years if not decades, and that were economically vital for maintaining the health of British broadcasting are often only covered as footnotes – if at all.

If one focuses on the more popular histories, some of which have been produced by those that worked in the industry, or associated industries, sometimes in the form of autobiographies, the situation is similar. Peter Black, who worked as the television critic of *The Daily Mail* in the 1950s and 1960s, produced two volumes – *The Mirror in the Corner* (1973) and *The Biggest Aspidistra in the World* (1972), the former about the coming of television in Britain and the latter about a personal celebration of fifty years of the BBC. Throughout these works, there are a fair number of references to America, its system, personnel and programmes, but they are usually employed as part of wider debates about aspects of British television and British programmes, rather than as the main focus of attention. For example, Black talks about how the turn towards producing television series by the BBC, in particular *Z Cars*, was partly 'a straightforward adaptation of American techniques as displayed in the Hollywood film series, such as *Bonanza*' (ibid.: 211). This is the same for many of the other work written by those who worked in the industry. American programmes are mentioned, there is interest and a concern, but there is little concerted analysis of their role in British television.

It might be argued that these works, sometimes covering between fifty and eighty years of broadcasting history, with a primary focus on the British broadcasting context, have little space to touch on such extraneous programmes and issues in much detail; this is true. But it does still raise the question of why, over the range of work that exists, there is so little analysis of the role of such imports – imports that have been of economic and cultural importance for the system over many years, and that are ingrained in most people's memories of watching television in Britain – and the way they have influenced British television production and scheduling practices. It is as if domestically made programmes are British television while American programmes, mere interlopers. Where they are mentioned, it is part of particular discourses that tend to view television and American culture in certain ways: with programme production lying at the heart of creativity in television and America signifying the 'other', that which is alien to British television. American productions are viewed almost with suspicion, unable to bring anything of value to British television or British culture.

To help bring some clarity to the following overview, I will divide it into three: I will begin by focusing on the extension of the BBC's monopoly to television and the coming of ITV (pre-war till the Pilkington report), before looking at the duopoly (late 1960s till the early 1980s) and the age of plenty (mid-1980s till the 1990s). While I have made these analytical divisions using accepted notions of change in British broadcasting, see for example Ellis (2002), it must be noted that, in reality, the way American programmes have been used, the way British broadcasting has developed and the debates which have arisen over time tend to spill out of such divisions.

2.3   Historical re-evaluation

In this overview, I will be exploring the developing relationship between the American and the British television systems, the debates about American television and American programmes and their differing uses on British television. This I will do by re-evaluating existing coverage and reassembling this in a narrative more focused around the role of American programmes, while also reflecting on how such histories have tended to cover such issues. This should not be viewed as an exhaustive history but should be treated as a contextualising chapter, a way of understanding the main economic, political, social and cultural developments affecting broadcasting over the last fifty years.

2.3.1 The television monopoly and the coming of ITV

In the 1930s as developments in television became more strident, the BBC argued that it was the natural home for this new broadcast medium. The government, in response, set up the Selsdon committee in 1934 to consider who should run television. The committee, as others would in the future, looked abroad, including to America, for examples of how television was being developed by international rivals (Briggs, 1965: 583). The development of television was not just a question of cultural production but industrial and technological developments and international rivalry; British television developments were seen as being as advanced as America's, and others in the field. The question was, How to keep this advantage? With the support of the Selsdon committee's report in 1935, the BBC was able to consolidate its control over television and in 1936 started the world's first high definition television service (ibid.: 582–622). The BBC, a national public service broadcaster, was confirmed as the proper authority to develop and protect this new national resource in a similar way that it had for radio. Indeed, according to Briggs, its successful start before the war had led to 'not only the first regular television service but also the best television service in the world between 1938 and 1939. The United States was well behind' (ibid.: 621–2).

In 1943, the Hankey committee was set up to consider television's development after the war. It concluded in 1944 that 'the future public television service should be entrusted to the BBC as the sound broadcasting authority' (Briggs, 1979: 180). Though, it must be noted, Hankey did listen and take account of arguments that sponsorship, as developed in nations such as America, offered another possible way of organising television (ibid.: 182). Developments in America, and fear over the extension of commercial broadcasting in Europe, played an important role in the evidence collected by the committee. In this embryonic period the concern was less over direct American programme imports than the competitive advantage that the American television industry might gain in the post-war world, including, what everyone would hope would be, the newly liberated Europe and the possible effect of allowing the development of a commercial form of broadcasting within Britain (ibid.: 184–5).

In 1946, the BBC re-started its television service with the very same *Mickey Mouse* cartoon it had ended pre-war transmissions with (ibid.: 197). While many felt that the BBC's monopoly over television and radio was secure, a debate was again (re-) surfacing in the late 1940s about whether this should change. While the Beveridge Report of 1951 more or less backed the BBC maintaining its monopoly, this did not placate all. Indeed, a minority report was produced by Selwyn Lloyd, which argued for the introduction of commercial radio and television (ibid.: 389–90). A number of MPs, supported by the entertainment industry, manufacturers, such as Pye Radio, and advertisers, such as J. Walter Thompson, pressured for change (Jenkins, 1961: 17–19; Thomas, 1977: 33; Curran and Seaton, 1997: 162). They saw a need to break the BBC's monopoly to allow the quick development of television, both to appease audiences and to support British industry. One group, increasingly eager for the development of a more commercial broadcasting system, were the powerful advertising agencies, some of which were American or had American linkages (Briggs, 1979: 366). Manufacturers and advertisers were aware that to help sell their goods advertising on radio and television would be essential; this became more important for such groups as Britain began to experience a consumer boom in the mid-fifties. However, some viewed the role of American advertising companies with some suspicion, seeing their role as an attempt to open British society to a more American-styled commercial culture (Christopher Mayhew cited in Jenkins, 1961: 19).

It would seem that much of the debate that arose in the forties and early fifties was informed by what had and was happening in America – the paradigm of commercial broadcasting (Hilmes, 2003a: 2); indeed, for some it was the vision of what would happen to British broadcasting unless carefully regulated and controlled (Seymour-Ure, 1993: 68). Throughout this period politicians and broadcasters alike went across the Atlantic to witness how commercial broadcasting was operating in the United States. Beveridge, for example, sent 'pairs' of committee members to the United States on fact-finding missions (Briggs, 1979: 204–5). Many did not like what they saw, or heard about third hand (Sendall, 1982: 15). Indeed, the debates about commercial broadcasting were fuelled by the 'way American commercial stations had covered the coronation' (ibid.: 19). The coronation in America had been interrupted by adverts featuring J. Fred Muggs, a chimpanzee, who, at one stage, was 'mockingly' crowned (Seymour-Ure, 1993: 121). Some were also worried about the lack of diversity on offer in America; for example, Earl Jowitt 'cites examples of eight stations in one US town all showing the same ball game' (Sendall, 1982: 49).

America, in this sense, was a mirror of what Britain might come to look like culturally if it succumbed to popular (American) culture (Beadle,

1963: 79). If some saw British culture as a distinct culture, a mixture of Arnold's sweetness and light with the authentic working-class culture that Hoggart describes, American culture was all that was crass and popular, pandering to the needs and desires of the masses; many critics, politicians and broadcasters feared this 'shiny barbarism' (Hoggart, 1957: 193). However, in the late forties and early fifties, with few American television imports on British television, and with the accepted low standard of many of these, the fear was less of a sudden direct influx of American television, than of the creation of an American-styled commercial broadcaster pandering to the lowest common denominator.

After a degree of political jockeying, and after a tightly fought debate, the government passed the Television Act of 1954. This allowed for the creation of a commercially funded channel but in a controlled, regulated form with public service responsibilities; in this way the commercial threat was supposedly contained. The Act set up a new authority, the Independent Television Authority (ITA), legally the broadcaster, which was to contract commercial firms on a regional basis to supply programmes and run the network; the channel, after some debate, was to be called Independent Television (ITV), though some disagreed that it could be independent if owned by private firms (Sendall, 1982: 38). The ITA was to oversee the network, to bring it into being and to make sure it followed the regulations outlined within the act (ibid.: 59–67). Commercial funding was to come from spot adverts clearly separated from the surrounding programmes; the dominant American form of sponsorship was spurned because it gave sponsors too much control over the programme's content (ibid.: 98–103) – though, throughout the 1950s and 1960s, there was a move in America towards spot advertisements as the dominant form (Boddy, 1993: 155–67). The concern expressed in debates about the television bill over the use of foreign films and programmes was to be settled by the ITA. According to Sendall (1982), there were three linked worries: the import of programmes 'from the much derided commercial TV stations in America'; 'to protect the jobs of British programme makers' and, lastly, to encourage the development of a British programme-making industry, 'capable of significant export earnings in the English-speaking world' (ibid.: 51). It was eventually agreed by the contractors and the ITA, by a gentlemen's agreement, that use of imports was to be limited to 14 per cent or below, a level that the BBC also came to follow (ibid.: 106–9).

In 1955, the first franchises of the new ITV network began broadcasting, initially only in the London area but this soon spread to the midlands and the north; in the regions early broadcasting included

Associated-Rediffusion, Associated-Television, ABC Television and Granada TV. Initially they 'copied much from the BBC and [were]... firmly attached to the notion of "improvement" in broadcasting' (Williams, 1998: 163). However, as a financial crisis began to grow, the different companies making up ITV started to move the so-called 'serious programmes' to off-peak periods and replace them with programmes more likely to attract an audience, replacements which included a number of American programmes (ibid.: 164; Sendall, 1982: 326–9). While it is true to say that the BBC had used some American material before the war, and had shown a limited number of American telefilms and series in the late forties and early fifties (for example, *Hopalong Cassidy* was being shown in the afternoon slot in the late forties, though it was to be shown in the evening slot in 1949 – the 'first Western that has ever been scheduled for an evening showing' [T6/144/ 1, 26 September 1949]), the amount that began to appear on ITV, after the initial hiatus, was something of a revelation; this shift in programme policy was driven, as Segrave notes, by the need to fill hours quickly, to attract audiences and advertisers while still constructing a production base. ITV companies, therefore, began to purchase and use a large number of filmed American series in prime-time slots (1998: 49–53); these were, however, scheduled with a mix of popular and more serious domestic productions.

The ability of ITV, and later the BBC, to buy such programmes was the result of changes in the American television system. Increasingly, with attempts by the US networks to create a more commercially orientated television system new types of programmes began to appear (Boddy, 1993). Increasingly, after some initial teething problems, the studios and independent producers started to produce programmes more suited to the needs of the networks; these were mostly long-running series, often up to thirty episodes per season (Cantor, 1971: 16) which, with a sustained presence on the screens, were able to build audiences over a long period of time, a feature which many of the shorter British series or one-off plays could not duplicate. With their costs covered in the United States and being shot on film, these series could be sold on to other broadcasters and at a price that undercut local productions; this was a source of revenue quickly exploited by American networks and distributors.

As Briggs and Sendall both highlight, within a year American programmes came to dominate the top-twenty rating chart for London, ITV's initial area of operation, for example *Dragnet, Gun Law* (a.k.a. *Gunsmoke*), *Frontier Doctor, Fairbanks Presents* (an NBC-commissioned programme made in the UK) and *Assignment Foreign Legion* (Harbord and Wright, 1992: 11). These imports were programmes that large numbers of viewers chose to watch, where they had the choice, and which the BBC and ITV found hard to produce themselves; for example, 'British television could produce nothing to approach them [American comedy shows] for style or suitability to television' (Goddard, 1991: 75–89). As research showed in 1958, many people numbered American-commercial styled shows as their favourite, 'men gave their highest preferences to sport, plays, news, travel, variety, documentaries, *westerns* and current affairs... Women put plays, news and *quizzes* top... Young people were more interested in films, *crime* and *quizzes* than their elder' (emphasis added in the original – Seymour-Ure, 1993: 156).

The American programmes acquired by ITV, and initially in smaller numbers by the BBC, were mostly American comedies and crime and Western series; these latter programmes were long-running episodic series made with high production values, often re-utilising stories and characters made famous by Hollywood, in a style that fuelled the imaginations of viewers. These American programmes offered a glimpse of a consumerist future, an escape from the last days of the empire and the austerity of post-war Britain; these were a cultural form increasingly sought by the youth of the day and large numbers of the working classes (Hoggart, 1957).

These programmes were designed for commercial scheduling techniques. As a CBS report noted in 1950,

> they can be scheduled at times that are best for their own maximum growth; and once established, they can be held at strategic points throughout the week's schedule, in time-periods that then become 'anchor-points' in the winning of a great network audience. Carefully placed throughout the schedule, these anchor-points naturally attract other audience-seeking programs. (Cited in Boddy, 1993: 95)

They were formulaic, so viewers would know what they would be watching in advance, though the story would be different each week; and were made in huge numbers, compared to most British shows. Because they could occupy the same slot for a considerable amount of time, and were of regular lengths, broadcasters were able to use them to build schedules with a regularity in them; viewers would eventually become used to where to find them in the schedule; these programmes offered a known quality, unlike one-off plays; they could be used, alongside similar programmes, to attract and keep audiences over the evening. The commercial type of scheduling, increasingly adopted by ITV (Sendall, 1982: 325), ran contrary to the BBC's traditional practice of making different length programmes, making them few in number and placing them in juxtaposition with different types of programmes; often the BBC would even fill gaps between programmes with the infamous potter's wheel. The BBC, it would seem, were not making the most of their programmes (ibid.).

However, it must be noted that the use of imports was not solely the preserve of ITV; to compete, the BBC began to increase the number of American comedy, police and Western series it was acquiring (Segrave, 1998: 27). Sendall illustrates this when he compares a similar week of programme schedules of the BBC and ITV, showing that the BBC screened only slightly less American material than ITV, the opposite to how some on the Pilkington Committee would view the situation (Sendall, 1983: 98–100). By looking at figures provided in a BBC report of the time, it can be seen that their use of American imports had been increasing from the end of the 1950s and into the 1960s to similar levels of usage as ITV: 10.07 per cent in 1957, 11 per cent in 1958, 10.02 per cent in 1959, 10.96 per cent in 1960, 13.06 per cent in 1961, 12.49 per cent in 1962, 12.86 per cent in 1963 and 12.08 per cent (BBC1) and 12.15 per cent (BBC2) in 1964 (T16/29S, 15 January 1965). Indeed, in the early 1960s it was *Dr. Kildare*, a US import, which was the most watched BBC programme (December 1961 and January 1962; Harbord and Wright, 1992: 128–9).

Accompanying the rising popularity of ITV and the heightened profile of American programmes on both channels, there was increased public criticism. For some, the problem was inherent in commercial television, it was there to pander to the lowest common denominator, and the use of American programmes was the result of this; for others, there was a worry about certain genre, the crime series and Western, and their depiction of violence. The fact that most of these series were from America did not go unnoticed. For example, Sendall quotes from the *Darlington Northern Echo*, which criticised Tyne Tees, one of the ITV companies, over the use of American programmes, '[t]he company policy has been ... to give the public what it wants. This is the natural result of its commercial nature. The bulk of its time has been consequently devoted to American serials, give-away shows, variety and drama' which, it continued in another article, leads to 'a sense of unease' (cited in Sendall, 1982: 8). However, most were more critical of the general commercial nature of ITV, for example Briggs mentions the attacks led by *The Spectator and Manchester Guardian* in January 1956 (1995: 13). For many, as Briggs notes, 'commercial television continued in many minds to be identified with Americanization' (ibid.: 28). The worry was less about American programmes dominating British television than about the creation and effects of a commercialised television service.

Against the background of the increasing success of ITV, supposed problems of falling ratings at the BBC, the heated debates about ITV's reliance on too many popular programmes and its increased use of American imports, the government set up the Pilkington Committee in 1960 to examine the state of broadcasting. One of the main expected outcomes of the subsequent report would be the allocation of a third channel. Both ITV and the BBC had their own ideas of who should run such a channel and how it should be funded. The committee included one particular commentator on cultural matters, Richard Hoggart, who had, in his seminal work *Uses of Literacy* (1957), been critical of the incursion of American culture into Britain, something he referred to as 'shiny barbarism' (ibid.: 193). The committee heard many submissions of evidence from those arguing for the right of the public to watch what they wanted to those that thought the government should protect the public. *The Observer* chose at this time (1960) to publish a memorandum to the committee entitled *The Use of Television*, a play on the title of Hoggart's work, *Uses of Literacy*. It noted, among other things, that the top ten programmes for the week ending on 18 September 1960 was dominated by ITV companies, indeed there were no BBC programmes in the list. The American series *Riverboat* and *Cimarron City* came, respectively, 1st and 2nd, while another, *77 Sunset Strip* came 6th (*The Observer*, 1960).

The resulting committee's report vindicated the BBC and proposed that it should run the new channel, what would become BBC2. For ITV, however, it proposed substantial changes. The recommendations of the committee included the proposal that the ITA should run the network and commission the contractors for programmes (Briggs, 1995: 294–303). In this way, the committee hoped that the popular, and American, tendencies found currently in the system could be contained. Many were up in arms about the report. Maurice Wiggins, in an article entitled 'Going the Whole Hoggart' suggested that the attempt to 'make the ITA into another BBC [was] the hopeless last resort of men who fundamentally fear the operation of a free society' (*The Observer*, 1962). While the government took on some aspects of the report, for example the allocation of the third channel to the BBC, the drastic restructuring of ITV did not occur (Briggs, 1995: 303–8).

However, not all the references to American television and its relationship with British television are negative. Some works highlight the two-way nature of this relationship (Miller, 2000). For example, as American programmes introduced new types and forms of programmes to British audiences and broadcasters, and with the creation of new production facilities and the steady rise of advertising and licence revenues, programmes began to be produced that could, in some way, substitute for some of the imported programmes. For example, the format of *Z Cars*, a popular hit of the sixties, was, according to John McGrath, inspired by *Highway Patrol* (Laing, 1991: 127). Indeed, following on from the early success with *Robin Hood*, ATV, a British broadcaster, began to create American-styled series, partly aimed at the American market, that were successful on both sides of the Atlantic (often referred to as mid-Atlantic shows) (Caughie, 1991: 39), for example *The Avengers* and *Danger Man* (see Miller, 2000). Miller also argues that some of these British shows helped to innovate American programmes which, a decade later, came to dominate British screens, for example *The Forsyte Saga* feeding into *Dallas* (ibid.: 165–7). Such references illustrate how, early on, British television producers, like those in radio before them, saw the United States as a useful resource for programmes and programme ideas, some of which could successfully be assimilated into the British system – for good or for bad. Sendall also touches on another element in this relationship, the flow of personnel; for example, Rai Pundy, who worked at one stage for CBS NY, was then engaged as an executive producer at STV (1982: 207). For ITV, attracting commercial expertise was important to their success.

While it might be argued that the popularity of American programmes at this time was short-lived, the annual ratings for the period 1957–1964 give the impression that there were only a few huge American hits, for example *Wagon Train* and *Rawhide* (Harbord and Wright, 1992: 14–35); if one looks at schedules from the time one can see that ITV, the channel dominating the ratings in this period, was not networking all of its programmes, thus the regional popularity of some American shows was not always translated into national viewing figures. In some respects the true popularity, as expressed by ratings, was hidden by the way the system was operating at the time. However, as BBC and ITV geared up their production bases, as the initial public excitement of seeing American programmes waned and as ITV and the BBC, post-Pilkington, moved into a new relationship, often referred to as the duopoly, offering a mix of serious and popular domestic productions, the prominence of American programmes declined.

It must, however, be noted that while the histories about this period mention the popularity of American programmes and the success reflected in the rating charts for both the BBC and ITV, they do not suggest that British television was Americanised. Briggs, for example, mentions that 'British TV, however, remained essentially British, not American or Americanised. The top rated BBC programmes in the schedules for 1959 and 1960 were not American programmes but British ones, for example, *Hancock's Half Hour* and *Whack-O!*' (Harbord and Wright, 1992: 143). Most comedies were British, not American (Crisell, 1997: 96). American programmes might have played an important role but this has to be put in perspective, the BBC and ITV still produced most of the programmes they showed and, as television matured, as more money went into production and as they developed their creative skills, American programmes were increasingly substituted by British ones.

However, the financial stabilisation of ITV and the development of popular British series did not mean the end of American programmes on British screens but, instead, they began to take on new, less prominent roles. For example, as the number of hours broadcast increased from the 1950s onwards, with all government restrictions ending in 1972, American programmes began to be used to fill up the less popular outer reaches of the schedules (Potter, 1989: 70–1). Indeed, it is interesting to note that between the years 1965 and 1975 no US programmes appeared in the annual top-twenty rated programme charts; though, when American shows were shown in peak slots, they sometimes made the monthly charts; for example, *A Man Called Ironside* (a.k.a. *Ironside*) was one of the higher placed BBC programmes in the late sixties and early seventies (Harbord and Wright, 1992: 134–70). It would seem that as the system matured a balance was reached. British programmes dominated peak time, supported by some American shows to add something different to the schedule, while other American programmes were used to help fill up the increasing non-peak hours (Briggs, 1995: 952–3).

2.3.2 The duopoly: From economic despair to Dallas

The seventies was a volatile time for the UK, economically, socially and politically. After an early economic boom in the 1970s, with a sudden steep increase in oil prices the UK's economy went into recession; this would be a decade remembered for its strikes, unemployment, electricity cuts, petrol shortages and violence (Markwick, 1987: 188–91). It was a period when the United Kingdom seemed to polarise geographically and socially; it was a time of national tensions, with the troubles in Northern Ireland, developing nationalisms in Wales and Scotland and ideological clashes, between the right and the left. The swinging sixties, white heat of technology and rebirth of Britain after the fall of the empire were replaced by pictures of the government going cap in hand to the International Monetary Fund (IMF). Hyperinflation was eating into savings, unemployment was rising and workers were reacting by demanding large pay rises. 'Prices, on average, trebled during the 1970s' (Potter, 1989: 5).

While the 1970s, overall, were to be good to ITV, it started the decade with a downturn in its revenue (ibid.: 18–19); it was not helped by a decline in popularity as, from the late sixties, competition from BBC2 grew and the growth stemming from the roll-out of ITV coverage tailed off (ibid.: 18). While generally, throughout the 1970s, ITV's income grew, it was a period of rising costs. Most of the country got caught in a spiral of high inflation, wage claims, strikes and then higher inflation; the situation was no different at ITV. Costs for all types of television production were rising at an alarming rate, not helped by the switch to colour production. At times the cost of production was actually increasing faster than advertising revenue. The cost of drama production between 1975 and 1979 trebled (Potter, 1990: 221). This did not mean that ITV companies shied away from the production of such programmes, only that finding co-production partners or achieving a successful overseas sales was increasingly an important part of the picture (ibid.).

While at this time ITV might be viewed as storing up financial problems for another time, of having high wages and being generally overmanned, in many ways the seventies was a time when its reputation as a producer of good quality, serious programmes was established; indeed, for some, it seemed as if 'the BBC imported American soap operas to bolster its ratings while ITV took the lead in news and current affairs coverage' (Potter, 1989: 3). The contractors were spurred on to invest money in these rather expensive programmes because of a government levy, introduced in the 1960s due to the exceptional profits being made at that time. These programmes, if of the right sort, could then be sold abroad and any profits gained would not be liable to the levy – which was only paid on advertising turnover, not on profits gained elsewhere (ibid.: 30).

The BBC found the seventies less amenable, while its costs also increased its income proved to be less elastic. While it received a number of increases from the government in the licence fee, these were often late in coming and usually quickly undercut by high inflation. As Michael Swann remarked, 'we were forever either having just got an inadequate increase or preparing the ground to try to get another increase' (cited in Briggs, 1995: 1003). While there was some respite from financial pressures with the income generated from the increasing take up of colour licences, this would only last for so long – indeed, by 1986 saturation point was more or less reached (Graham and Davies, 1992: 204). The BBC was also not helped by ITV pushing up the going rate for labour and, in the early seventies, the abolition of restrictions on the broadcast day.

In 1972, the limit on the number of hours that could be broadcast each day was rescinded (Potter, 1989: 70–1). The ITV companies saw such developments positively. Such a move provided more time in which their non-networked programmes could be shown, as well as more time in which, importantly, advertising time could be sold. Indeed, as Potter points out, the '[s]hortage of airtime had now become more crucial than shortage of money' (ibid.: 30). However, the ITA were worried about how these extra hours would be filled, and therefore called a 'special meeting of their Television Safeguards Committee to air the implications of de-restriction in relation to the quota of foreign material and the number of feature films and programme repeats' (ibid.: 74). The existing limits would be maintained, 'adapted where appropriate, but not eroded' (ibid.: 72). The BBC, however, was more worried because of the financial burden more hours would place upon its stretched finances. As it was, the number of hours it broadcast did not increase immediately.

Throughout the early 1970s, American programmes, such as *Star Trek, High Chaparral, Kojak* and *Mission: Impossible*, continued to play an important, though often understated, role throughout the schedules of the BBC and ITV. Though, as Lealand notes, as competition increased between the BBC and ITV at the end of the 1970s, American programmes came to be used more frequently in peak-time slots, for example *Charlie's Angels, Hart to Hart, Dallas, The Six Million Dollar Man* and *Starsky and Hutch* (Lealand, 1984: 14). While these programmes were relatively cheap to buy (ibid.: 24), they were also proving themselves to be popular with audiences, often managing to appear in the annual and monthly top-twenty rating charts of that time. Indeed, for some of the months they were the most watched, for example *Dallas* was number one in April 1980, and, as Potter points out, *Starsky and Hutch* was attracting not only huge audiences, but was ranked high on the appreciation indexes (Potter, 1990: 141–2). For the BBC, the position was particularly striking, with American programmes providing their highest placing in the charts on some months. For example, in January 1978 *Starsky and Hutch* was 19th with 14.1 million viewers, the only BBC programme in the top-twenty for that month (Harbord and Wright,

1992: 145). For the BBC, this reliance on American material and domestic soaps and quizzes was brought on by a financial squeeze on its resources and increased competition with ITV (Lealand, 1984: 14; Williams, 1998: 172–3); ITV, however, while using some American imports, were more financially stable and generally had the more successful domestic programmes. For example, for the year 1978, on average, ITV programmes took 17 places of each monthly top-twenty programme chart (Harbord and Wright, 1992: 145).

It would seem that some American programmes of this time had a content, style, form and cultural cache that were popular with the mass audience – a popularity that is still evident by the continuing nostalgia of many for the American programmes of that time. While British productions of a similar genre were being made, for example *The Sweeny* and *The Professionals* were of the same police genre as *Starsky and Hutch*, these were neither as glossy and as fast-paced as the American programmes nor made in the huge numbers that gave them a sustained presence. For example, over 7 years only 57 episodes of *The Professionals* were made while over 5 years 92 episodes of *Starsky and Hutch* were produced (Cornell *et al.*, 1993: 259–60; <http://www.tv.com/starsky-and-hutch/show/81/episode_listings.html> accessed on 16 June 2005).

In many ways British producers and broadcasters were still caught up in a system that privileged serious programming – single-author texts, short serials and historical drama – often made in short runs with a form of realism that was not that appealing to mass audiences (Paterson, 1998: 59). While the single play had started the decade in a strong position, by the end it was in terminal decline; the drama series was increasingly viewed as 'the staple item of television fare' (Potter, 1990: 220–1). It could be argued that far from American shows being unable to compete against domestic equivalents, as some suggest, if given the right slot, they could (Paterson, 1998: 58).

By the end of the seventies, as the importance of US material in both ITV and BBC schedules grew, there was increased competition for sought-after films and television programmes (Potter, 1990: 299). Such imports were now playing a vital role, both in prime time and other periods, for both ITV and the BBC. Indeed, for Lealand, their role at this time was more important than in the 1950s, when they were shown not so much in prime-time but often in the early, pre-peak time slot (Lealand, 1984: 13–14). For ITV, 'programmes acquired from overseas accounted for some 15 per cent of each company's total output and included popular networked series from the USA' (Potter, 1990: 12). As Paul Bonner notes in relation to a public spat between Kevin Goldstein-Jackson and Granada over films and television acquisitions, such imports were seen as being important for the economic viability of ITV individual companies's programme schedules (Bonner and Aston, 1998: 31).

The growing competition between ITV and the BBC over such imports is illustrated by the battles over the rights to *Dallas*. *Dallas* was a prime-time soap that, for a number of years, was very successful, not just in Britain, where it was shown on the BBC, but around the world. It was as if *Dallas* came to signify not just a prime-time hit, which it was, but the increasing commercialisation and internationalisation of television. After its initial successful run on the BBC, attracting a regular audience of 13 million people (ibid.: 80), there was a need in 1981 to renegotiate the contract for *Dallas*. Many of the ITV executives understood that its scheduled slot, right in the middle of ITV's valuable network output, was costing them dear (ibid.). So, when negotiations began between the BBC and WorldVision, the owner of the programme rights, Bryan Cowgill (Managing Director of Thames) and Michael Grade (Programme Director of LWT) broke an unwritten agreement (soon to be put on paper after this event) that the BBC and ITV companies would not compete in a bidding war over the renewal of the rights to a programme (ibid.: 81–3).

The onscreen world of the corrupt and double-dealing *Dallas* oil family now seemed to have been replicated in the real world. ITV executives, worried at what this might mean for their own attempts to renegotiate American programme contracts, piled the pressure on Cowgill and Grade to give way. Initially they held firm but, eventually, they withdrew from the fray and the BBC renewed its commitment to *Dallas*. Five years later, the same tug of war over *Dallas* was staged again. This time Thames, one of the companies whose personnel sought previously to buy the rights, managed to buy them. The other ITV companies, along with the IBA, pressured Thames to give the rights back to the BBC. Eventually, in a humiliating climbdown, leading to the resignation of Bryan Cowgill, the rights were handed back to the BBC (ibid.: 97). Such a struggle over the rights for an American programme signalled, for some, the growing competitive tensions between ITV and the BBC. Such a public battle led some politicians – for example, the then Home Secretary, Leon Brittain – to question, 'why should a broadcasting service funded by a tax on the public... squander its resources in providing fare that is indistinguishable from the run of material provided by commercial Television' (cited in Williams, 1998: 173).

However, while prices for such programmes and films had been kept in check for some time, thanks to the BBC and ITV both agreeing not to compete for renewals of programmes, with such competition increasing between them, and with new competition appearing, this was changing. While the coming of Channel 4 (C4) in 1982, which used a number of American imports such as *Cheers*, fitted within the duopoly structure – ITV even acquired overseas programmes for C4 – other developments in cable and satellite television on the horizon would seem to herald the end of the comfortable duopoly, increasing demands for American programmes and, signalling, what some feared would be, the eventual domination of British screens with American-styled programmes: Wall-to-wall *Dallas* (ibid.: 243).

However, the relationship with American television, even in this period, which saw heavy use of imported programmes in prime time, was not just one way. For example, by the 1970s the larger ITV companies were managing to successfully sell a large number of their programmes abroad. Indeed, as Merlyn Rees noted in a speech in 1976, in the previous year ITV had exported £14 million, five times that of the costs of ITV's imports (cited in Potter, 1989: 262). Thames even took control of an American broadcaster's schedule for a week to showcase its programmes – though some American critics were not that enamoured (Potter, 1990: 67). Thames was also successful in this period in selling formats, mostly comedy, to American companies, including *George and Mildred* (Thames), which became *The Ropers*, and *Man About the House* (Thames), which became *Three's Company* in the United States (ibid.: 66; Steemers, 2004: 110). ITV companies were keen to develop different forms of overseas sales, as this revenue stream was not affected by the levy. However, for some companies, ATV in particular, making programmes tailored partly to the needs of the American market, was frowned upon. For the IBA, ATV's constituency was, first, its British audience (Potter, 1990: 39, 337) and, even though ATV had won the Queen's Award to Industry for Export Achievement in 1967, 1968 and 1971 (ibid.: 5), it was to find itself under attack during the 1980 franchise round due to its neglect of this region (ibid.: 336–44).

The historical narratives that cover this period, the late 1960s till the early 1980s, start with little coverage of American programmes but end with them in centre stage. While they were being used in the 1960s, there was less controversy because of the strength of domestic programmes. Only in the late 1970s and early 1980s, as certain American programmes began to be shown in peak times and attracted large audiences on both BBC and ITV, was there heightened coverage. Much of this is within discourses around violence (*A-Team* and *Starsky and Hutch*, for example) (Potter, 1989: 141), worry about their domination of the national viewing charts and an impending cultural invasion. Though, as Christopher Dunkley (1985) has argued, while the BBC and ITV were fuelling this fear of what would happen in the future, as they wanted to gain support from the government at this time, they were actually using large amounts of American programmes.

2.3.3 The age of plenty: The multi-channel environment

While the start of the eighties saw the introduction of a new terrestrial public service channel, C4, that complemented the existing duopoly system, it was to end with the creation of a new television provider, a powerful new satellite company, BSkyB, created from the merged Sky and BSB channels (Bonner and Aston, 2003: 432–4). Seemingly, the time of the relatively cosy duopoly that had existed between the BBC and ITV was ending, or at least was in crisis (Williams, 1998: 171–92). Throughout this period, as production costs continued to rise, as the number of hours broadcast increased, for some channels moving towards around-the-clock broadcasting, and as competition became more intense, American programmes yet again took on new roles. Increasingly, the main terrestrial channel came to rely less on American imports than on domestic productions. Some saw this shift related to the lack of suitable popular programmes to attract a mass audience as well as a realisation that domestic shows were more popular than bought-in programmes (Segrave, 1998: 225–6; Steemers, 2004).

Increasingly, the two main channels, ITV and BBC1, which were still attracting a large mass audience, relied on domestically produced programmes to compete in the peak hours, with only an occasional American programme, for example BBC1's use of the *X-Files* in prime time in the 1990s (Jennings, 2003: 113). The majority of imports, mostly American, tended to be used in the expanding off-peak slots (films continued to be shown in all periods) (*The Times*, 1995; Phillips, 1997). For example, on Wednesday, 7 October 1992, BBC1 and ITV showed no American programmes between 6 p.m. and midnight – apart from a made-for-TV film on ITV at 9 p.m. However, Thames (ITV) filled up its late-night schedule by showing *Kojak*, at midnight, *America's Top Ten*, at 1 a.m. and an American comedy, *Three's Company*, at 5 a.m. (*The Times*, 1992). The prevailing logic, at least for peak-time scheduling, was that domestic programmes were more popular than similar imported material, they could be controlled by the broadcaster, so could not easily swap to another channel, and they could be tailored to the particular needs of the channel, for example *East Enders* saw its output increasing from 3 to 4 episodes a week as the BBC sought to milk its success (Bignell, 2004: 263).

Another reason for the BBC's shift away from using American programmes in peak time was the political criticism of a public service broadcaster relying too heavily on American programmes (Williams, 1998: 172–3). To continue to keep a claim to the licence fee, the BBC had to show that it was not acting as a commercial broadcaster, but was offering a diverse range of quality domestic programmes. It was meant to be the cornerstone of British broadcasting, and not a commercial channel constantly seeking high ratings. Even now, when the BBC competes to buy American programmes, questions are raised whether this is what it should be doing with the public's money (Gibson, 2005f).

While the main channels in the 1990s began to push imports into off-peak periods, the smaller terrestrial channels, BBC2, C4 and, later in the 1990s, Channel 5 (C5), began to use a number of the quality American programmes that were appearing from the early 1980s, such as *Cheers*, *The Cosby Show*, *Hill Street Blues*, *Twin Peaks*, *Star Trek: The Next Generation*, *The Simpsons*, *Buffy the Vampire Slayer*, *CSI*, *Joey*, *Charmed*, *Angel*, *Nip/Tuck*, *Friends*, *Frasier*, *24*, *House*, *Desperate Housewives* and *Lost*, as important scheduling cornerstones to attract niche audiences, though sometimes of a considerable size (Crisell, 1997: 199, 238–9; Ellis, 2003: 95–8). For example, the double bill opener of *Lost*, screened at 8.30 p.m. on Wednesday, 10 August 2005, gave C4 audiences in excess of 6 million, more than either BBC1 or ITV1 (Gibson, 2005a).

Channel 4 had been set up with a remit to provide for 'tastes and interests not generally catered for by ITV' (cited in Born, 2003: 778). One way those at C4 interpreted this was by 'bringing an ironic sensibility to television's past, recycling old shows such as *I Love Lucy* and *Sergeant Bilko*' (ibid.). However, it also began to show a number of contemporary American programmes that could play in peak time, around which an evening's schedule could be planned that could attract reasonable audiences, programmes such as *Roseanne*, *Cheers* and *Hill Street Blues* (Bonner and Aston, 2003: 132–3). As competition increased, as more channels came on stream in the 1990s, some at C4 argued that it should seek to target the sought-after youth and ABC1 audiences, rather than a whole range of minorities; the emerging American quality dramas and comedies were seen as a rich vein of programming that could help them achieve this (ibid.: 779).

Channel 4 soon established itself as the terrestrial home of many of the quality American shows, however, over time, Sky and later C5 have adapted their strategies to also use these types of programmes to attract similar niche audiences. Increasingly, programmes such as *Homicide*, *ER*, *Friends*, *The Simpsons*, *Desperate Housewives* and *Lost* are attractions around which other shows, often domestic, could be and are scheduled. Such programmes fitted C4's brand of serving up good quality, slightly innovative cutting-edge dramas. C4 was helped by the support of many television critics who, once so dismissive of American imports, slowly came to praise these new shows (Strinati and Wagg, 1992: 72; Collins, 2000). These programmes, shown on C4 in and around prime time, were, for some, becoming cult and 'must-see' programmes (Crisell, 1997: 238–98; Segrave, 1998: 157; Williams, 1998: 243). Such that, for much of the time, many of the most viewed programmes on C4 were American imports. For example, for much of the late 1990s *Friends* and *ER* frequently appeared in C4's most viewed list (<http://www. barb.co.uk>) and more recently *Lost* and *Desperate Housewives* have attracted large audiences (Gibson, 2005a).

Since the sixties, BBC2 had used American imports, sometimes to good effect, often seeing these then switch to BBC1, for example, this happened with *High Chaparral* and, in the 1990s, *X-Files*. Like C4, BBC2 was not seen as a mainstream channel – it was a place for innovative programmes, programmes aimed at minorities, which might include those that were seen as part of the public service remit, and events that would disrupt the schedule of BBC1, for example political conferences and sporting events. However, it had to work within a certain budget while still attracting an audience at least comparable in size with C4's. American films and programmes were one way of balancing these needs. As more 'quality' American productions appeared, these were used by BBC2 to target certain niche audiences; for example, with the development of the 6–7 p.m. slot on BBC2, aimed at a younger audience. On 7 October 1992, BBC2 showed *Star Trek* at 6 p.m. followed by the DEFII slot, starting with *Wayne's World* at 6.50 p.m. (*The Times*, 1992). Such a time slot, throughout the following fifteen years, has often been filled by a number of American programmes, for example *The Simpsons*, *Star Ship Voyager* and, later, *Buffy the Vampire Slayer*, primarily aimed at a youth audience; indeed, audience research has shown that it has succeeded in attracting a young male audience (Brown, 2002). Sometimes the offerings have been innovative programmes gaining critical kudos – *X-Files*, *Seinfeld* and *24* – and occasionally they are the most viewed on BBC2. For example, *The Simpsons* was, until it moved to C4, one of the more popular programmes on BBC2 (see http://www.barb.co.uk). However, while the number of American programmes shown has been limited compared to Sky or C5, it now seems to be decreasing.

Channel 5, the last analogue terrestrial channel to appear, started broadcasting in 1997 (Fanthome, 2003: 137–48). Unlike the other terrestrial channels, its public remit was virtually non-existent, though what there was of it has caused it some problems (ibid.: 200–3). Its programming budget, while larger than some current satellite channels, was limited, originally set at, compared to the other terrestrial channels, a low £110 million (ibid.: 139). C5 attempted to win viewers from ITV and BBC by 'making the schedule easily navigable, based around key appointments to view, a stripped and stranded policy, and aggressive complementary scheduling' (ibid.). Initially, many saw its programme mix as being fairly downmarket, relying on soft porn programmes, American imports and cheap quiz programmes (ibid.: 160–1). Indeed, at one stage its channel controller, Dawn Airy, called its programming policy as the 'Three Fs' – Football, Films and Fucking (Born, 2002). This, however, was to change. Increasingly, American programmes, still relatively cheap to buy but increasingly coming with critical kudos attached to them, began to play an important role on C5 as it sought to follow a more upmarket programming strategy. Using programmes such as *CSI*, *CSI Miami*, *The Shield* and *Law and Order* in prime time, often mixed with domestic documentaries, C5 has tried to present itself as a place to see good quality detective, law and order styled programmes (Fanthome, 2003: 162). With a good critical reception it has tried to drop its more dubious reputation as a 'soft porn channel'. With its latest acquisitions, *Joey* and *House*, bought at considerable expense, it seems to be hoping that it might emulate C4 and its successful association with *Friends* and *ER* (Deans, 2005). Such American programmes are still, relative to producing them, cheap to buy, though the prices are increasing, especially for the more sought-after series. With their huge number of episodes, many have become fixtures on C5's schedules. Though it must be noted, since becoming fully owned by RTL, Dan Chambers, C5's director of programmes, has 'promised to reinvest more in homegrown commission' (Gibson, 2005g).

While the initial burst in enthusiasm for satellite in the early eighties had been replaced by a push towards cable, by the end of the eighties, with the launch of BSB and Sky, this was to change. While the early low-powered satellites used cable systems to re-distribute their television signals to customers, the new satellite channels were designed to be Direct to Home (DTH) (Bonner and Aston, 2003: 427–34). The government, keen to encourage the development of the industry, placed a requirement on the official DTH service to use a new untried technological standard, D-Mac, and to purchase a British satellite. The initial attempts to create a public service–national service satellite broadcaster, first awarded to the BBC and then to a consortium of

21 British companies, failed. The second attempt saw British Satellite Broadcasting (BSB), a new company with some form of public service remit, winning the contract (ibid.: 430–1). Then, as if a replay from the 1930s, a Luxembourg-based broadcaster, Sky, switched from using a low-powered satellite, to deliver its programmes to cable networks around Europe, to using a medium-powered satellite, to deliver a DTH service aimed solely at the British market. Unlike BSB, Sky was using a cheaper and more flexible satellite service, relying on the PAL system, a standard already in operation. The subsequent battle led to a merger, to some a takeover of BSB by Sky, creating a new company, BSkyB (O'Malley, 2003a: 59). The new threat to the British television system was no longer, as it had been viewed in the past, from American programmes shown on national channels, but from a non-British-based, non-regulated commercial broadcaster, run by an Australian company, News Corp, owned by a newspaper proprietor well known to the British establishment, Rupert Murdoch (Bonner and Aston, 2003: 433–4). At first few were worried about BSkyB. It could only be received by those with a suitable satellite dish, which few had; it had hardly any programmes that people wanted to see, it was losing money and was expensive to subscribe to. By the mid-1990s this had changed, partly helped by BSkyB's winning the rights to televise English Premier football (Horsman, 1998: 92–102). By 2005, it was a profitable system that dominated the delivery of satellite channels in Britain.

The new satellite and cable channels that were appearing had few resources for dedicated domestic productions and even fewer viewers than their terrestrial competitors; therefore, with only limited supplies of British ready-made programmes being available, they often relied heavily on substantial amounts of American material throughout their schedules (Crisell, 1997: 222). For example, if one looks at the output of BSkyB, LivingTV, Paramount or a whole host of other satellite and cable channels, most of the programmes scheduled are American, which are usually the most popular; for most of 1999–2000 SkyOne's top viewed programmes were dominated by American programmes – *The Simpsons, Buffy the Vampire Slayer* and various science-fiction programmes (<http://www.barb.co.uk>). However, not all these channels use American programmes – some, either owned by or with relationships with terrestrial broadcasters or large British producers, were able to show repeats of British shows. For example, UK Gold had a close relationship with the BBC. These channels offered a form of second-run television, similar in some ways to the way syndication market operates in America.

For these channels, the attraction of American programmes has been fourfold: they are relatively cheap to buy, they suit commercial scheduling techniques, they are popular and, lastly, while in the late 1980s most of the imports were of a low quality giving the channels a dowdy image, now many of these programmes are loved by the critics and, from this, the channel gains some kudos; for example, the Living TV with the *L Word*, FX with *The Wire*, BSkyB with *24*, *Nip/Tuck* and *BattleStar Galatica*. Even those that depend more on repeats are now able to schedule shows that, since being shown on other channels, now have some public exposure, critical acclaim and, occasionally, a fan base; for example, FX scheduling shows such as *King of the Hill*, *NYPD Blue* and the *X-Files*, and Paramount Comedy showing, *Frasier, Ally McBeal* and *Seinfeld*.

Not to be left out of the move towards a multichannel environment, many of the terrestrial channels began to set up their own cable and satellite channels. At the start of 2001, at the very moment that C4 was being pressured by the Independent Television Commission (ITC) to reduce its reliance on bought-in programmes, it launched a new digital channel, E4, which relied heavily on many of its successful US imports (Collins, 2001). Programmes, such as *Ally McBeal, ER* and *Friends*, initially made popular on C4 were now having their first run on E4; in many ways C4 seemed to be, in American television parlance, a second-run channel, at least for much of the American material. While C4 continued to compete with BBC2, E4 was positioned to compete with SkyOne (Fanthome, 2003: 780). Having a pay-TV channel allowed C4 to fully utilise the various distribution rights that most programmes are now bought with – off-air and pay-TV rights (ibid.: 783) – though E4 is to become a free-at-point-of-use advertising-funded channel. It would seem that American programmes are again attractions in their own right; they have become the reason to subscribe to a channel and are no longer just 'televisual polyfiller' (Brown, 2000).

The BBC and ITV have, in a similar way to C4, launched a number of new digital channels. However, the BBC channels, BBC3 and BBC4 (initially called Choice and Knowledge [O'Malley, 2003b: 88–9]) have tended to show mostly domestic productions, made up of some repeats and a limited number of new commissions and art house films. Though, it must be noted that American programmes have been used by the BBC to try to lead audiences from the analogue to the new digital channels; for example, *24*, shown on BBC2 on Sunday nights at 10 p.m., was ending just as the next episode started on BBC3 at 10.45 p.m. ITV2 and ITV3 have made use of a range of programmes, American and British, which ITV has the rights to; for example, ITV2 shows such American programmes as *The Late Show with David Letterman* and *3rd Rock from the Sun*, while ITV3 shows such American programmes as *Chicago Hope* and

LA Law. The use of these American repeats helps keep the costs down for the channel while still being able to attract an audience. Indeed, it has, in the past, marketed the fact that it shows American programmes at 10 p.m. every night.

2.4 Conclusion: Historical discourses

The role of American programmes on British television has, in various ways, been omitted or downplayed by many broadcasting histories. Most have tended to focus on the national context – British broadcasters producing programmes for British audiences. Where they have provided coverage of issues relating to American television and programmes, it is often infrequent, dispersed throughout the text, lacking depth, often only naming the odd American programmes and usually framed within and by particular types of narratives or discourses, including concerns over the erosion of British culture, depictions of violence, economic and industrial competition and the loss of ownership and control of terrestrial channels.

However, American television, as a concept, an example of the commercial and as an 'other', has played a long and important role in the debates that have occurred in Britain about broadcasting, and in the shape and form taken by the broadcasting regime. Likewise American programmes have a long history of being acquired by British broadcasters, playing an important economic and cultural role for most channels; they have provided popular programmes at relatively cheap prices, programmes that, relatively, came in long series, with very high production values and, often, well-known stars. They have over the years played all times of the day, from early morning, late night, in the afternoon and, prominently, in prime time. As the types of programmes produced in America have changed, so too have the needs of British broadcasters and the roles American programmes have played in the schedules. Even though these roles have changed, they are still important. Many of the new and smaller channels rely on these American imports to attract audiences, and to provide a full service on a limited budget. American programmes might not have as big a profile as they have had at other times, or to attract as large an audience as they once did on British television, but they are still part of British television.

While I have only been able to present in this chapter a rather limited historical overview of the changing use of American programmes, it does illustrate the need to re-evaluate their role on British television. While such programmes have played an important part in British television history, and while much of this is touched upon and covered by existing histories, it is often dispersed with little in-depth analysis. This overview, while it cannot completely correct this deficit, can, at least, help delineate the changing role played by American programmes over time; it helps provide a context, an understanding, in which to situate the following chapters. I will now, in the next chapter, focus on the importance of economics in explaining the role of American programmes and their use by British broadcasters.

3
The Economic Rationale: Push and Pull Factors

3.1 Introduction

In this chapter, I will be exploring the importance of economics in understanding the reasons for the international trade in programmes and, in particular, the use made by British broadcasters of American programmes. I will begin by outlining the main preoccupations of economics, one that focuses on the operations of the market, the chief mechanism for achieving efficiency. While some economists argue for a logical, detached understanding of any economic activity, I will take the view that the political, social and cultural context is always important – that the market can only exist where rules, regulations and codes exist; these come into place because of, not in spite of, the existence of society. Therefore, understanding the economics behind any activity also requires an understanding of the political decisions made in relation to the needs and wishes of that society – an understanding and concern that, in some ways, has been forsaken by classical economics since the 19th century (Mosco, 1996: 47–52).

After exploring the main concerns of economics, I will relate these to the broadcasting activity, looking at economic reasons why and how broadcasting is organised as it is, the cost factors and financial decisions that play a role in the construction of the schedule. This will be followed by an analysis of what I will call the pull factors, the reasons for buying in programmes, and the push factors, why broadcasters seek to sell programmes. In the last two sub-sections, I will explore how the dominant political-cultural view of broadcasting has, since the 1980s, been replaced by a more economic, market-driven one, spurred on by the potential offered by new forms of technologies. I will end by looking at the appearance of global media operations and the way they are seeking to operate in a number of markets; for some, a move away from the notion of a national division of labour, where certain nations' broadcasters dominate the trade of certain genre of programmes, to a more international division of cultural labour, where some large media companies produce and broadcast on a more global basis.

3.1.1   A general definition of economics

To begin, I wish to reiterate Garnham and Locksly's useful definition of what constitutes the study of economics: 'economics analyses the ways in which human societies allocate the resources at their disposal among different social activities and different social groups' (Garnham and Locksley, 1991: 8). This allocation, for economists, should be done as efficiently as possible. To be efficient, commodities should be produced at the lowest possible cost; all goods that people value more than they cost to produce should be made; and all goods should be consumed efficiently, such that everyone whose 'valuation exceeds the cost of supplying it should end up consuming the good or using the service' (Koboldt *et al.*, 1999: 54–5). If this happens the whole of society benefits: resources are used efficiently and goods provided as cheaply as possible. For many economists, this is usually best achieved by, what Adam Smith called, the 'invisible hand of the market' (Smith, 1937 [orig. 1776]). If there is a fully competitive market, then, all things being equal, products should be offered at the lowest cost (Koboldt *et al.*, 1999: 55). Entrants will enter the market to produce all goods for which there is demand, at a price level more than production cost; and all consumers valuing such a product at that price will purchase it. In many ways, this is an idealistic view of the workings of the market, but it is one that is an important concept in economics.

However, economists also accept that a market can sometimes fail to provide the efficiencies or benefits noted above. For example, certain markets might be deemed to be natural monopolies (Pennant-Rea and Crook, 1986: 149–50). This means that if more than one company attempts to supply a service or goods in that market then the price will go up for all. Traditionally this sort of argument has been applied to infrastructure that usually requires huge investment, for example bridges, roads, railways, cable and telecommunications networks. Another example would relate to those industries in which there are barriers to entry. Such barriers might include the need for large amounts of investment to enter a particular form of business (Seldon and Pennance, 1965: 293). In both these markets there is thus a tendency towards monopoly or oligopoly – a sector dominated by one or a few large companies, respectively. Such dominant firms, economists would argue, do not tend to work efficiently for, with little competition, they have less incentive to price their goods at the lowest level possible; while they are inefficient, they can still make a profit as they can use their dominant position to increase prices.

Equally, some economists accept that some activities cannot just be measured in terms of individual needs. Some activities have wider social, cultural and political impacts; they have externalities. They have effects beyond the consumption of the product, which could be positive or negative. For example, some view some films as promoting violence, a negative externality, therefore governments have tended to operate forms of censorship or regulation over what films can be released and who can watch them. Likewise, some goods or services can be viewed as merit goods/services. These are goods or services that are directly beneficial to the wider society and the individual and therefore should be promoted, perhaps with public funding (Hoskins *et al.*, 1997: 84–5; Koboldt *et al.*, 1999: 56). An example of which could be education. The market, working through individual decision, will not always allocate enough resources in these merit goods or services for the benefit of society.

Therefore, it has usually been accepted that, in both these cases, of market failure and where there are externalities or merit goods, some form of state interventions is necessary (Pennant-Rea and Crook, 1986: 149–51, 156–7). Such interventions can take a number of forms: the state or an appointed public body could intervene to provide the goods or services; or, a rule-based system could be set up. A rule-based system would be one where a limited number of commercial bodies (an oligopoly) or a single commercial body (monopoly) is allowed to operate but would be overseen by a regulator imposing a set of rules. In this way the state will attempt to organise a particular sector in a way to try to help the market work properly and to reach certain economic and social outcomes.

I will now, by interpolating these ideas into the area of broadcasting, explore how governments have, in the past, made decisions on the allocation of resources in this area; such decisions, dominated by social, political and cultural concerns, have determined the form taken by broadcasting, its underlying philosophy and objectives, and its financial underpinning and structure. Not that the economic importance of broadcasting to the wider economy, or its inherent industrial nature, was forgotten, but they have taken second place in many societies till recently. It is within the resulting regimes that broadcasters have, in creating their television outputs, come to experience, to various degrees, pull and push factors, tendencies to purchase from and to sell programmes abroad.

3.1.2 The allocation of broadcasting resources

One of broadcasting's main resources, the airwaves, has, from the start, been viewed as finite; a view that has been reinforced by governments who, reserving much of the airwaves for their own uses, have allocated only a small amount to broadcasting. As noted above, one method of allocating resources efficiently, of making sure that a service is delivered at the lowest cost, is by the operation of an open competitive market (Garnham *et al.*, 1987: 3–5). However, with the airwaves being scarce, with a limit on the number of possible broadcasters that can enter and operate in the market, broadcasting could be taken to be a natural monopoly; a true competitive market could not develop and there would be a tendency for a monopoly or oligopoly to develop. Governments have therefore had to decide how to allocate these resources in a controlled and beneficial manner. Some have allowed a sole regulated broadcaster or public broadcaster to operate the service (monopoly), for example Britain, while others have allowed the service to be offered by as many competing broadcasters as the spectrum allows, overseen by a regulator (rule-regulated oligopoly), for example America.

Beyond the problems of broadcasting tending towards monopoly, broadcasting has also been viewed as a merit good, having cultural, political and social benefits. Therefore most societies have had another reason to intervene and place some form of public interest requirement on the broadcaster(s) – a requirement to offer a range of programmes, to offer a service to all sectors of society, to treat the viewer as a citizen, to invest in domestic productions and, more generally, to play an important cultural, social and political role within the life of the nation (Graham and Davies, 1992: 171–3). Though, in some societies these requirements have been less onerous them in others, perhaps regulating broadcasters in a lighter fashion to work, more generally, in the public interest. For those societies, more used to the state playing an active role in the life of the citizen, it has been easier to accept broadcasting being delivered by a state-run, or public, broadcaster, for example Radiotelevisione (RAI) in Italy (Sartori, 1996: 134–72); for other societies, less use to state interference, broadcasting might be offered by a regulated commercial sector, a rule-regulated system, for example with the Federal Communication Commission (FCC) in America (McChesney, 1994).

While governments take decisions on the way broadcasting should develop, whether by way of a public service or rule-regulated system, there is also a question of how it should be funded; how the resources of the public, beyond the airwaves, should be allocated to the broadcaster. Broadcasting can be funded in a number of ways, through taxation (general or hypothecated), licence fee (to some a hypothecated tax), subscription, sponsorship, advertising, pay-per-view, private and public donations, charity events and audience drives; it could, of course, also be funded by a mixture of these. Each form of funding raises different questions and problems for the broadcaster, government, society and the public. These problems relate to economic concerns of whether the form of funding is efficient and whether it provides any feedback between the viewer and the broadcasters; technical question of whether it can easily be collected; political questions of fairness: should all contribute, only those that can afford it or those that directly use it; and cultural questions of whether the methods of financing provide enough funds for the broadcaster to deliver the desired quality and diversity of service (Graham and Davies, 1992: 167–221).

Different societies have chosen different funding methods, combined with different sets of public service or regulatory requirements, depending on the existing technologies and their economic, political, social and cultural environment. The initial means of financing television have tended to be taxation, licence fee, sponsorship, private/public donations and advertising. However, many economists have been critical of these forms of funding because they provide little direct feedback between the choices of viewers and the broadcaster. With the advent of new technologies, the ending of the scarcity of the airwaves and ideological-political shifts, there have been moves towards forms of funding that allow more feedback between the two: pay-TV (subscription) and pay-per-view forms of funding (NERA, 1992: 92–161; The Communications Market, 2004: 8). As NERA notes,

> [m]any economists support subscription television because it creates a clearer link between viewers and broadcasters (i.e., consumers and producers). It is argued that viewers' tastes and preferences...can best be expressed within a system which allows the viewers themselves (rather than advertisers or politicians) to choose which programmes or channels to pay for. (1992: 93)

One of the main concerns relating to the operation of national broadcasting is whether the resources allocated will provide enough funds to allow for a quality national service and for a healthy production sector; it is generally accepted that such a service should be dominated by domestic programmes, programmes that can represent and help (re)create the nation's culture (Garnham *et al.*, 1987: 26). For many societies, the national role of broadcasting is very important, especially with the dominance of America and other regional powers over other media areas such as film, news agencies and advertising (Tunstall, 1977). Often, therefore, there is a reluctance to allow too much foreign input into or control over the service, whether in terms of ownership or programmes. This might be enforced by a quota or regulations, or by the general remit of the broadcasting company (Hoskins *et al.*, 1997: 18–19, 97–8).

However, television broadcasting is an expensive business, few nations can afford the necessary finance to fill all their hours with expensively made domestic productions. Therefore British broadcasters, even with government pressure and intervention limiting imports and the encouragement to use domestic productions, have tended to use some foreign programmes. In doing so, they weigh up the economic situation, the amount of domestic production they want and can afford, the programmes being offered to them on the international market and their prices, the competitive nature of the national market they operate in, the perceived demands of the audience and the type of regulations or public remit they operate to. While it is a complex question of what is bought in and how it is used, for most broadcasters acquired programmes are now part of life. I will now move on from these rather abstract discussions to explore, from an economic perspective, the changing financial context of British broadcasters as they seek to create the television commodity.

3.1.3   Creating the television commodity

While it might seem obvious that the television commodity is the television programme, it could also be thought of, as Garnham *et al.* argue, as the wider schedule: 'The definition of the broadcasting commodity will vary as between the broadcaster, the programme maker and the viewer. An independent producer may see an individual programme as the commodity while a broadcasting organisation may define the commodity as the totality of scheduling over a season and beyond' (1987: 6). For the broadcaster, the aim is to construct a programme service that will attract audiences, fulfil public service requirement and satisfy advertisers, all within the resources available; they create a 'flow culture' (Miège *et al.*, 1986), '[where] a range of items is assembled into a constantly renewed stream which is sold to consumers as a whole' (Garnham *et al.*, 1987: 11).

The cost of providing a full television service, day in and day out, is huge. It requires not only the fixed costs of the transmission network, the studios and office buildings, security, technicians, sales and administration teams and the like, but also variable costs relating to programmes; the more hours that are provided, the more these costs increase. These costs typically vary depending on the type of programme; for example, drama programmes invariably cost more than current affairs (an average of £500,000 to £154,000 per hour respectively in 1998; Graham, 1999: 21). The reasons for these variations are many: the different level of staffing required for a production, the amount of editing time needed, the cost of talent, the number of expensive sets and costumes, whether film or video stock is used, and if it is shot in a studio or on location.

Over time the total cost of providing a television service in Britain has increased. For example, according to Garnham *et al.*, the expenditure spent on BBC television increased from £231 million in 1979 to £554 million in 1985 (1987: 31–3), an increase, for the period of six years, of 42 per cent. The reasons for such an increase in expenditure, beyond a wish to improve the quality of the service, can be divided into three: first, while inflation occurs in the general economy, it has tended to rise quicker within broadcasting; this is partly due to the intensive use of labour, the successful demands for pay increases and the traditional lack of competition in the area. For William Shew, from 1986 to 1991, the average rise in programme costs in Britain has been 2 per cent in real terms (1992: 68). Second, costs have increased with the ongoing need to employ and invest in new technologies, for example the introduction and use of video machines, colour cameras and now, digital technologies; though, using such technologies have produced some savings. Third, broadcasting has slowly moved towards a 24-hour culture; many channels now broadcast around the clock. To fill these hours more programmes are required, whether domestic or imported, new or repeats (Garnham *et al.*, 1987: 16–19; *TV, UK Special Report*, 1991: Table 3).

Currently the main terrestrial British television broadcasters are transmitting around 8000–9000 hours per channel per year (BBC1's output of networked programmes was 8554 hours in 2003/2004: BBC Annual report and Accounts 2003/2004; ITV companies, as they transmit throughout the night, require slightly more, around 8700 hours). While some of this is made up of relatively cheap-to-produce domestic programmes, including reality shows, quizzes, current affairs programmes or repeats, some are made of more expensive drama productions that can cost over £500,000 per hour. According to the BBC's Annual report 2003/2004, the cost of factual programmes was on average £110,900 per hour, entertainment programmes £200,600 per hour, current affairs £117,600 per hour; this compares with £518,300 per hour for drama. For ITV, the costs of programme production are considered to be slightly higher, C4 about the same and C5 less than average (Fanthome, 2003: 145–6). For satellite and cable channels, like Sky, lower still.

While for drama productions, in terms of audience share or advertising attracted, the expenditure might not always appear worthwhile, more people might watch and enjoy a cheaper genre of programming, for example a quiz show, other factors are at work. Drama might bring in a sought-after audience, it keeps certain fixed assets fully utilised, brings professional pride to the broadcasters working for the organisation, it brings kudos to the channel, and placates the regulator who might be wary about channels that rely too heavily on popular programming; it might also create a product that can be sold abroad. Indeed, some companies will lose money on a domestic commission, believing they can make it back through later sales.

> we make *Inspector Morse* at a price. We do not get that back from the network. The network don't pay it. They pay us far less, collectively to screen that programme than it does for us to make it. Therefore we have to sell it...in order to recoup the money and then eventually show a bit of a return on it, make it into a profit. (Childs, 1992)

While broadcasters might seek to make up any 'losses' on their most expensive programmes, for example with drama, through future sales, the rights are not always automatically theirs to exploit. In these situations, the broadcaster, as the commissioner, will usually only partially fund the programme, expecting the owner of the rights to make up the cost of production through future sales (Hoskins *et al.*, 1997: 76). This is known as deficit financing, and has tended to be more prevalent in the US than the UK. In this way, the broadcaster attempts to constrain the cost of expensive programmes when they know they are only buying a number of limited showings of the programme.

If broadcasters were to spend the same average amount for every hour of the broadcast day, they would struggle to meet the expenditure they incur in peak hours; they would especially find it hard to provide for the more expensive forms, such as drama. For example, it cost some £812 million for BBC1 to provide a programme service in 2003/2004, which would make, approximately, an average spend of £95,000 per hour; an amount which, if spent on each hour, would still allow the BBC to provide a full service, but not one where the programmes would have the same associated quality that they have when, at certain points in the day, hundreds of thousands of pounds are spent per hour (calculated from BBC Annual report and Accounts 2003/2004).

Broadcasters therefore, as they create a schedule, take decisions of where to target their resources; where in the schedule to spend more and, consequently, where to spend less; what types of programmes to commission; what to repeat; and what to acquire. They usually try to spend more money in the peak hours when most people are available to watch, and less at other times of the day when fewer people are around (Tunstall, 1986: 36). However, it must be noted that certain times of the day, the afternoon for example, can still attract a sought-after audience, and therefore require adequate resources – for example the American networks find this a profitable period. Overall, broadcasters are worried that if they fail to target their resources at peak times, they might lose the audiences as they might switch to channels with more attractive and higher quality programmes or to more fulfilling forms of entertainment, for example videos, electronic games or the Internet. It also does not make sense to spend hundreds of thousands of pounds on a programme scheduled at a time that few can watch. Broadcasters, overall, prefer their flagship productions to be watched, to attract audiences and to garner critical acclaim: '...where you are spending money you make sure it reaches the biggest audience...so you wouldn't put very expensive programming in the afternoon...you wouldn't put new drama at five o'clock because a lot of people aren't home' (Hills, 1992). Broadcasters therefore target resources at particular moments, usually spending above the average on peak-time hours and below the average on non-peak-time hours.

However, other factors come into play in establishing a schedule mix beyond the targeting of resources. For example, while, mostly, expensive drama productions will be shown in the peak hours, other, relatively cheap forms of programmes, will also be scheduled at this time because they are popular with audiences – for example, quiz shows like *Who Wants to be a Millionaire* (ITV), reality programmes like *Return of the Chef* (C4), documentaries like *Seven Natural Wonders* (BBC2) and comic series like *The Office* (BBC2), which have all run in peak hours. Public service commitments and regulatory rules will also cause broadcasters to weigh up what is being offered and when it is shown, which has consequences for when resources are being targeted, what programmes are shown and for what size of audience; for example, the almost perennial discussion about whether *Panorama* should be returned to its old peak-time slot on Monday evening, or continue in its current late-night Sunday slot. This is not a debate about cost and targeting of resources, but about the public service role of providing a certain form of programme at a time when a large number of people might watch. Broadcasters are also aware that they have to make sure that they must provide an acceptable service at all hours of the day. If not they risk public and governmental criticism, or even some form of censure from the regulator for not providing a full and proper service. Another strategy to save money, to attract audiences and to 'give the schedule a rest' has been by using imports – both films made for theatrical release and films and programmes made for television.

3.1.4   Imports: The pull factors

For all broadcasters, various pull factors are at work, leading to a need to look towards buying and using imports; though such factors are not the same for all broadcasters and do change over time. Such pull factors might include a lack or weakening of revenue, increased competition, the need for variety, the need for niche programmes for which adequate resources are not available, the lack of production facilities and demands from audiences. Imports of programmes are particularly attractive to buyers because the price asked is usually low, being less than the production cost (Garnham *et al.*, 1987: 25; Hoskins *et al.*, 1997: 72–3). For example, while *Variety* estimated the production cost for an episode of *Dallas* in 1983 as $850,000 (Garnham *et al.*, 1987: 76), the BBC was paying approximately $50,000 (£29,000) in 1985 (Hoskins *et al.*, 1997: 74). Such programmes, especially if they can attract a fair-sized audience, offer channels economic efficiencies. As Nossiter notes, for the BBC between the years 1983 and 1984, the differences 'in the hourly cost per viewer between bought-in programs at one end of the range and drama at the other is of the order of 0.5 pence and 6.0 pence, trivial when expressed that way but more critical when expressed as a ratio of 12 to 1' (1991: 113–14).

The reasons why prices are so low are because they do not relate to the cost of making the programme but to what the market can bear. Therefore the price will differ from market to market; what is usually referred to as 'price discrimination' (Hoskins *et al.*, 1997: 69–72). While sellers will usually want to push the price of their products up as high as possible, unless they are seeking to gain a long-term hold on the market by way of undercutting competition in the short term, buyers will do their utmost to keep prices low. Indeed, according to Jeremy Tunstall, the aim of American distributors was to initially sell American programmes cheaply and then, once the competition disappeared, to raise prices. However, for some thirty years, Britain has been a buyer's market (monosphony) and prices, until recently, have tended to stay low (Tunstall, 1977: 42–3). Where there is competition, however, prices tend to be higher. Indeed, as Hoskins *et al.* point out, '[m]arkets with a single broadcaster paid about 55 per cent less than markets with competing broadcasters' (1997: 79).

Such relatively low priced programmes offer broadcasters a var.. benefits: first, they can help fill up the increasing number of hours in the broadcast day, especially the off-peak periods for which little money is often allocated. For example, BBC2 and C4 have used old American imports, such as *Bilko* or *Bewitched* in late night, afternoon and morning slots, which has helped to keep their spending down. Second, certain imported material can attract large audiences in the peak hours for a low outlay. For example, *Starsky and Hutch* was often shown in the 1970s in a 9.30 p.m. slot on Fridays, often gaining a high audience rating for the BBC (Harbord and Wright, 1992: 145). Third, increasingly, the smaller channels find that they can use quality American imports in and around peak hours as a way of attracting sought-after audiences; for example, *House* (C5) or *Sopranos* (C4). Fourth, some imported material, even if shown out of peak time, can attract a fan following. For example, *Seinfeld* often shown fairly late on BBC2 attracted a loyal fan base, though they used to complain about the way the BBC kept moving the slot around (Kelner, 2000). And fifth, the sheer length of American series allows them to be shown in ways that British ones are unsuitable for. For example, the BBC, Sky and now C4 have all stripped *The Simpsons* across their weekly schedules.

Indeed, American imports have, for a long time, provided British broadcasters programmes they have occasionally found difficult to finance; they have provided another option. As Gerald Beadle, in the 1950s, in a report on 'British and American film in BBC Television programmes' noted, '[m]y own view is that they [American televisual productions] provide an element of entertainment and realistic story telling which it would be difficult, and sometimes impossible, to achieve any other way. They are a method by which we employ somebody else's production resources, and so relieve the pressure on our own' (T16/599/1, 11 June 1957). Bought-in programmes are important in allowing a more flexible response from broadcasters at times of change.

There is, however, a limit on how much imported material the terrestrial channels can or will use. The limit might be set as an official or unofficial quota, the result of an agreement with the regulator; it might relate to how much imported material the broadcaster believes the audience will accept; there might also be a need to limit imports so that the production resources of the broadcaster can be fully optimised. On the other hand, some of the newer channels, operating outside the public service regime, and which are part of large global media organisations, might seek to take advantage of synergies offered by using large amounts of imported material from other parts of a connected media empire.

3.1.5   The question of sales: The push factors

The public good nature of television programmes and films is important for broadcasters and producers, as it means that a television programme, if of the right sort (one in demand) and captured with the right technology (on video or film), can enter into a new market for further exploitation after its initial showings (Koboldt *et al.*, 1999: 55–6). Unlike many other industries which put similar levels of resources into manufacturing each product they sell, for example to produce each car requires comparable amounts of material, labour time and energy, with programme or film production most of the resources, which are often very high, are invested into the initial production, as a kind of research and development cost; this, in a way is comparable to a prototype. Subsequent copies are, however, made relatively cheaply (Hoskins *et al.*, 1997: 31–2). For example, the cost of producing each episode of *The Sopranos* might be over $1 million but to create a copy to be sold in another market might cost only thousands of dollars.

The broadcaster that commissions a programme will often write down, amortise, the cost of the production over its first and second showing; though, for the most expensive productions costing a million dollars or so an hour, this can only be done in the larger markets such as the US (ibid.: 40–2). The broadcaster or rights owner will then try to sell the programme on to other markets, both domestic and foreign. As the costs have mostly already been covered, this can be done for little extra cost, beyond the general costs of marketing and duplication. Almost all the money gained from sales will be profits (ibid.: 79). With the higher costs of some forms of production, such as drama, there is often increased pressure to seek overseas sales; indeed, the investment decisions, of whether to go ahead with a production, might be influenced by the possibility of sales in other markets. Broadcasters are therefore very keen to keep the rights to such programmes so they can continue to exploit them over time. However, in some cases, sometimes because of regulation, for example the FinSyn rules in the United States (now revoked), the broadcaster might not own the rights to all the programmes they have commissioned. If this is the case they will usually only pay a percentage of the production costs. They, the broadcaster, reason that the producer or rights holder can make up this deficit financing by future sales (ibid.: 75–6).

America, for some, has come to dominate the world market in certain programme genre because of various comparative and competitive advantages (Garnham *et al.*, 1987: 51–2). These relate to the sheer size of the American market (turnover in 2004 for the four large networks was,

NBC \$5.1 billion, CBS \$4.45 billion, ABC \$4.45 billion and Fox \$2.41 billion (Higgins, 2004)), where American broadcasters are able to invest huge amounts in programmes and films with the knowledge that most of this will be covered in the domestic market, and to the expertise built up in the production of particular genre that the international market finds attractive, for example America has become known for its expensively made tightly scripted action dramas such as *24* and its comedies like *Friends*. It might also be because of the critical mass of talent and expertise that Hollywood, also the unofficial centre of world film production, has access to and California's climate which offers an advantage as it allows all year round outdoor production (Hoskins and Mirus, 1988: 506–7). Likewise, it could be argued that America benefits from a cultural advantage, such that 'the universal popularity of American entertainment abroad [lies in] its "genius" for tapping deeply and broadly into the common elements of experience that bind humanity together' (reference to Tracey [1985] by Cantor and Cantor, 1986: 5–12). Some have discussed this idea in relation to the cultural discount that affects programmes when they are consumed in other cultures. American programmes, because of the dominance of English and the general spread and acceptance of American culture in many market, has a low cultural discount, and are therefore often more popular than other imported programmes (Hoskins and Mirus, 1988: 32–3; Collins, 1990: 52–73). While other nations can make similar programmes to the American broadcasters and producers, it might not be economically worthwhile. An old adage is illustrative here: All nations can grow bananas but, for some nations with the right climate, the amount of resources they need to put into growing them is a lot less than those nations that will require heated glasshouses (Collins, 1990: 152–3). It is better if a nation concentrates on what it is good at, and to import what it is not good at from those nations that have a comparative advantage in those areas.

It could therefore be argued that a form of division of labour has appeared in the international programme market, where different national broadcasters/producers dominate the production of programmes in certain genre; for example, Britain in historical drama and comedies, America in action series, made-for-TV films and comedies, Mexico and Brazil in telenovelas and Japan in animation (Nordenstreng and Varis, 1974; Steemers, 2004: 3–4). Different nations, because of certain cultural and economic advantages, perhaps also backed by political and military power, have come to dominate the supply of certain programmes (Alvarado, 1996: 68–9). While for some, this division is viewed in terms of a form of cultural imperialism with the western nations selling their programmes and films on to the third world, for others regional markets are becoming more important, markets where regional producers have and are developing and exploiting comparative and competitive advantages (Cunningham and Jacka, 1996: 181–2).

For these reasons, the push factors in the American market, which have tended to be stronger than the pull factors, have led to American broadcasters, producers and rights holders actively seeking to sell their programmes around the world. One of their key markets – partly because of its size, use of a similar language and culture and, from as early as the 1950s, the existence of a commercial broadcaster – was Britain. It was a market American media firms were keen to break into, though, as noted above, for many years, with the dominance of cultural-political concerns over too many imports and strong domestic production, the broadcasters' use of American programmes has been limited. However, as I will now cover, this started to change from the 1980s.

3.1.6 Return of the economic discourse

For the first sixty years of broadcasting in Britain the role of the market has been some what muted; generally the dominant view has been one of broadcasting as a public service and broadcasting as a cultural activity. Broadcasting was a scarce resource, a public resource, there for the betterment of the nation; it was there to entertain, but also to educate and inform; it was a national asset producing and circulating a national culture and, for these reasons, most of the official committees set up by the government of the day, for example the Sykes Committee, the Crawford Committee, the Selsdon Committee, Pilkington Committee, Annan Committee, have frowned on the development of too commercialised a service and, linked to this, too much foreign involvement, whether in terms of ownership or cultural imports; broadcasting was not a market like any other. However, since the eighties a more economy-driven discourse has become more important. For some this move towards 'an economic focus should serve as a healthy antidote to that bias in favour of cultural questions divorced from economic ones, which was established by previous committees of inquiry' (Garnham *et al.*, 1987: 2).

The eighties was a time of the rolling back of the state, the rise to dominance of Thatcherism with its neo-liberal view of the world (Thompson, 1984). With Thatcher's dislike of the welfare state, of public bodies such as the BBC, the government in the mid-1980s set up the Peacock Committee (Hearst, 1992: 70). This was a committee, which included two economists with free market leanings, Prof. Alan Peacock and Samuel Brittan, whose main stated objective was to look in detail at the funding of the BBC (O'Malley, 1994: 92–7). Indeed, to look radically at the licence fee and what might replace it, though it interpreted its remit in a wider sense, partly alluded to in its original brief, and looked at the whole sector. However, much to the surprise of the government, it rejected the introduction of advertising onto BBC, suggesting that, in the long term, subscription would be the way forward. It then proposed, by way of three stages, the introduction over time of a more market-driven broadcasting system (ibid.: 107).

The first stage would see the development of satellite and cable services and the BBC's licence being linked to the retail price indices (RPI); stage two would see many different forms of broadcasting and finance, allowing the replacement of part of the licence with subscription. The third stage would see the creation of a fully commercial market in broadcasting (ibid.). By the last stage, the public service role in broadcasting would be provided by some form of grant body or rump BBC. The report went on to recommend, as part of this development, that C4 should be allowed to sell its own advertising time, ITV had been doing this till then in return for funding their service, therefore allowing some competition in television advertising to develop and, by allocating ITV franchises by way of an auction, to provide the public a return from the use of the airwaves as well as forcing ITV companies to become more efficient.

For some, this report, along with others, such as the Hunt report on *Cable Expansion and Broadcasting* (1982), signalled a turning point, as the public service view of broadcasting began to be supplanted by a market-dominated view. As Goodwin notes, the way the report framed

> the future of broadcasting as a whole in terms of the market was a fundamental theoretical break with all previous official reports on broadcasting in Britain – including Annan – all of which had stressed public service as their central organising principle. (1998: 78)

No longer was the cosy duopoly of the public service broadcasters, the BBC and ITV, providing a protected public service for the citizen, going to dominate. The aim was to create a system able to serve the viewer as a consumer, to introduce the market into broadcasting, to allocate the resources of broadcasting in a more efficient way, and to reduce, eventually, the public service delivered element of broadcasting. This new system would operate with few controls and regulations, providing less what the government wanted than that demanded by the viewer, as shown by what they would pay for. As the 1988 White paper noted, 'viewer choice, rather than regulatory imposition, can and should increasingly be relied upon to secure the programmes which viewers want' (Home Office, 1988: 5).

While foreign influences, in particular American broadcasters and their programmes, had been looked at warily by most of the earlier committees, for example see the debates around Beveridge and Pilkington, this was of less concern to Peacock. Indeed, they even recommended that American firms should be able to own cable companies in Britain (O'Malley, 1994: 113). The language was less one of cultural invasion, of cultural imperialism, and more one of opening the broadcasting system up to competition, to offering what consumers wished to see (buy).

> Our own conclusion is that British broadcasting should move towards a sophisticated system based on consumer sovereignty. That is a system which recognises that viewers and listeners are the best ultimate judge of their own interests, which they can best satisfy if they have the option of purchasing the broadcasting services they require from as many alternative sources of supply as possible. (Peacock Committee, 1986: paragraph 592)

As Graham Murdoch also notes, the Cable Authority, set up as a 'light touch' regulator by the Cable and Broadcasting Act of 1984, stated in its first annual report 'that, since "cable was not designed as a public service" . . . the amount of foreign programming allowed – "could be left to market forces to decide"' (Cable Authority, Annual Report 1986, cited in Murdoch, 1994: 161).

This is not to say that fears about American ownership or Americanisation (also read this for commercialisation) of British broadcasting had gone away. Indeed, the 1980s was to see a public debate about the possible Dallasification of British screens (Collins, 1990: 151–2). The fear was that, with technological developments allowing more channels to appear, with increasing pressures to compete, and with financial resources spread too thinly, the resultant channels would rely heavily on American programmes. Christopher Dunkley (1985), however, suggests that this moral panic was partly fuelled by the BBC and ITV, and its supporters, wishing to use such fear to maintain public support to protect the duopoly. Indeed, it should be noted that the BBC and ITV were, throughout the 1980s, actually using a sizeable amount of American material in prime time (ibid.: 100–1).

With the shift from a public service–dominated system to a dual system, one where public service and regulated broadcasters sat side by side with weaker regulated commercial broadcasters, and with an ideological shift towards the market ideology, it was accepted that some channels would rely heavily on American programmes. This would be acceptable as long as the main terrestrial channels were still able to produce domestically most of their programmes; there was also some hope that, over time, such channels would invest in domestic productions. However, recently the concern has been more about the range, type and quality of domestic programmes being made and shown in peak hours rather than about imports (Beavis and Ahmen, 1998; Robinson, 2004; Wells, 2004b).

However, for the BBC, the main public service broadcaster left operating in a more market-orientated environment, there has been an ongoing debate about what its role should be. For some, such as the Peacock Committee, the BBC was an outdated institution that should, eventually, be replaced by a new grant body. For others, while there is still an important role, the BBC should be pressured to become more efficient, to cut costs and employees, and to use more independent production. Indeed, in the late 1980s with the appointment of John Birt, attempts were made to shake the BBC up with such strategies as Producer Choice; for some, the BBC seemed to be behaving more like a business than a cultural institution (Born, 2004: 97–128, 101–5).

However, by the late 1990s, with a change to a Labour government, while it would seem that the dual system has been accepted, the BBC has come to be seen as an important cornerstone of British broadcasting, there to uphold the quality and standards of British broadcasting in a sea of competing commercial broadcasters (Graham *et al.*, 1999). This can also be seen in the recent Green paper (2005), which sets out a new take on the public service remit, one where the language of the market, at least for the BBC, has been toned down. Indeed, the new definition of public service offered by the paper suggests that there is little room for popular entertainment and, therefore, it should not compete for expensive foreign (American) imports (Gibson, 2005f). It would seem that public service broadcasting increasingly means national broadcasting and national production. Then again, broadcasters, public and commercial, still have to operate in the real world; they have to balance their public service commitments against their financial limitations. American programmes, and the attractions of the American market, will, therefore, continue to play some role for public service broadcasters, and a larger role for commercial broadcasters, at least for the foreseeable future.

3.1.7 The economics of the new environment: The rise of the New International Division of Cultural Labour

Since the 1980s, with technological, economic and political changes, the television environment in Britain has transformed dramatically. Over the last two decades as satellite and cable technologies began to develop commercially, the supposed limitations of the finite space offered by the airwaves have ended (Bonner and Aston, 2003: 387–434); space was even found on the terrestrial airwaves to allow a new channel to be launched in 1997, Channel Five (C5) (Fanthome, 2003: 49–59). While the initial offering of new channels were fairly limited, originally there were between 5 and 20 additional services, depending on the platform, they later expanded for those with digital satellite, cable or terrestrial services, to number in the hundreds (O'Malley, 2003a: 59). So rapid and profound have the changes been that Sky, one of the newer service providers, using medium-powered Astra satellites to beam their signals to British homes, has become a major force in British broadcasting with a turnover of £1906 million in 2003 (The Communications Market, 2004: 8). Most analogue terrestrial broadcasters have countered by offering their existing channels via these new platforms as well as offering new supplementary channels, for example BBC3 and BBC4 (O'Malley, 2003b: 88), E4 and Film4 (soon to be joined by More) and ITV2 and ITV3. The importance of these new forms of delivery can be seen in the fact that in multi-channel households the share of terrestrial channels now stood at 58.4 per cent compared to 41.6 per cent for non-terrestrial channels in April 2005 (<http://www.barb.co.uk>).

However, while it is accepted that audiences prefer domestic productions, many of these new channels have come to rely fairly heavily on bought-in programmes, mostly American. This is partly due to the high costs of originating programmes, the lack of good quality supplies of British programmes and the relatively small turnover of most non-terrestrial channels. For example, while the BBC allocated £2233 million to its TV service, ITV spent £1634 million (at 2002 prices), C4 £608 million and C5 £242 million (The Communications Market – Television, 2004: 8, 22–3), the rest of the broadcasters, of which there are many, mostly operate on £10 million or less per year (ibid.: 29); though Sky has a turnover of nearly £2 billion, overall it spends very little on domestic productions with some £1.2 billion being spent in 2003 on films and sports rights (ibid.: 24). Some of these new cable and satellite channels have, however, been able to get access to some British programmes; for example, Granada in 1996 sold programmes to Sky to start up channels such as Granada Gold Plus (Crisell, 1997: 241), and the BBC has also, through a number of commercial tie-ups, for example with Pearson and Flextech, allowed access to its programme libraries, with channels such as UK Gold (Crisell, 1997: 236; Horsman, 1998: 102–4).

All broadcasters when launching a channel from scratch are faced by huge initial costs. They must find a headquarters, employ staff, set up the advertising or subscription offices, market the channel, pay for a means of distribution, buy stocks of programmes or create facilities for the production of programmes, all before any revenue has come in. For example, according to Christine Fanthome, it had cost C5 by the end of 1996 some £86 million for administration, set-up and retuning costs (C5 had to pay for the retuning of videos in the UK which operated on the same frequency as C5), even before the launch of the channel in 1997. Indeed, the channel was still losing money for some six years after its launch (2003: 188). Therefore many channels, at least in the initial phase, will buy in, often in package deals, existing programmes. Even ITV, started in the 1950s, used some American programmes, very successfully, in peak time for a number of years (Wheatley, 2003: 78). However, with pressure from the regulator and with the development of their own production centres, ITV's use of such imports declined; likewise Sky, started in the eighties, bought in a large number of American programmes, often in competition in the early years with BSB, pushing prices up (Horsman, 1998: 52–4). However, while BSkyB now, as a group, has started to make money, with little or no real pressure from any regulator and with a smallish audience for SkyOne, has invested little in domestic programme production – while its spending on programmes was second highest to the BBC, most of this went on sport and film rights (The Communications Market – Television, 2004: 24).

Of course, this is not always the case for all channel start-ups; for example, existing domestic broadcasters can use their existing infrastructure and library stocks to help support setting up their own channels without relying on too much bought-in material; for example, BBC2 was launched off the back of the BBC's existing plant, assets, programme stock and so on. E4, likewise, has been supported by C4 in terms of programmes, personnel and financing. However, E4 has also been very reliant on using a number of American programmes to attract audiences (Born, 2003: 787). Indeed, C4 and E4 have used the attraction of some such programmes, along with other domestic programmes, to lead viewers from one channel to the other; for example, the scheduling-marketing strategy based around 'first look', which allows a viewer to catch the next episode of a programme shown on C4 directly after on E4 is often used with American programmes such as *Desperate Housewives*.

As the British context changes, as the pull factors alter, so too has the American context and related push factors. Increasingly, American networks and television producers are facing more competition at home. New networks, such as Fox, WB and UPN have appeared, alongside numerous satellite and cable channels, such as HBO, A&E and MTV, which in some cases are rivalling the old guard, NBC, CBS and ABC (Perren, 2003: 107–12). As the American market has become more competitive, as the regulation protecting and limiting the networks' control over programmes has gone, as more broadcast licenses have been issued and as new technology has allowed the appearance of more channels there has been a period of realignment. Since the 1990s, in a number of waves, mergers have occurred leading to the creation of a small number of global media giants, most with a foothold in the American media market (Holt, 2003: 19–23). These have increasingly looked towards the potential of the deregulating markets, especially in Europe and East Asia – one of the most important markets being the UK.

However, rather than just continuing to concentrate on producing programmes for the American market and then trying to sell these on to European and British broadcasters, American media firms have also sought to develop new strategies, strategies backed by the American government, which has been trying to open up the trade in services (TIS), first via GATT and now by the World Trade Organisation (Miller, 1996). American media firms have for a long time developed media relationships with other countries, for example American networks have had links with South American nations for some time (Parks, 2003: 115), but this time they are developing and expanding their channels on the world scale, supplied with a mixture of American products, regionally produced material and more localised programmes. To develop and nurture such channels (brands), they have, in differing degrees, set up regional headquarters and employ staff who have local knowledge; they have entered into co-production arrangements with other producers and broadcasters to share costs and engage with local government agencies as they seek to develop their operations. They are increasingly restructuring their businesses from one mostly focused on America, with some sales abroad, to one operating around the globe, though all are linked through the American-based corporate headquarters. What Chalaby calls 'the creation of a network of local channels around a core broadcasting philosophy... [l]ocal channels share a concept, brand, part of their programming and library titles, resources and infrastructures, and teamwork, but develop according to their respective environments' (2005b: 56). It is no longer a simple case of an international division of labour, where a small number of nations produce the cultural products of the world, but a 'new international division of cultural labour' (NICL). As Miller and Yúdice suggest,

> [j]ust as manufacturing fled the First World, cultural production has also relocated, though largely within the Industrialised Market Economies (IMECs). This is happening at the level of popular textual production, marketing, information and high-culture, limited-edition work, because factors of production, including state assistance, lure culture producers (2002: 76).

For some, these developments are similar to other developments that seem to signal a shift from a Fordist to a post-Fordist system of production (Cunningham *et al.*, 1998: 177–8). So, for example, we see the creation of global companies, like News Corp, Viacom, Liberty Media and Time Warner that, while they are incorporated in one country, operate in many others. For example, News Corp have created a system of production that while centred on America, with the Twentieth Century Fox studio and the Fox television network providing some of the content, it also uses local or regional headquarters to understand local cultural and political sensibilities and local production centres to create a more localised output. So, for example, News Corp has Sky as its British-aimed broadcaster, Fox as its American broadcaster and Sky Italia as its Italian broadcaster (Chalaby, 2005a: 7). Such global concerns adapt, change and tailor their production on a worldwide scale, some more than others, they no longer just produce and package output in the dominant nation from which they then export. As Straubhaar notes, '[t]o achieve greater popularity among local audiences some channels have begun to translate and adapt their U.S. channels to the language and cultures of regional audiences' (1996: 291).

Increasingly, a number of media firms, especially the large American firms, treat television as a global operation, one where companies operate in many national and regional markets; however, they do not just sell pre-made programmes, and they are not creating a homogenous culture which is then imposed upon other cultures, but are also involved in production, marketing and engaging with these local and regional markets, there is 'an active interplay between global, national and local' (ibid.: 294). The days of national gatekeepers, whether broadcasters, politicians or cultural critics, trying to protect some idea of national culture have gone; increasingly they have to be aware both of the global pressures and the needs of the local culture (Miller and Yúdice, 2002: 104–6).

Conclusion

For some fifty years, the economic discourse around television broadcasting in Britain has been somewhat muted. This is not to say that
broadcasting's economic-industrial role was not recognised from the start –
most British governments have always seen the broadcasting industry as
an important part of the economy – but that they have tended to focus
on its cultural, social and political role. While an economic view of television broadcasting would seem to suggest that buying imports is always
cheaper than producing the programmes, the government has since the
start placed an expectation that broadcasters would use a large
percentage of domestic programming; broadcasters were expected to play
an important part in the cultural life of the nation (Blumler, 1992: 7–42).

However, while the economic discourse was subdued at the level of
policy, those working in broadcasting were more aware of the economic
and financial pressures at work. British broadcasters have found that
they operate in a context where, over time, costs have increased, often
without reciprocal increases in income, where the broadcast day has
expanded, where investment in new technologies has had to be made
and where new channels have had to be funded; it is a world of changing demands from audiences, critics and politicians, and of pressures
placed on broadcasters to develop a diverse range of programmes,
serving a range of informational, educational and entertainment
needs. Within this context, as broadcasters make decisions about the
construction of their output, as they have balanced up their wish to
commission programmes from domestic sources with their particular
financial constraints, they have often also looked for sources of relatively cheap but popular bought-in programmes. These 'pull factors'
have been stronger for some broadcasters, and weaker for others; they
have also changed over time depending on the context of the home
market, the level of competition and the finances of the broadcaster in
question.

Though it must be noted that this is not a one-way relationship,
British programmes and ideas have also been bought and used by
American broadcasters, as well as by others around the globe. For
example, from the ATV and its mid-Atlantic series in the fifties (Osgerby
et al., 2001: 18–20), to the BBC's early attempts of co-production with
The Third Man and *Royal Canadian Mounted Police* (T16/599/1, Spicer,
1959) and Thames selling the format of *Man about the House* to ABC
(Steemers, 2004: 90), to the latest co-productions such as *Supervolcanno*
(shown on 13 and 14 March 2005).

However, because of competitive and comparative advantages, American broadcasters have come to dominate the trade of certain genre of programme production. Such advantages include the sheer size of its market, which has allowed the average spend on programmes to be high and their cost to be amortised domestically; the utilisation of the creative mass of talent centred in Hollywood; the production-friendly climate of California; and the length of series produced and their commercial slickness (ibid.: 40–3). With high costs, the tradition of deficit financing and the production of programmes on film, 'push factors' have led American rights owners to seek to exploit their products abroad. As the costs of such programmes have been covered in the US, and because of the monopsonistic nature of the early British market, prices paid by British broadcasters have historically been low, though still bringing a profit to the American distributors.

The international programme market has, in many ways since the 1950s, come to be structured in terms of an international division of labour. American production, focused on Hollywood, was able, through its comparative and competitive advantages and through political pressure, combined with the needs of recipient broadcasters, to dominate the trade in certain genre of programmes. Many television channels, throughout the world, from the 1950s to the 1980s, showed similar American programmes, comedies such as *I Love Lucy*, action series and Westerns, such as *Rawhide*, and soaps such as *Dallas* and *Dynasty*. While the American distributors were happy with their expanding market, they were less happy with the prices they were receiving for their products (Tunstall, 1977: 43). However, while most broadcasters bought in some programmes, in the main most wished to substitute these with their own when they could – programmes which were mostly more popular with audiences, but definitely so with governments and critics wary of the American dominance of the international television market.

However, by the late 1980s, with the coming of new channels, new ways of distributing channels, and with de- or re-regulation, the economic structure of the industry has changed. If a form of international division of labour characterised television in the early period, where certain nations dominated the market in certain genre, some have argued that a global organisation of television is developing – a new form of an international division of cultural labour. While the first form saw American rights holders selling programmes at low prices to national broadcasters, the new era is one of large media firms seeking to operate branded channels around the globe – channels that combine American (global), regional and local programmes, and that organise at the global level but operate at the local level.

For some, these global tendencies are leading to or continuing the American dominance of the media of many nations; American culture is destroying national cultures, replacing them with a homogenous American-world culture, with the dominant lingua franca being American (Tunstall, 1977; Boyd-Barrett, 1979; Lee, 1979). However, others have argued against such views, as Straubhaar notes, '[s]ome previous assertions about the role of globalisation in cultures, that it leads to the homogenisation, the more or less automatic erosion of national and cultural differences, and domination of all by U.S. productions, have been modified by recent theorization' (1996: 294–5). While American programmes do flow around the international market, there is local and regional competition. Programmes are not finished text – they can be changed in use, they can be nationalised, re-edited or placed in certain positions in the schedule which change their meaning (ibid.: 288–9). Also gate-keeping policies, by regional bodies and government, can limit or mollify the influence of American firms in favour of the indigenous culture (Chadha and Kavoori, 2000: 428–9).

Therefore, it can be argued that there is a need, at least on one level, to understand the role and development of the trade in programmes, and their use, within an economic discourse. If we want to understand the role of American programmes on British screens, there is need to explore the reasons why broadcasters in Britain import programmes, the pull factors, and why those in America attempt to sell their programmes, the push factors. There is also a need to comprehend how these factors change over time, changes that are linked to various economic, political, cultural, social and technological developments. Indeed, as the broadcasting markets around the globe go through a period of de- or re-regulation and as more and more commercial channels appear, it would seem that the push–pull factors that once characterised the American–British relationship are now changing. Increasingly, American media companies have set up their own channels in the British context, and they are bringing American programmes direct to the British public, something I will look at in more detail in Chapter 7. I now wish to move on to explore how, from the viewpoint of British broadcasters that buy and schedule American programmes, they perceive of the market they operate in, which programmes they select to buy, why and how they use them.

4
Broadcasters as Active Mediators

4.1 Introduction

In this chapter I will explore the experiences and perceptions of the British broadcasters who buy and schedule American programmes. These broadcasters are ideally positioned to give an insight into the processes at work in the selection and use of imported programmes. However, I will argue here that they are more than witnesses; indeed, rather than think of them as passive conduits, their actions directed and determined by wider economic forces, we should conceptualise their roles in a more dynamic way, though still constrained in the degree of autonomy they can exercise (Cunningham and Jacka, 1996: 53–4). While they are guided, limited and constrained by the wider socio-ideological-economic-industrial context and discourses within which they work, it is they who chose which programmes to buy and how to use them; they stand between the wider forces, value and meaning systems, and the actual decisions made; forces do not buy programmes, broadcasters do. It is they 'who are making decisions based on their understanding of domestic audiences, channel require-ments, scheduling practices and the prevailing television environment' (Steemers, 2004: 18–19).

In approaching an understanding of such roles we must, however, realise that these broadcasters work and make their decisions within a particular cultural-industrial discourse, one which has been dominated by a derogatory view of American imports and, by implication, the role of those that buy and use them (Tunstall, 1993: 103–4). 'British TV regulators, legislators and channel controllers have long had a kind of Gresham's Law of Entertainment as one of their main anxieties – a fear that bad entertainment will drive out the good. "Good" has tended to be equated with British-made...' (ibid.: 104). Within such a discourse, those working in production, in the supposed creative roles, have argued strongly that British broadcasting is the sum of its own domestic output. The success of British television should be judged on how well its domestic productions work, whether in terms of delivering to the public service remit, critical acclaim, audience figures, industry awards or sales abroad, and not on how well imports work for the channel (Tunstall, 1986: 31). Likewise, the success of a channel stems from the creative-production staff and not with administrators, accountants or programme purchasers (Curran, 1979: 252–3; Curran and Seaton, 1997: 222; Steemers, 2004: 29); indeed, in the past, the BBC had been described as being run by and for programme producers (Tunstall, 1986: 197; Tunstall, 1993: 1). It is against this backdrop, this widely held view of imports and the role of buyers and schedulers, that I will now explore the perspectives and experiences of those that are involved in buying and using American programmes; those that, in some way, shape the use of American programmes on British screens.

4.2   Active mediators: Context of decision making

To begin to understand the perspectives of those working in buying and scheduling roles within British broadcasting, we need, first, to understand the context within which they work. To undertake this I will focus here on exploring how the industry is structured, the different types of organisations that exist, their raison d'etre and the mixture of roles and functions that exist in broadcasting organisations and their different levels of historical reliance on American programmes. Earlier, such an understanding would have been simple, all those working in broadcasting in Britain worked for, in a variety of roles, one broadcaster, the BBC. This was a Public Service Broadcaster, the underlying ethics and ideology of which, in many ways, broadcasters came to understand and share (Tunstall, 1986: 197). However, this does not mean that they all had the same views about every aspect of broadcasting and how it was developing (Beadle, 1963: 40–2; Burns, 1977).

Even with the introduction of ITV in the 1950s, the public service nature of broadcasting remained. ITV might be commercial, but it operated under a complex regime of regulations (Sendall, 1982). However, over time the environment within which broadcasting was developing became more competitive and complex. By the 1990s a dual broadcasting system had been established, one where regulated and public-run broadcasters were joined by weaker, regulated broadcasters. If one now surveys the broadcasting landscape, one can observe a hugly diverse range of television channels operating in Britain – ranging from terrestrial broadcasting channels to channels delivered by satellite and cable; some channels using analogue and others, digital technologies; and some free at point of use, others charging a subscription or pay per view. While a few of these are run by integrated broadcasters that produce, broadcast and own most of their own programmes, such as ITV and BBC (Tunstall, 1993: 6–10); some operate as broadcaster-publishers, like C4: broadcasters that have no production base commissioning others, often independent produces, to make their programmes; a large number of the newer television channels are, what Tunstall calls, packagers (ibid.: 7); they produce and commission few programmes of their own and rely heavily on programmes bought in, often in large numbers, for example the Living Channel or SkyOne. Though, sometimes, they are buying programmes from a related company, for example SkyOne buys a number of programmes from Twentieth Century Fox, both of which are owned by News Corp.

Broadcasting companies and television channels can also be understood by way of their underlying raison d'etre. Some have, for most of their existence, been public service broadcasters, like the BBC, while others are commercial broadcasters regulated to carry out some elements of a public service commitment, ITV for example; they are there to work in the public interest, offering a diverse mix of programmes for all audiences (for an overview of the changing PBS concept, see Scannell, 1990: 11–29). Others are pure commercial operations there to make money for their shareholders, for example SkyOne (for the background to Sky see Horsman, 1998). These latter channels are unencumbered with public service commitments and will do their best to schedule popular programmes at times most likely to attract their target audiences, according to a particular market model.

Those working in the sector will be situated in one of three functional areas: production, broadcasting (including programming and planning) and sales/distribution. Some companies will embrace all three areas, and some, such as the packages, might incorporate only the broadcasting function. Those involved in buying American programmes are usually associated with the broadcasting function (programming and planning), working closely with those that assemble the schedule: the schedulers, controllers or directors of television, though sometimes these roles overlap. In some of the organisations where domestic programmes dominate, they will only be acquiring and scheduling a limited number of programmes, for example with ITV and the BBC.

In other companies they might have an important role finding, selecting and buying a range of imports that will fit well with the commissioned programmes in and around prime time, for example with C4 or C5. For many of the newer channels, they might have to provide the majority of the channel output, in both peak and off-peak times; their roles here are to create, through a mixture of bought in programmes and a few domestic productions, an affordable popular schedule, for example, SkyOne or Living TV.

For the rest of the chapter I will explore by way of interviews undertaken in the early 1990s, the views and perceptions of those working as buyers and schedulers at a moment of great change in British broadcasting (Born, 2004: 294). This will be supplemented by other sources, interviews, memos and secondary sources. The aim is less to provide a concise and complete analysis of their views, there is not enough space available here to do so, or a complete overview of changes in their perceptions, rather than to indicate a number of ways in which they view the programmes they buy and the way they seek to use them. This highlights the important role they play and the insight they can provide of the complex processes at work in the area. As Georgina Born notes, in relation to scheduling, 'An art as much as a science, scheduling condenses all the complex logistics of television. In the alchemy of scheduling, long-term and high-level strategic objectives must somehow be transformed into a continuous and successful broadcast flow – into gold' (ibid.).

I will divide this analysis into two main sections, the first, 'Buying American programmes', where I will look at how broadcasters, purchasers in particular, understand, read and acquire such programmes and, in section two, 'Assimilating American programmes', I will explore their views of how and why American programmes are used as they are, how such programmes become part of British television and affect those programmes scheduled around them and how American imports are viewed as influencing domestic production. Through such analysis, I will explore how important such roles are in the way American programmes are assimilated into British television, some of the ways these roles are changing and what factors and forces continue to constrain and direct their autonomy.

4.3   Buying American programmes

As suggested in earlier chapters, programme purchasing can be thought of in terms of an economic rationale. Many television channels cannot afford to, or do not wish to, fund the production of all the programmes they provide; one option is therefore to purchase relatively cheap ready-made programmes from external sources. America, as noted earlier, has tended to dominate the sale and distribution of fiction programmes through the international market. Because of their domination of the market, and their ability to offer large amounts of well-produced programmes at low cost, they are a vital source of programming for those broadcasters without the resources to produce their own. The American distributors try, and are sometimes able, to cajole, encourage and pressure foreign companies to buy their programmes in large amounts, to agree to take output deals, indeed, acquire large packages of programmes offered to them. For some, this domination replicates the economic and political power of such nations, a form of media or cultural imperialism (Schiller, 1969).

Such views often suggest that the programme buyers have little autonomy; the process is very much one-way, they have little control over what is offered or over the terms. While one must accept that, at the macro level, the domination of international trade of certain genre by a number of nations could and might occur, we should also be aware of the processes happening at this meso or middle level; of what happens at the market level (Steemers, 2004: 17–19). We should be aware that those who buy, chose and use such programmes do so in a way that might not only benefit the dominant selling market, but also the domestic (buying) market and its television channels.

In this section I will concentrate on the way British buyers enter into negotiations, judge, come to value and buy American programmes. As I do this I will explore the way broadcasters are informed and guided and interact with the sellers, the market, other broadcasters and the economic-cultural needs of their channel as they come to value and understand the programmes they are buying. As they undertake this, while they are pressured to both work and react in certain ways, they also exhibit a degree of constrained autonomy or choice.

4.3.1 Buying programmes: Packages

Many of those working in broadcasting view the buying of programmes as a commercial rather than a creative act. It consists of purchasing a finished commodity – a television series, serial or a single programme – as much as one buys any commercial product. Buyers have little input into the programme itself and are usually acquiring it for economic necessity; it is cheaper than producing it domestically. The programme distributors, as with those working in film, are often viewed as trying to exercise power over the buyers as they try to pressure or 'encourage' broadcasters to buy their product and to increase the prices paid.

One practice that illustrates the supposed nature of this 'relationship' is the use of packaging, or volume selling. Here a distributor will often package a popular sought-after programme with other programmes, a practice also associated with film selling. For Segrave, this is a form of block-booking, 'whereby potential buyers who expressed the desire to buy a hot series or film for their stations were forced to buy it in a block of other material, much of which they didn't watch' (1998: 16). As Jane Dromgoole, C4's controller of acquisitions, wrote in 2004, '[t]he Americans have always loved their bulk deals, obliging non-US broadcasters to buy a broad package of TV shows and movies in order to secure the hit comedy or drama they really want'. For some broadcasters such a practice suggests a disempowerment of buyers, with a requirement to take products they would not necessarily want.

> One of the big problems with American programming is that there are three big distributors, and they are increasingly determined to do great big package deals...if you want this you've got to buy ten other major series at the same time...We've just managed to buy a series of *Wayne's World*, but we've had to buy other things that we will never end up broadcasting as part of the package. (Tony Moss, 1992)

However, for the programme buyers, the buying–selling relationship is a dynamic site of negotiation. It is where they try to use their skills to construct deals for the benefit of their channel. They see the package deal as a way for distributors to try to pressure them to take more material, but one that can be mitigated. They do not feel that distributors are always able to force their product on them.

Generally most thought that the majority of the material could be found a slot and so were not a complete waste of money. Also, with the cost of such imports generally being fairly low, even if programmes were bought that could not be used, this was not a huge problem. The question was less the weak position of British buyers in regard to the American distributors, but more of how they select and use the programmes. As one C4 buyer noted,

> Some of the deals done to pick up the long established comedies involve taking other material at the same time; they are sold as a package. In order to get *Crosby* picked up, or *Roseanne*, I might pick whatever Viacom has produced as a new series. Because there is no

way I'm going to say 'Sorry Viacom I don't want *Crosby* or *Roseanne* this year if you want us to take all that new stuff you've made this year'. And they know that, so we actually get material that in an ideal world I wouldn't have bought... But we haven't so far been stuck with anything... I am conscious that as the purchaser I can't buy something that will just sit on the shelf. (MacDonald, 1991)

Many of the buyers deflect questions about their buying of packages by preferring to talk about and propagate rumours about what their competitors have paid or had to take to get a particular programme, 'Channel Four had to buy a lot of crap that they never broadcast to get *Cheers*...' (BBC Programmer, wishing to remain anonymous, interviewed by author). It was as if they were trying to reaffirm their abilities as buyers – while others might occasionally fall into the trap, they do not. However, generally, they felt that British terrestrial broadcasters would not just buy anything and would always be willing to walk away; that still there was more supply than demand, '...the UK will remain a buyers' market for US material generally... there is much more material made in the US than there is the capacity for the existing channels in the UK to transmit' (Lenventhal, 1991).

While, for the smaller channels there were a few programmes over which they would compete, '...what we are talking about is competition for the better, or best shows' (ibid.), on the whole, they felt that they were still in a position of power with the distributors, and were able to play an active role in choosing programmes wanted for their channel. Those working for the newer cable and satellite channels saw themselves, partly due to the lack of financial freedom and their reliance on bought-in programmes, as being less able to pick and choose, indeed that they relied on buying in bulk.

I think the difficulty, really for us, is that putting together some of the major film deals with the majors, the Hollywood studios, most of those companies produce television programmes as well, and in some of those deals is an on going commitment to taking television programmes from these companies. So, we have the choice of what is there and available but, none-the-less, it is a definitely yearly value amount that we have to take.... (Boulton, 1992)

Those working for newer channels, like Sky, saw bulk buying as an efficient way of gaining the amount of material required to fill their schedules, including some popular programmes. Such a buying practice was also useful at developing and maintaining a relationship with a buyer, which is important as more channels compete for some of the better programmes. Indeed, Sky recently has been negotiating an output deal with HBO, one where Sky would take most if not all of HBO's output. On the plus side, this could mean Sky would gain all of HBO's hit shows for the UK market; on the negative side they might also have some less popular series and serials. For the terrestrial channels this kind of deal is an anathema to British broadcasting and its traditional strength in domestic production and the way it usually cherry picks American programmes (Dromgoole, 2004).

4.3.2 Market knowledge

While most purchasers saw themselves operating with some autonomy, and especially those in the larger broadcasting organisations, from a position of strength, some did note the way they were affected by the differences of, and changes occurring in, the supply market over which they have little input or control. In particular, they saw American television following its own trends and producing programmes to their own requirements. As a BBC purchaser illustrated in terms of changes happening within American market:

> the trend at this moment is definitely towards a youth/younger audience. Now that's been partly brought about by the rising profile of Fox broadcasting...they have made a very definite play for a younger audience, and that is reflected in the kinds of shows...we are being offered. (Macshire, 1993)

It would seem that as the needs of the American market have changed so too have the dominant programmes being made, from the action adventure series and prime-time soaps in the 1980s towards comedy series, quality drama and youth-oriented programmes in the 1990s and, more recently, a decline in popularity of comedies. These are changes that buyers sought to have knowledge about as they tried to keep on top of the market.

Another related concern facing buyers is the cancelling of recently acquired programmes that are under-performing in the American market; for example, *Firefly*, a programme created by Joss Whedon, which was being shown on Sky in the UK in 2004, was soon cancelled by Fox after only 9 of 13 episodes were aired after a disappointing American season (<http://www.scifispace.com/html/firefly.php>, accessed 30 June 2005). Thus purchasers spoke of having to take the apparent success of a programme in the American market into account when acquiring a programme:

> [we need] ... the confidence that a show is likely to run for a long time or, possibly, has already run for a long time, is a very positive factor in its favour ... it creates a stronger presence in the schedule if you know you can sustain a particular programme in a particular time slot over a reasonably long period of time. (Howdon, 1992)

This suggests that the international programme market is not a buyers' market in the traditional sense because the real buyers are, in the first case, the US networks.

One way British broadcasters attempted to maintain a relationship and knowledge of the American market, was by visiting America in May or June to see programme pilots, new series and to meet American broadcasting representatives. As one broadcaster noted, 'we generally tend to focus, when we are talking about American series, on really two points in the year, which are around May and June. Which is when the new American series, which will appear on the American schedules in the autumn, are being presented for the first time, or at least their pilots are' (BBC buyer, Macshire, 1993). However, as Leslie Halliwell, ITV buyer for the 1970s to the 1980s, suggests, they went 'largely as a courtesy to sellers. We go, usually knowing what we want' (cited in Lealand, 1984: 24). Likewise, Alan Howden, at the BBC, also noted that as it was a buyer's market and with the BBC being so large that it attracted sellers, there was little real need to go to America, but that it was useful to sign contracts and to meet representatives of the distributors, networks and producers (ibid.). However, with more channels competing to buy particular programmes, and with the need to pick up all the required rights, for example free to off-air, pay-TV and pay per view, the need to have complex negotiations means increasing importance in face-to-face contact (Wells, 2003; *The Guardian*, 2004).

Purchasers therefore are aware of having to take account of market differences and idiosyncrasies, by becoming more active in their surveillance of the market – understanding which programmes are being successful with particular audiences and those around which some kind of critical acclaim is building. This does not necessarily mean that more programmes are bought, but that time and care is spent buying what fits the needs of the channel. As one broadcaster noted, '[i]n a few weeks' time, we will be heading out to LA to preview the US network's autumn collections ... we're going to examine the merchandise very carefully before selecting any new additions to the Channel 4 wardrobe' (Dromgoole, 2004).

4.3.3   Categorising the programme market: Lingua Franca

Buyers consistently spoke about American programmes in certain ways, using similar terms, categories and specific examples, in a way creating and sharing a common language of labels and understandings of what was on offer; these included: 'glossy soaps' such as *Dallas* and *Dynasty*, though this is 'not a genre that plays in peak time any more'; the 'action series' and, the sub-category of, 'cop shows', such as *Starsky and Hutch* and *Miami Vice*, which are 'not being produced any more'; the 'hospital drama', for example *ER*; the 'quirky programmes', such as *Wild Palms, X-Files or Quantum Leap*, suited for 'niche audiences'; the 'must-see' or 'breakthrough' programmes, 'those around which there is a buzz', which are getting some critical acclaim, such as the current hit *Desperate Housewives*; the 'half-hour comedies', like *Friends, Cosby* and *Frasier*; and more mainstream popular programmes such as the 'chat show', for example *The Oprah Winfrey Show*.

> When you analyse it...[y]ou've got your one hour drama series, some of which are in the soap arena...night time soap or day time, some of which are cop shows and that sort of fair, most of the half hours are sitcoms, there has been a gradual incursion, especially in the Fox network, of reality based shows. (Boulton, 1992)

The buyers utilise a commonly held set of categories and definitions, often developed within and by the industry, to divide up and understand the programmes being offered by the international market – this is shorthand for associated values. Such terms provide a means by which broadcasters can quickly classify a programme; it allows them a way of comparing programmes with others in the genre, it allows them to think and talk about programmes in terms of the needs of slots and channels; it provides a means to easily communicate with others working in the industry, especially between the schedulers and channel controllers/directors of television. In a way, such a common language, and its particular associations, is a kind of lingua franca of broadcasting, helping British broadcasters to impose a framework onto the programmes being offered by American broadcasters and distributors. An understanding linked to the way British schedules are organised, the way different programme genre are valued and the way the British broadcasters view American programmes.

4.3.4   Buying for a channel and slot

Buyers, when discussing how they bought programmes, would mention that, increasingly, they always bought for a slot, that they never just bought programmes on the hoof, it was all considered. Buyers work for different media organisations, which sometimes operate a number of TV channels, each of which has a particular identity. Buyers were aware not only of the identity and needs of their channels but of others out there in the same market. They therefore would often talk about programmes in terms of their 'fit' with a channel's identity – for example, some programmes were spoken of in terms of being a Sky programme (popular), a C4 programme (innovative) or a BBC2 programme (quirky), depending on the type of programme. They were thus aware of what types of programmes channels tended to look out for; for example, C4 and BBC2 were spoken of as 'channels which looked for quality programmes' that could add to the channels' standing and that could add to their creative identities.

Programme buyers approached the programme market with a sense of what they were looking for. They were not going there just to buy programmes offered to them by the distributor. They had a sense of the needs of their broadcaster and used that as a way to filter, sort through and select what programmes they would be interested in.

> I think in the past both ourselves and ITV, we would simply buy what took our fancy, in terms of what was really good, we would buy a whole stack of shows. We would think about where they would go later. I think TV schedules have changed, that you are identifying slots now, and saying we just need to look for programmes that will fill this kind of slot. (Macshire, 1993)

He went on to illustrate this point further by talking about how programmes were purchased with a particular youth slot in mind on BBC2,

> under Janet Street Porter we have a very identifiable youth strand that provides us with another opening for a certain sort of programming...we have the *Fresh Prince of Bel Air*, that plays very successfully in Janet's strand. So we have seen a couple of shows that we think might be of interest to her that come up in the autumn. (Ibid.)

Programme buyers would usually know whether there was a need for a show to run in peak or off-peak times, whether it was to target a mass popular, youth or niche audience, and if a short or long run would be more appropriate. They would, usually, have some inclination of what genre was preferred and the form, for example, made-for-TV film, a cop series, a half hour comedy, a reality TV show or a medical series, and whether it would be able to fit a 30 or 60-minute slot. This is not to say that, on occasions, they might see a programme they would want, but for which they were not originally looking. As Mari MacDonald (1991), C4 film and programme buyer, noted, '[t]he budget is structured in such a way that I have an x amount for x number of slots, so I have an idea of what I need to buy. I have to see if the American programmes produced will fit a specific slot. Alternatively if something wonderful pops up I will probably buy it in its own right.'

4.3.5   Aesthetic decisions

When broadcasters look at the programmes they are interested in buying, they make judgements about its style, quality and form. Purchasers, working within the British broadcasting industry, and living within a particular cultural and social context, view, understand and value American programmes from a British perspective. As such, in interviews, they would often compare and contrast American and British productions, often in terms of aesthetics – their style, production values, story lines and the type of creativity and innovation they offer.

While American programmes over the years have been spoken of as being slick, glossy, well produced and having high production values, not all liked the form taken. For example, Leslie Halliwell has, on occasions, been rather derogatory about the style of some American programmes being shown on BBC and ITV in the 1970s and 1980s:

> Even the more watchable American series in recent years, like *Streets of San Francisco, Kojak, Starsky and Hutch* and *Barnaby Jones*, are assembled by computer. Exactly 50 minutes; the right proportion of badinage between the stars; the right amount of chase footage; the right amount of scenic city background. The story, and the acting, come second best to these sponsor-orientated necessities. (Halliwell and Purser, 1985: xiii)

However, since the 1980s, as American production, at least in some genre, entered what some have called a second golden era, most buyers have felt that many American programmes bought by British purchasers are now of a good 'quality'; that some of the programmes have tight well-written scripts: 'American comedies are good, they are well scripted...they are tighter scripted than a British comedy is' (C4 buyer); that some are different and stand out, '*Quantum Leap*...[is] a nice quirky show from the States, which also shows a sign of quality. As opposed to that kind of mass produced, popular programming, that we have been use to' (Baxter, 1992); that America is able produce good fantasy programmes, '...the British have never been that good in doing fantasy television like the Americans' (Shivas, 1992). Indeed, that many of the programmes have a pace or rhythm that many programmes in Europe lack.

> I think the European style of doing things is a lot more leisurely, I'm always aware that the pace of the European drama production, feature film or what ever, is always more leisurely than the Americans, the Americans...[have a] tremendously fast style of presentation. It isn't always appropriate but which is always very exciting. I think audiences have come to expect that. And a European production takes longer to establish and develop the characters...well people enjoy that but I think it is more difficult to get people to stay with it. I always think that the first twenty or thirty minutes of a mini-series, or series, are quite crucial. (Slater, 1992)

Some British broadcasters even accepted that certain American programmes are more innovative than British programmes, and that some are more able to tackle certain issues in a way that British programmes have been unable to achieve so far, '*Fresh Prince*, which is a youth black teenage show, is unlikely to have emerged in Britain in a way. There is a sort of confidence about black comedy, and about black humour in America, there is a style, there is a certain style about comedy in America that is different and interesting' (Moss, 1992).

While some of these programmes were seen as offering something additional to British television, of being able to find a place in the schedules, this is not to say that all necessarily liked the programmes on offer, or the style in which they were made. One BBC buyer, discussing the content of American programmes, suggested that, '[t]o be honest we don't really need to have the perspective of LA Lawyers, or New York cops', some went even further to describe a lot of it as 'crap'. Seemingly the role of the buyer was to select the best examples from the, 'huge amount of material out there. British television only really creams off the best American series' (MacDonald, 1991).

4.4   Secondary encoding: Assimilating American programmes

I now wish to look at those broadcasters involved in scheduling programmes; those that are involved in a process of assimilating American programmes into British television schedules. This process is not the same as the initial encoding, which relates to how the dominant preferred meaning is encoded into television programmes at the time of production, or the way a programme is produced with particular rhythms or segments of coherency for a specific supertext, but how, through the scheduler's decisions, the programme form will alter as it is assimilated into the schedule; how American programmes, through the way they are scheduled and shown will work differently in the British context than in the American one. Therefore such a process plays an important part in the way British audiences consume, understand and experience American programmes. Those in the scheduling roles will have to decide whether to edit the programme, if a series then in which order to run it, when and where to schedule the programme(s), and between which programmes to schedule it. By placing the programme in an earlier slot than shown in America, they might change the programme from being defined as adult to one thought of as part of children's television; for example, *Buffy the Vampire Slayer* was used on BBC2, at least before the late-night uncensored version appeared, in a much earlier slot in the UK than in the US to target a younger audience (Hill and Calcutt, 2001). They might put the programme on later than in America, allowing it, perhaps, through access to a limited audience, to take on a cult status. For example, *Seinfeld* ran at various times in the late evening on BBC2, unlike its more prime-time slot in the United States, gaining a small but vocal fan base (Kelner, 2000).

4.4.1   Nationalising American programmes

For many years, there has been a view that if too many American programmes appeared on British television it would affect British television's character and, in a wider sense, British culture. However, the fear has lessened as it is now accepted that British audiences prefer domestic productions and, overall, at least on the main terrestrial channels, the amount of American material being used has declined; though some might argue that as British broadcasters have sought after exports the domestic programmes have become more Americanised (Steemers, 2004: 211–12). However, those working in the scheduling areas suggest that, to a certain degree, American programmes and films can be presented as part of a national flow, they can be assimilated – a situation helped in Britain by the shared language with America, the supplier of most imports:

> We integrate American TV in a way that doesn't appear to undermine the fact that it is a domestic channel. Where it is a much more obvious invasion [is] when X something is going out in a different language. But I think the perception is more important than the reality. We perceive it to be a British show...whatever the percentage of American output we perceive it to be our own channel. (Moss, 1992)

Implicated within this discourse is a suggestion that the cultural specificity of the national televisual service is not necessarily the result of the origins of programmes but is also created by the presentation and mix of the overall flow – its balance and how it was scheduled and presented to the audience; in fact that some bought-in programmes, shown on the same channel, in the same slot, over time, become fixtures, national institutions:

> it's there for more than half the year. So there is a regular run which viewers can get the habit of regularly watching it. And know it will be there most weeks in a fixed time slot. *M*A*S*H* for many years operated on BBC2 on the same basis. It stayed in the same time slot regularly for years and years. So the audience knows where to find it. (Howdon, 1992)

In a way the suggestion is that there should not be an automatic fear of imports, they do not impose on a British culture but become part of it, and that they should therefore be judged more on their merits. Sometimes they could even add to the character and identity of the channel. As Jane Dromgoole, the controller of C4 acquisitions wrote, 'Channel 4 has become known as the home of top US programming. It's a point of distinction that has been carefully nurtured over many years by hand picking the best shows to suit the Channel audience and brand' (Dromgoole, 2004). Though, in an article published in the same year, Kevin Lygo, C4's director of television, was quoted as saying that, 'Channel Four used to be the only place where you saw a certain type of US programme and that just won't be the case going forward. The distinctiveness won't be there; though the best of the US remains...with *Six Feet Under*, *The Sopranos* and *The West Wing*'

(Gibson, 2004a). As a number of smaller channels have started to follow a similar strategy of using popular quality American programmes, C4, to differentiate itself from these, might, if it has enough resources, come to use more domestic programmes, as BBC1 and ITV1 had started to do at the start of the 1990s.

4.4.2   Filling the gaps

Sometimes American programmes are bought to complement those being made in Britain or to fill a gap in supply. For example, British broadcasters bought Westerns in the 1950s and 1960s, cop shows in the 1960s and 1970s and the glossy soaps of the 1980s to fill either an existing need or demand or one that came to develop. A more recent example was the use of American sitcoms in the 1980s, which some working at C4 spoke about at some length. They saw the programmes coming out of America at the time as revitalising this genre, a genre that had fallen on bad times in Britain. The hope seemed to be, for some, that some of the American practices would innovate the genre in Britain, but they accepted that the essence of British comedies would, somehow, be maintained.

> Historically the reason why Channel Four has a lot of half hour comedies, for they have had them since the beginning, is that partly they were something the other channels were not doing at all. Nobody wanted to pick them up, like *Crosby*. So the channel could get access to that material and cover an area of programming not being covered by the other television stations. And a lot of viewers discovered they were in fact quite good programmes. American comedies are good, they are well scripted ... they are tighter scripted than a British comedy is. (MacDonald, 1991)

Other programme genre which seemed to be dominated by American imports include some niche areas for which British broadcasters do not want to or cannot afford to make the right-styled programmes to fill the demand; for example, teen programmes such as *Buffy, Angel, OC* and *Dawson's Creek*, and science-fiction programmes such as *Star Trek: The Next Generation, StarGate* and the like – though some limited attempts have been made by some channels to produce similar-styled programmes like *Hollyoaks*, the new *Dr Who* or *Spooks*. Such American programmes, with long runs and a fair amount of marketing and publicity, either about the star(s) or original film, come to attract a mixture of existing and new fans. These programmes are often used by the smaller channels, C4 and C5, as part of a strategy of aiming at niche audiences, rather than going head to head with the larger channels, ITV1 and BBC1. For example, SkyOne uses *StarGate* in an early slot to attract a niche audience of male fans, and C4 uses *OC* on Sunday afternoons to attract a youth audience.

4.4.3 Adding value: Themes/blocks/new uses

American imports, over time, have been used in different ways to support domestic programmes or to increase their own value to the channel – for example, screening them within seasons, theme nights, their use in blocks and stranding or stripping them across the schedule (Fanthome, 2003: 139–40). As one purchaser mentioned, concerning the use of imported material to help build themed evenings by supporting domestic material,

> [W]e are looking all the time for thematic concerns in the schedules all the time...theme nights [like] Wet and Windy, the Horror night, the Food night. And we keep on presenting them one or two films for that...but always at the behest...they are bringing the ideas to us, and they're saying what can you do to support us from underneath and basically help them get an audience, if it comes down to it. (Baxter, 1992)

In this way, often fairly ordinary, old or little-known films and programmes can be placed within an attractive theme, with other better known programmes, including domestic productions, that will provide an overarching text within which to watch them, for example *Starsky and Hutch* weekend or the *Soap* weekend. They can be marketed in a way that will attract people to the whole evening; they will be given a new meaning or slant, depending on the theme of that night. In a way, this is a means of adding value to American programmes or using their value to create something greater than the parts.

Likewise, some American programmes have been used to create and support long-established blocks of programmes, such as a comedy hour, zone or evening. American programmes are particularly suitable because, as they are made in such long runs, they can sustain a block for most of the year, thus providing an anchor point for other shorter series.

> I think if you ask the other commissioning editors, they would be horrified...but in a sense it is true. The comedies are, to a sense, building blocks...it is in fact a combination of American and British

comedies... on Friday night the ten o'clock comedy is paired with a ten thirty British comedy... and on the Wednesday the *Golden Girls* is now pair with a British comedy *S & M*. (MacDonald, 1991)

It could be argued that many American programmes, because of their continued presence on British screens, not only supported British productions but also became part of the culture of British television, part of the larger megatext. For example, *Cheers* will always be thought of as being linked to the early days of C4, *M*A*S*H* with BBC2, *CSI* with C5, *The Simpsons* with Sky and the *A-Team* with ITV.

The time slot within which they are scheduled can also define a programme. They can be put into slots that have certain associations, for example programmes shown in BBC's 6–7 p.m. youth slot might loose their adult feel or might be viewed in a more ironic playful way. Programmes might also be shown at different times than they were originally produced for, for example *Buffy* and *Angel* were used in the United States in an 8 and 9 p.m. slot, respectively, aimed at an older audience while in Britain, on C4 and BBC2, they were initially used in earlier slots offered to a supposed younger audience (Hill and Calcutt, 2001). Also, schedulers might use older American programmes to attract new audiences, 'Channel 4 became the first channel systematically to mark television's coming of age as a medium by recycling its canon, shows such as *I Love Lucy*, *Sergeant Bilko* and *The Munsters*' (Born, 2004: 46). In this way, the original use for which a programme was designed can change when used within another market, within another context.

4.4.4 Learning from American television

While purchasers and schedulers spoke about the way American programmes are assimilated into the British schedule they are also aware that they, through the programmes they buy and use, are helping to change the way British programmes are produced and the shape and form of the schedule – in a way changing the face of British television. Many felt that British broadcasters were taking on production practices that were similar to those already developed in America – British broadcasters are increasingly producing series in longer runs, using teams of scriptwriters, thinking more about the needs of the schedule and generally creating slicker types of production. This is not to say that all broadcasters agree that this is happening with all genre or for all channels or, if it is occurring, it is more because of commercial pressures than some form of Americanisation.

One ITV commissioner spoke about how, a number of years ago, his then company, London Weekend Television (LWT), took a series of decisions to change its drama output in a way that could be construed as a form of Americanisation. A move towards using film to create a more expensive, 'high quality look'; something which audiences had increasingly got used to with the imports of American films and filmed series. In some ways such a response was an attempt to create a domestic product able to compete with American imports and demands from audiences.

> LWT took a strategic decision and cut entertainment programmes and went into drama. Such drama was, and is, shot on film – look at *Poirot* for example. It has a classy high quality look. Something people were getting used to via the big blockbuster Hollywood films. Such production values were appreciated by the audiences... [t]o a degree it was an Americanisation of values, production values... Thus we had no studio work... all filmed. (Plantin, 1991)

A BBC programmer also noted that such changes were happening and, for him, were because British broadcasters were learning from American television and programmes. It was not so much something forced upon the British producers than something taken up by them. In this way, American productions offered a model:

> British programmes in the last ten years have converted themselves from being rather static studio bound productions to being essentially done in the same surface way as American films. They are shot on film, they are edited in a crisp fast way, the writing is in the style of film writing rather than theatre writing or play writing, and the on screen effect is instantly more palatable to the audience... I don't think it's been caused by increased competition, I think it's more caused by professional programme makers seeing how successful the American movie making, story telling method is, and copying it. (Howdon, 1992)

As Andrew Quinn suggests, British broadcasters have to learn from the Americans if they are to survive, '[w]e must emulate the American system, where they commission treatments, do a pilot, commission production and start transmission all in the same year' (1991: 2). In some ways, it is the producers and commissioners, those most closely associated with the creative production side of broadcasting, that cast these developments in a more negative light. They tended to frame such discussions in a comparative sense, of how superior British productions are compared to American ones, and how American practices were undermining all that was good with British television. Those broadcasters, who acquire and schedule programmes, while aware of such a view did not feel they were pressuring producers to change, and if they were it was required because of the new market-driven environment. They felt British broadcasting was not really endangered by Americanisation, though it was being changed by competition. However, over the last ten years or so it would appear that some of the roles of American programmes have, at least on the larger terrestrial channels, been taken over by similar British programmes. Some broadcasters and commentators have spoken, for example, of *Spooks* having a similar style to *24*, the new *Dr Who* being reinvigorated by fantasy/sci-fi programmes from America such as *Buffy the Vampire Slayer* and shows like *Cold Feet* being similar to *Thirty Something* and *Friends*; others have also noted attempts by the BBC to follow a similar approach to *The West Wing*, with programmes such as *The Key* and *The Project* (Joseph, 2002; Sherwin, 2002).

As noted above, there was some discussion over whether changes that were happening in scheduling were the result of a form of Americanisation or were generally being driven by the onset of a more competitive regime. Such changes included the practices of stripping (showing in the same slot each weekday) or stranding programmes (showing similar programmes in the same time slot on different days) (Fanthome, 2003: 131–40), for example *The Simpsons* has been stripped by the BBC, Sky and Channel 4; ordering more episodes of successful series, for example two more series of *Dr Who* have recently been ordered – each 13 episodes long; of not taking risks, of dropping failing programmes and honing a schedule to attract the required audience, for example when *Survivor* was not attracting the expected audience, ITV quickly moved to cut one of the scheduled slots and to move the remaining programmes to a later slot (BBC News, 2001). However, some felt that while these were practices that had developed in the US over the last fifty years, they were obvious practices for a broadcaster to develop if it wished to survive in a more competitive market. The question was less one of American pressures and influences than of commercial need.

Broadcasters are becoming more commercial in their thinking. And I think that the viewing public are wanting more. In the case of Sky television...it's bringing in a sort of American/Australian style of programming to this hallowed area of the UK that has always had

BBC, BBC2, C4 and the ITV network, which has never really programmed . . . aggressively and commercially. (Murphy, 1992)

Others, however, argue that such developments, especially in certain genre, are alien to British television. While it seems acceptable for American productions to be made in huge batches, this fits the needs of their commercial system. British productions, generally, still played an important cultural and creative role and, as such, programmes were spoken of as crafted pieces of work, the result of particular writers who would not be able to keep up that kind of output without a reduction in quality. One broadcaster mentioned an attempt to increase the number of episodes of a particular British production to break into the American market, which in his eyes was a failure:

I think the attempt to do a lot of *'Allo 'Allo* actually resulted in a decline of the standard of the programme. They tried to do 26 I think, partly due to a potential American sale. I don't know whether it came off. So they tried to just reel them out; and actually they are not as good. (Hills, 1992)

It was suggested that with schedules being constructed with the need to attract large audiences, which relied on using a succession of successful programmes made in huge numbers, the tradition of risk-taking, whether in supporting a programme to build an audience over a number of seasons or in the need to push the barriers of creativity, as much as they ever existed, would be undermined, '. . . it needs the confidence and commissioning process . . . [for] people [to] . . . take a gamble. I was responsible for *All Creatures Great and Small*. We commissioned series 2 and 3 before 1 was on the air. Now people don't operate like that now. They don't take those risks' (MacDonald, 1992).

4.5 Conclusion

It could be argued that, for sometime, the most powerful voices heard within the broadcasting discourse have been those of the producers and commissioners. They have articulated a view that national broadcasting is defined and depends on domestic programmes and that they, as the producers of such programmes, should be, by extension, accepted as having the most creative and most important roles within the industry. They are, in this way, essential to what British broadcasting is. This belief propagates a hierarchical view of broadcasting – at the top sits production, within which those that make the British programmes reside, followed by the commissioners/controllers, those that order programmes that play an important part in the identity of the channel, and the controller/scheduler/director of television, who assemble and plan the national schedule. The least creative, and therefore least important, part of this hierarchy, are the programme buyers; they merely buy ready-made programmes, what Gerald Beadle called 'canned programmes' (Beadle, 1963: 119–30), which are often part of large packages. As one purchaser spoke about how those involved in production thought about programme acquisitions,

> They are wanting all the time to show that they are makers of programmes, and our stuff sort of demeans that or belittles that capacity of their making, because obviously...they can just say its just bought in...They will just pat each other on the backs for anything just made in the BBC, and...even though the audience figures for anything we put on, of the success of *Quantum Leap*, which is a very successful series...they will never discuss that because its bought in. All the years I've been here I have never know them discuss anything that we have put on, even if it is a series, or a season of films, a one-off event. (BBC purchaser, wished to remain anonymous)

Therefore, the dominant broadcasting discourse has often viewed the process of buying programmes as being rather passive, with much of the power, economic and cultural, lying with the Americans – the main distributors and producers. The buyer was thought to have a limited role, they were there to try to buy useful material cheaply, to keep the programme stock up to date and to make sure that the channel bought a good number of the blockbuster Hollywood films. If a purchase was a success, if it attracted a large audience or gained critical acclaim, the buyer had no real role in this; those praised would be the original producers or those like the channel controller, as Maggie Brown, in an interview with Jane Root, Controller of BBC2, notes that she was, ' "incredible proud" to be screening the thriller/crime drama, *24*, bought from Fox and now attracting 2.9 million viewers' (2002). Likewise, for many years those working in scheduling were seen as either merely putting together the essential units of broadcasting, the programmes or, lately, interfering with the creative art of producing programmes as they demand longer runs and a more commercial crafted piece of work.

However, as I have illustrated and argued in this chapter, those working in the purchasing and scheduling areas do play an important and active role – in some ways they too are creative. Indeed, for John Ellis, scheduling is where the power in television increasingly lies (2002: 130–47). It is important that they purchase programmes that will help attract audiences and bring kudos to the channel; that they select programmes that shape and uphold the brand of the channel; that they choose programmes that can revitalise British television, programmes that often become seen as part of British broadcasting; that they will create the appropriate mix of domestic and imported programmes for their channel and will exploit the value of imports in suitable slots; and that they will do their best to assimilate these imported programmes into British television. In this way they have an important role in defining the identity of the channel, as a C4 broadcaster noted, '*Sex and the City, The Sopranos, Six Feet Under and Angels in America* have been among the channel's most admired and talked-about programmes of recent years...' (Dromgoole, 2004).

We can therefore conceptualise the role of those buying and scheduling American programmes in terms of active mediators, buying and assimilating such programmes into the British output. They read, understand and use programmes from the position of a British professional broadcaster; they place them within the schedule, the supertext, in such a way as to blend them to become part of the output of that channel. In a sense they are 'nationalising' the American programmes. While the discussion and analysis above, does not necessarily show that they manage this successfully, it does start to indicate how they perceive and experience buying and using American programmes, how they view their relationship with American distributors and other British broadcasters, how and why they select certain programmes and how they incorporate them into British television. I will now extend this analysis in the next chapter to focus on how American programmes interact with and work within British television schedules.

5
The Black Art: Scheduling American Programmes

5.1 Introduction

In this chapter I will turn my attention to the way in which American television programmes become part of British schedules. I will argue that only by analysing how they are assimilated into British television's output, rather than by just looking at the programmes in isolation, can we start to develop a full understanding of the role taken by American programmes on British screens. In this way, American 'texts', while still identifiable as such, are on another level, dynamic, still undergoing change as they are incorporated into and interact with a schedule; in this way their meaning and role are partly the result of the moment of broadcast – their position in the temporal and spatial dimensions of the schedule.

To help focus and direct this work, my analysis will draw on and utilise four linked concepts: the text, supertext, megatext and the wider context (Browne, 1984; Houston, 1984; Gripsrud, 1995: 125–6, 129–31). In some ways, these divisions echo those used by Raymond Williams in his study of programme flows – these being close-, middle- and long-range analysis (Williams, 1979). In my first level of analysis, which overlaps with Williams's close-range analysis (ibid.: 111–18), I will use the concept of the text to refer to the named programme that is produced, sold, bought, marketed and scheduled, this would also include adverts, announcements and trailers. When a text is shown in another television system, its form will often be changed or adapted to help its successful assimilation. So, for example, American programmes are sometimes changed as they are used by British broadcasters; this can be by re-editing programmes, perhaps because of the worries over their violent content, or by changing the larger text, of the serial or series, by not screening all the episodes or showing them in a different order to suit the needs of the channel.

My next level of analysis will be that of the supertext, which, in some ways, fits with Williams's medium-range analysis of flow and 'sequence' (ibid.: 100–11). Here, I will focus, as Williams did, on actual examples of what is broadcast. This can include programmes, announcements, news slots, trailers, silences and, on commercially funded channels, adverts and sponsorship messages. The question that must be asked is whether this supertext, this additional material, is important when trying to understand the role and meaning of American programmes or can it, in some ways, be stripped out to provide a clearer analysis of, what has been called, the programme proper? (Gripsrud, 1995: 131–2) Taking the view, as I argued in Chapter 1, that the programme must be understood in relation to the schedule it is shown within, I will explore here how American programmes interact with the British supertext and how this affects their meaning; how viewers watching an American programme do so within a British schedule, where they will make different connections between the programme and the other surrounding elements that American viewers would have experienced in the American context. One way of thinking about this is in terms of meaning and experience of television coming out of horizontal linkages, linkages between programmes, segments and other inserts shown before and after (vertical linkages will refer to those linkages happening across channels).

My next level of analysis will focus on the megatext, a level of analysis that fits with Williams's long-range analysis of sequence and flow (Williams, 1979: 97–9). Here Williams concentrates on exploring the planned and advertised progression of programmes, the schedule, to see what insight this can provide in relation to the organisation of the 'television flow'. In a similar way to Williams's analysis I will look at how the use of American programmes in British schedules has changed over time and how this relates to developments in the wider broadcast environment. This work will draw from an ongoing analysis of television schedules dating from 1946.

In my last level of analysis, that of the context, I will focus on how broadcasters engage with a public discourse that exists around television as they seek to shape a programme's narrative image. This they attempt to do via secondary text such as press releases, websites, videos sent to critics, trailers and advertisements – usually found in magazines, newspapers and hoardings and broadcast on television and radio (Ellis, 1982: 24–5). While such a study allows us to comprehend the changing public discourse around American programmes, it also allows an understanding of how British broadcasters try to marry the image and understanding of American programmes to their needs.

5.2   Exploring the role of American programmes on British screens

5.2.1   The dynamic text

While there is a popular conception that there is such thing as a finished, uncensored authentic programme, whether an individual episode or a series/serial, in reality they change in form and length depending on where and when they are screened. This can be because of the interactions between texts situated within a supertext, as I will explore in the next section, or it can be because the programme or series is physically altered in some way. These alterations might lead to a different experience or meaning being made of the programme. I will now look at two examples of how and why a text might be changed and how it can affect the viewers' experience of a programme or series.

5.2.1.1   *Re-editing the programme*

An acquired programme might well be edited or changed before its broadcast. Dialogue, visuals, music or whole scenes might be eliminated. This can be for myriad reasons. It might be to cut the programme to fit a particular time slot, to make it more acceptable to national cultural sensibilities or to limit regulatory and legal interventions; this latter concern often relates to problems over gratuitous violence or the representations of sexual behaviour. For example, ITV edited violent scenes out of *The A-Team* when it was moved to an early slot on Saturday afternoon (Bonner and Aston, 1998: 106). Such cuts will change the text; it will be different to other versions, in length and possibly in terms of the programme's potential meaning to audiences. While changes made to a programme could be fairly minimal, with little effect on the coherence of the programme, perhaps only altering one or two scenes, they can also be fairly major, affecting the overall meaning or slant of the programme or even the series as a whole.

American programmes, as they are made for a different broadcasting environment without the usual interaction between British commissioners and producers who understand the needs of the domestic system, are particularly susceptible to re-editing. A recent example of this, which has been fairly well documented, has been with *Buffy the Vampire Slayer*. This series, which is fairly violent, with various vampires, demons and the like being killed in various ways in virtually every episode, as well as having implicit and, sometimes, explicit sexual references, has been edited to different degrees by the BBC, Sky and, more recently, by C5.

To explore one example, the BBC, unlike the American networks, decided to show *Buffy*, not at 8.00 p.m., but in an early evening slot at 6.45 p.m. This, while allowing the series to develop a larger and younger following, meant it had to be cut to make it more acceptable for this time (Hill and Calcutt, 2001). Hence, the *Buffy* programmes shown on the BBC at 6.45 p.m. were often different, in length, to versions shown in the United States, on other British channels and those now available on DVD. Some, such as Vivien Burr (2005), have argued that these edits have actually changed the sense of the programmes, often making them more ambiguous, or even confusing:

> In the edited final scene … [of 'Smashed'], Buffy throws Spike against a wall and kisses him. As she lifts herself up onto his body, we fade to the credits. What we do not see is Buffy quite clearly initiating sex in a very direct way, unzipping Spike's pants (this is heard rather than seen) and lowering herself onto him. The act of sex that follows is brief, almost brutally physical, and without joy. Viewers of the edited version, while they may guess that sex took place, are not faced with some potentially uncomfortable questions.

Interestingly, because of complaints, by those including viewers, fans, and by *The Guardian*, the BBC relented re-screening each new *Buffy* episode later at night in an 'unedited' ('uncensored') version (Hill and Calcutt, 2001). Similar problems were faced by the linked series of *Angel*, which was shown both on Sky and C4. While it was shown in a later slot on Sky, 9.00 p.m., on C4, at least initially, it was shown at 6.00 p.m., which, some argued, was a completely unsuitable slot for such a dark and violent programme. Because of this, again, it was cut and therefore changed. While the series was produced with an older youth audience in mind, and was scheduled by Warner Brothers (WB) for this audience, British terrestrial broadcasters targeted a much younger audience (Hill and Calcutt, 2001).

Another way a programme might be transformed is by changing the audio track in some way. One example has been with *M*A*S*H*, which when shown in America was with a laughter track but when shown on the BBC, this was omitted. This, for some, altered the feeling and experience of the programme. In the British screening, where the viewer laughs with the actors, the comic element is downplayed with the darkness of the show, a programme about war, being more apparent. While in the American showing, the programme appears more like a comedy, trivialising the war, as the viewers laugh with the laughter track at the actors. As one fan notes, '[t]he BBC bought a US comedy series – effectively a sitcom that just happened to be based in the Korean War – and rather than just playing the original version, they decided to remove the laughter track and let the audience decide what was funny' (Estall, 2002). By deducting the laugher track the whole feeling of the show was changed. British broadcasters, wishing to shape the programme to British sensibilities and the needs of the channel, took the decision that it would play better without the additional laughter track.

5.2.1.2   *Reordering the American series*

One of the commercial advantages of episodic series, those series with no necessary connections between the different episodes, beyond the cast, has been that they can play in any order or with episodes left out with little loss to the overall sense of the series – unlike a serial where, with an on-running story, all episodes need to be shown. This allows distributors to be able to sell such programmes on into markets with a range of different regulations, laws, morals and censorship rules with little problem: if offence is caused by an episode, it does not have to be shown (Cantor and Cantor, 1992: 15). An example of this is with *Star Trek*. During its numerous early runs on the BBC, a number of episodes were not shown, 'The Cage', 'The Empath', 'Whom Gods Destroy' and 'Plato's StepChildren', at least until the early nineties (*Freedom Party*, 2003) – the reason given by the BBC was that they, or at least a number of them, were unsuitable for children (T66/6/1, Memo BBC TV Press Office, 1976). Because these are free-standing shows, with no or few story lines running between them, the general public did not notice the programmes' non-appearance. For fans, however, this was not the case and the BBC, for some twenty years, was pressured to show these episodes, which it did, eventually, in the early nineties.

However, there are times when the omission of some episodes, or the mixing of the order of the series, is more obvious. This is particularly true for many of the new drama series that mix ongoing story lines throughout a series with others played out within an episode; for example *ER* or *West Wing*. Therefore, when C4 dropped three episodes of *Angel*, 'Somnambulist', 'Expecting' and 'I've Got You Under My Skin', some have suggested that it was a little confusing to the viewer (Hill and Calcutt,

2001). Also, with series like *The Simpsons*, which the BBC would show in no obvious order, it could, again, be perplexing to audiences because of the way the animation style has changed throughout *The Simpsons'* history. '[A]t one point the earliest story of them all ("Simpsons Roasting on an Open fire") was followed a week later by the 61st episode ("A Street Car named Madge")' (Williams and Jones, 2005).

British broadcasters make decisions on how and when to show a series and, sometimes, on which episodes will be excluded. At one level this might just mean that viewers in Britain see less episodes of a series than audiences in the United States or are available on DVD. On another level it could mean that the story lines of the series become confusing or are changed such that the experience of audiences watching the series on British television is different to those of an American audience – that the larger text, the series or serial, in a way, is altered as it is shaped for the needs of the British schedules.

5.2.2 Supertext: The broadcast

I now want to focus specifically on the way American programmes become embedded within and become part of British television schedules – how they become part of the temporal flow of the channel. To do this I will analyse and explore the different ways American programmes are inserted into the supertext and how they then interact horizontally with other text and programmes around them in the schedule. In this way I am suggesting that the experience of watching an American programme shown on British television is different to the experience of watching them on American channels – though, with commercial channels like SkyOne, which tend to use similar advert breaks and scheduling patterns to American television, the differences are not as much as they once used to be.

5.2.2.1 *Narrative residue – Commercial and cultural imprint*

When a programme is produced, it is done so with an awareness of the system within which it will be shown. It is created and shaped with particular rhythms to fit the needs of the channel for which it is commissioned; it is produced within and for a system that has particular ways of working, ways of constructing certain types of narrative flows. For Ellis, as discussed in Chapter 1, such moments of coherence might actually be smaller than the programme itself, what Ellis calls segments (1982: 116–26). So, for example, American programmes are usually commissioned for commercial channels with fairly frequent advert breaks. They are therefore designed with rhythms that suit these breaks and the commercial imperatives of the networks, an imperative to attract and keep audiences watching; for example, to do this, they usually start with a short prologue, a short piece of action or a scene setter, to make the viewer want to watch the programme, to hook them, before the first advert break, which often comes around after a few minutes. As noted by Delia Fine, Vice President of A&E, in relation to American compared to British programmes, '[I]n general we need a story to get going faster. We need a story to be faster paced from the beginning... here if you haven't hooked them in the first couple of minutes you're toast' (cited in Steemers, 2004: 116). Throughout the programme, before every advert break, there will be a narrative high or some kind of cliffhanger that is there to keep the audience watching for the resolution, to keep them watching the programme, the channel and, most importantly, the commercial messages.

However, while a programme is constructed for a certain system, for a certain type of channel, it can be sold on and watched elsewhere. So, for example, British broadcasters acquire and screen American programmes. However, most British channels and British programmes have different rhythms to American ones. For example, the BBC has no commercial breaks and where terrestrial channels like ITV, C4 and C5 do have them, they are shorter and less frequent than on American networks. For example, when C5 showed the first episode of *Buffy the Vampire Slayer* (19 March 2005), there were only two advert breaks, 12 minutes in and then another at 33 minutes; indeed, it was scheduled for a 50-minute slot rather than the hour slot it occupied in America. However, some of the new cable and satellite commercial channels tend to show American programmes in a similar way to how they are shown in their home market. For example, SkyOne, which tends to follow an American commercial pattern, has about five advert breaks per hour, after 6 minutes, 25 minutes, 44 minutes and 55 minutes into the programme and one at the end before the next programme begins; these are breaks which suit the narrative flows found in American programmes. For example, with *Dead Like Me*, shown on 22 March 2005, the first advert breaks comes when George (Ellen Muth), as a child, discovers that her parents are getting a divorce, the second as her mother remembers George's death and the next one just after a comic moment with one of the English characters. These moments provide hooks or narrative highs that are there to keep the audience watching over the advert break; by watching the next part we can find out more about George's parents, or how George died, or why she has decided to visit them.

Therefore, for American programmes, there is often a residue of the original commercial rhythm of the programme; one which might now clash, seem out of place or will interact in new ways with the surrounding British supertext – especially on public service or highly regulated commercial channels like ITV. For the terrestrial channels, advert breaks, if there are any, often appear in new places in American programmes and therefore the narrative high or cliffhanger is not always followed by an advert break. These highs might therefore be followed immediately by their resolution, often with a quick redundant recap reminding the viewer about what had happened before a now non-existent advert break. For example, *Star Trek*, when shown on BBC2, would occasionally reach a crescendo and would then fade out and then back in again, with the actors still in place as if nothing had happened; sometimes there would also be a recap of the situation. There would then be a resolution of the narrative climax provided before the fade-out. In America, an advert break would have occurred between the climax and the fade-in and recap. On BBC2, *Star Trek's* narrative stops and starts, its commercial rhythm, feel out of place, and certainly different to the flows found in other British programmes. At other times, British commercial terrestrial channels like ITV, will insert advert breaks into American programmes in relation to their needs rather than in the places used in America. This might mean such programmes will suddenly stop, for an advert break, with no narrative signal and return with no resolution or recap, which means that such programmes are not intertwined with the needs and flows of the British supertext in the way British programmes are and, therefore, might find it hard to hold onto its audience over an advert break. The American programme is experienced differently, at least at one level, than how it was in the original context of production.

5.2.2.2   Overlaps – Titles

Increasingly, when watching a programme in America, one will find the cast-list and titles at the end of the show being pushed to one side with a trailer for an upcoming show appearing on one side (a trailer used at the end is usually called End Credit Promotions [ECP]). The networks, worried at losing their audience, are promoting the next programme before the current one has completely finished. In a way it is an over-lapping of narratives, of extending the hold on the audience from the current programme and handing it on to the next scheduled programme; in this way, it is an attempt to keep the audience watching through the adverts – 'This is what's coming. If you want to find out what happens, stick around.' While some British channels, such as Sky and C4, are now using this technique with some programmes, this has been a fairly recent trend on British television (Beaumont, 2002). However, for the BBC, with no adverts, such devices are not used. For example, when *Cybill*, a comedy show staring Cybill Shepherd, was shown in the United States (CBS 1995–1998), it would end with this device being used. When the series was subsequently shown on the BBC, the titles were shown full screen with no ECP. The experience of watching the show on CBS and the BBC, at least at the start and end, is different.

As new commercial channels have come on stream, and as competition has increased generally in British broadcasting, some of these channels have developed a more commercial or even American feel; slowly the British supertext is starting to resemble, at one level, the American supertext. There is a feeling of more commercial rhythms at play at the micro level of the 'programme' and at the supertext level, of narrative patterns within programmes and narrative flows and segments stretching between programmes and across the evening. The overlapping of programmes through ECP, which some channels are now using, also adds a tempo to the schedule – 'quick, this programme is ending, lets hurry it up'; 'quick before people start to turn over we need to lead them into the next one'. There is no time to reflect on what has been seen, to think about what might be on next.

However, these developments are mostly found on the satellite and cable channels in Britain and less on terrestrial television. In some ways the pace of American life, of its commercial culture, while encroaching on British life has not yet completely taken over. The tempo of British television is still slightly more relaxed than American television; American television is one of movement, of never resting, of 24-hour broadcasting, of attempts to squeeze out lulls, of constant overlaps; British television, still has a slower rhythm, with more spaces and interludes between programmes.

5.2.2.3   *Commercial interactions*

We also have to remember that commercial channels in America show particular adverts and sponsor's messages around particular programmes, commercials which are usually produced to fit with the rhythms of American television and certain types of programmes. While for the viewer the programme and commercial message might appear distinct, this is the programme and this is the advert, at another level they might work symbolically together. For example, the experience of watching *24* would appear strange or different to an American viewer if shown without any advert breaks, or where the commercials are not American. When shown in America, *24* will be part of a supertext with fast paced adverts about mobile phones, electronic gadgets and cars.

When, however, *24* was shown on the BBC no commercial interactions occured, and therefore part of the experience of *24* is different to watching it in the States. While it is obvious where the break will come, there is no switching away to adverts that have been created to intermesh with the types of cars, gadgets that Jack Bauer has just been using. When American programmes are shown on the commercial British channels, while commercial messages do appear, and are some-times similar to the American ones, there is usually a difference. Many British channels clearly identify the shift form the programme to the adverts, which helps signal the end and start of the programme, and the breaks are not as long as they are in the States. Likewise the adverts' pace and rhythms are dissimilar; American adverts are often faster paced and more direct than British ones. Therefore, with differences in the ways of showing American programmes, with a dissimilar form of advertising culture, the experience of watching American programmes on American and British channels is different.

5.2.2.4   Linked and linking programmes

Some programmes, when produced, or scheduled, have been done so to allow some form of intertextuality, to encourage connections to be made between programmes and other cultural forms, meanings, associations or characters/actors (Collins, 1992: 333–6). For example, for a while *Buffy the Vampire Slayer* and its spin-off, *Angel*, were shown in America one after the other on Warner Brother. The two would, occasionally, be planned to interact, narratively, with a character leaving one show to appear in the following programme; or a phone call might take place in one, for the other side of the conversation to appear in the subsequent programme; or with story lines happening in the two shows occasion-ally intersecting. When initially shown on British television, the two programmes were shown back to back on SkyOne; this was, however, for a short time only. When they were subsequently screened on terres-trial television, BBC2 showed *Buffy* on one day and C4 showed *Angel* on another, there was no coordination between the two channels – though some fans argued that there should be some agreement between them (Hill and Calcutt, 2001). Because of this the intertextuality built into the programmes, and experienced by some watching the programme in America, was not so apparent to those watching them on terrestrial British television.

Likewise, programmes, which were not shown together in America, might be linked together when shown in the UK, or on subsequent showings in America through syndication. For example, C5 has been showing two programmes from the *CSI* franchise next to each other on Monday nights – in America these programmes, at least for their first runs, are usually shown on different nights in the United States. Therefore, on 22 March 2005, C5 showed *CSI: Crime Scene Investigation* at 9 p.m. followed by *CSI: Miami* at 10 p.m. While the characters and locations are different, the basic premise of the series is the same; viewers could start to link these programmes in their minds. Here we have one programme investigating murders happening in one place in America and then, after a short break, a similar group of detectives continue this elsewhere in America. The programmes, in this way, might interact with each other; the story lines and the segments in one might, in the mind of the viewer, be connected with the other.

Therefore to understand how the experience of an American programme works in the British context, requires, at least on one level, an understanding of how it is shown, embedded and watched within a specific schedule – indeed how it is embedded for each showing within each new supertext. One cannot just strip these 'other' elements out; one cannot forget the elements which exist around, and interact horizontally, with the 'text proper'.

5.2.3   Mega text

The megatext, as noted earlier, refers to the past and current histories and schedules of all broadcasters operating in that national environment. For Browne, the megatext is constituted by 'everything that has appeared on television' (Browne, 1984: 177). In this section, referring to schedules from the mid-1940s onwards, I will explore the changing ways in which American programmes have been used within British schedules. In many ways, there has been a tendency to use American programmes, most of which are long-running, action-based series, in a limited number of ways on British television – though some British programmes have also taken on similar roles. Throughout I will make connections between the different employment of American programmes and the changing broadcast environment.

5.2.3.1   Changing programme genre

The types of American programmes bought and used by British broadcasters have changed over time. Part of this change, of the types of programmes bought and used, is linked as much to what was being made in America for its own needs as to the needs of British channels. However, while, over some fifty years, there have been shifts in the programmes being bought, they have mostly been dominated by fiction – comedy and action series, serials and made-for-TV films. This has included police series, Westerns, doctor and military series such as *Raw Hide, Gunsmoke, Iron Side, Kojak, Starsky and Hutch, Hill Street Blues, ER, Homicide* and *Sopranos*; and comedies such as *I Love Lucy, Dick Van Dyke Show, Get Smart, Cosby, Cheers* and *Friends*. At moments when a genre has declined in popularity, another would often usually be in ascent and would take its place. So, for example, as the popularity of Westerns declined in the early seventies, and fewer were being produced in America, British broadcasters relied more on the existing and new American police and detective series, for example *The Rockford Files, Canon* and *Kojak*. As the action series, those such as *The Equalizer* and *The A-Team*, declined in popularity by the end of the 1980s, British broadcasters began to purchase more cerebral productions, such as *Northern Exposure* and *NYPD Blue*.

Over time, various programme genre have been used by different British broadcasters, sometimes quite successfully. Comedy series have been popular from the early days of television, from *I Love Lucy* and *The Burns and Allen Show* in the 1950s, *Dick Van Dyke Show* and *Bewitched* in the 1960s, *M*A*S*H* and *Happy Days* in the 1970s, *Cheers* and The *Cosby Show* in the 1980s and, more recently, *Frasier, Friends* and *Joey* – though they do appear to be in decline in the United States at the moment (Deans, 2005). However, the number bought and used have varied, depending on the genre's success and failure rates in both the American and British context; such that when comedy series are going through a creative patch in the United States more might be acquired and when British comedies are winning critical acclaim and are popular, less might be bought.

While some American variety-styled shows have been screened and were popular, for example *The Perry Como Show* (Harbord and Wright, 1992: 16), because of the relatively low cost of production, the live nature of some of these shows, links between broadcasters and British performers and the popularity of British productions, most of the popular shows have been made domestically, for example *Sunday Palladium, Val Parnell' Star Time*, and *The Rolf Harris Show*. In a similar way, quiz shows have tended to be produced domestically, but have, sometimes, been based on successful American formats, for example *The Price is Right* and *The Wheel of Fortune* (Moran, 2003: 118–21). In the 1980s and 1990s a number of American talk or chat shows screened by channels like C4 became popular. These tended to be less interview-based than involving audience participation and were, in a way, a revelation for British television viewers, for example *The Oprah Winfrey Show, Ricky Lake* and *Jerry Springer* (Crisell, 1997: 224–5) However, as these programmes are cheap to produce, and generally people prefer to watch domestic versions, many have now been replaced by British equivalents, for example *Trisha Goddard* and *Donahue*.

Documentary, current affairs and news programmes, because of their relatively low production costs, the subject matter, existing regulation and the still strong British public service ethos, have tended to be dominated by British productions or, increasingly, in the case of documentary/wildlife programmes, British-dominated co-productions. The few programmes of this genre that have been bought in do not usually work that well. When, for example, ITV showed the American current affairs programme Johnny Carson's *Tonight* (there was also a British programme called *Tonight*), it was not that popular with British audiences and was soon take off (Lealand, 1984: 18). However, in the new multi-channel environment, more American programmes of this ilk are being aired, often on American branded channels, for example on Discovery, CNN and National Geographic.

Lastly, American companies have, since the late 1940s, often supplied children's programmes or programmes used in the various children's slot. Hence, over the years *The A-Team, Munsters, Casey Jones, Party of Five, Top Cat* and the like have been used in the morning or afternoon slots; sometimes these are dramas and comedies, and sometimes animation. While American programmes are now used sparingly in terrestrial television's children's output, more are found on a number of dedicated children's channels, available via digital terrestrial, cable and satellite channels (though often using other sources, for example, Japanese cartoons), for example Nickelodeon, Discovery Kids, Jetix and Trouble.

While imported American programmes over the fifty-year history of television broadcasting have tended to be of a limited number of categories and genre, as new types of channels have come on stream and as broadcasters have more hours to fill, a greater range of American programmes and American-styled television channels are on offer. For example, CNN now offers the British viewer some US news programmes, Discovery offers American documentaries and C4 and C5 offer coverage of various US sports. However, most US programmes used on the main terrestrial channels are still predominately of the entertainment genre, and mostly made up of drama, comedy and made-for-TV films. There are few current affairs, news programmes, variety shows, quiz shows (though some British quizzes are often based on US formats) or talk shows being used on terrestrial channels, though some American ones were popular in the 1980s and 1990s. This is partly because these genre are very much culturally specific but also because they are relatively cheap to make or remake in Britain.

5.2.3.2   Prime time: The changing importance of American programmes

While complete agreement is not possible on exactly when prime time is, it is usually thought of as lying somewhere around 7–7.30 p.m. to 10–10.30 p.m. This is the time, traditionally, when most people watch or are available to watch, it is the prime moment. Traditionally, the earlier part of this period has been thought of as family viewing, which in Britain lasts till 9 p.m. After this 'watershed', broadcasters will usually show more adult-orientated programmes (Paterson, 1990: 30). However, as only 30 per cent of households now have children (National Statistics 2002–2003, <http://wwwstatistics.gov.uk>), and with the main terrestrial channels mostly aiming at the family audience, many smaller channels are now targeting their programmes at niche audiences, in particular the sought-after younger and more affluent viewers.

Back in the early years of broadcasting, when the BBC still had a monopoly, few American programmes were shown on British television, and when they were it was rarely in prime time. The BBC, at this time, would screen only a limited number of cartoons or occasional short films, most of which tended to be shown in the afternoon. For example, Westerns, such as *Hopalong Cassidy* and *Rin-tin-tin* films, were often shown on the BBC in the mid to late afternoon, though not particularly aimed at children who often would have been at school at these times, for example a *Hopalong Cassidy* film was shown on the afternoon of 21 July 1950. This, however, was to change with the move towards the production of filmed series in the United States and with the coming of ITV in Britain. ITV, launched in the mid-fifties, after a short hiatus, began to use a fair number of these filmed American programmes in and around the peak-time period. For example, between 20 and 26 December 1956, apart from films, the BBC showed no American imports, while Associated Rediffusion, an ITV contractor, showed the following American programmes in prime time – see Table 5.1.

From the placing of such shows in the heart of prime time, it would seem that ITV believed that they would be popular with British audiences, which audience figures of the time bear out. For example, for the month of December 1956, which includes the week above, according to the calculations of Harbord and Wright (1992), *Dragnet* was the second

Table 5.1 Scheduling of American programmes for the week beginning 20 December 1956

Thursday	20 December	None
Friday	21 December	8.00–8.30 p.m. *Dragnet*
		9.30–10.00 p.m. *Assignment Foreign Legion* (co-production with CBS)
Saturday	22 December	7.30–8.00 p.m. *Wyatt Earp*
Sunday	23 December	7.31–8.00 p.m. *I Love Lucy*
Monday	24 December	8.00–8.30 p.m. *Dragnet*
		9.30–10.00 p.m. *Assignment Foreign Legion* (co-production with CBS)
Tuesday	25 December	9.00–9.30 p.m. *The Bob Cummings Show*
Wednesday	26 December	None

Source: *Radio Times*, 20–26 December 1956.

most viewed programme and *Assignment Foreign Legion*, a co-production with CBS, was seventh in the London region (ibid.: 123). Sometimes, these programmes were aimed at families, those in earlier slots such as *I Love Lucy*, and sometimes at an older audience, such as *Assignment Foreign Legion* in its later slot at 9 p.m.

The practice of using American programmes in prime time, pioneered initially by the ITV companies, was soon to be taken up by the BBC (T16/29S, 15 January 1965). For example, by the end of the 1960s the BBC was regularly using various American imports in early evening and later evening slots. For example, in the week 26 October to 1 November 1968, the BBC showed *Rowan and Martin's Laugh-in* on BBC1 on Sunday from 9.55 p.m. till 10.45 p.m.; BBC2 showed *The High Chaparral* on Monday night from 8.00 p.m. till 9.35 p.m. (with a special recap for the following week's start of a new series); BBC1 showed *The Dean Martin Show* on Wednesday from 7.30 p.m. till 8.20 p.m. and showed *The Virginian* on Friday from 6.40 p.m. till 7.54 p.m. While these programmes did not ride high in the top-twenty audience charts, the BBC did not shy away from using such American programmes at this time.

The use of American imports by the BBC and ITV in the peak-time slots was fairly equal by the early 1970s. Both used a number of popular American series and serials, along with American films, in and around peak time spread throughout the week – see Table 5.2.

As it can be seen (Table 5.2), while, in terms of prime-time use on a channel-to-channel basis, American imports are restricted to only a handful of shows, they are being shown in key slots, often at the early

Table 5.2 Scheduling of American programmes
for the week beginning 10 October 1974

BBC1 showed in peak time
    Thursday *Tom and Jerry* 6.55–7.05 p.m.
    Friday *Ironside* 9.25–10.15 p.m.
    Saturday *Kojak* 8.40–9.30 p.m.
    Sunday None
    Monday None
    Tuesday *Mission: Impossible* 7.20–8.10 p.m.
    Wednesday None

BBC2 showed in peak time
    Thursday None
    Friday *M*A*S*H* 9.00–9.25 p.m.
    Saturday None
    Sunday None
    Monday *The Waltons* 8.10–9.00 p.m.
    Tuesday None
    Wednesday None

ITV (London) showed in peak time
    Thursday None
    Friday *Hawaii Five-O* 7.30–8.30 p.m.
    Saturday *Kung Ku* 7.30–8.30 p.m.
    Sunday *Planet of the Apes* 7.25–8.20 p.m.
    Monday None
    Tuesday None
    Wednesday *Police Story* 9.00–10.00 p.m.

Source: *The Times*, 10–16 October 1974.

stage or midway through the evening. These are important moments in the evening for attracting and keeping audiences. Also, if one wanted to watch American programmes throughout the week, during this period, one could, by switching channels, see one almost every day of the week, bar Thursday, where only *Tom and Jerry* was being played.

While in the early seventies the only American prime-time 'hit' on British television, if measured by the top-twenty monthly rating charts, was *Ironside*, later called *A Man called Ironside*, by the mid-seventies the number of programmes regularly appearing in the rating charts had, however, increased substantially, including *Kojak, The Invisible Man, Six Million Dollar Man, The Bionic Women, Starsky and Hutch, Charlie's Angels, Cannon, The Incredible Hulk, Roots* (mini-series), *Star Trek* (while only a repeat, it appeared in the charts late in the seventies helped by a long strike in the late 1970s at ITV) and *The Rockford Files* (Harbord and Wright, 1992: 137–45). Some American programmes at this time, used on certain nights, seemed to be acting as important tent-pole programmes, programmes that held up the schedule (Fiske, 1992: 102). They were being used in prime time because they were relatively cheap, suitable for commercial scheduling techniques, as they could dominate a slot for a long time, and were generally popular with the audience. For example, *Dallas* was, in 1980, in the top twenty of most watched programmes for 6 months, and was number one in April (ibid.: 147). While domestic programmes, which were mostly more popular than imports, were only made in short runs and therefore came and went, American programmes, made in longer runs, could remain in slots for a lengthy period.

By the 1990s, the prime-time use of American programmes by the BBC and ITV had declined. For political and programming reasons, they found it more advantageous to use domestic programmes; audiences preferred them and they produced less critical and political flak. It also made them more distinctive, making them stand out from the multitude of new cable and satellite channels which relied mostly on bought-in programmes. The smaller terrestrial channels, C4 and then later C5, used a number of American programmers in or around prime time, to attract sought-after audiences and to support their domestic productions. For other newer channels, such as Hallmark, Paramount Comedy and SkyOne, American programmes tended to dominate all periods, though the more popular and expensive imports were mostly scheduled in prime time to attract as large an audience as possible.

5.2.3.3   The outer reaches – Daytime and night-time

With the expansion of the broadcast day, for some channels now to 24 hours, and with the plethora of channels currently on offer, there are more hours than ever to fill. At any time there are hundreds of American programmes being shown daily on a multitude of terrestrial, or by cable- or satellite-delivered channels. American programmes are not just used by these channels in peak hours but also appear at every other possible time throughout the day, from early morning through to late night. With so much time to fill, many cable and satellite channels use bought-in packages of American programmes as a cheap way to run a service, even if they only attract a small audience compared to domestic productions; this is their market model. With the low price paid, the length of run and licences allowing multiple showings, American programmes are well suited to filling these outer reaches.

The use of American programmes by different channels in these outer reaches can, however, differ. On some channels the same programme or series are regularly shown throughout the day. If you missed an episode another one will be showing soon. Hence, ITV2, on 21 March, showed *3rd Rock from the Sun* at 9.25 a.m., 7.00 p.m., 7.30 p.m. and 11.30 p.m. Such channels are less about attracting a viewer by screening new programmes, but are a place where viewers can drop in, for a short period of time, to see a regular, a favourite; the viewer knows the types of programmes the channels shows, but possibly not what it is screening at a particular time until they tune in – though, as some channels strip programmes, showing programmes at the same time, or strand them, showing similar programmes in the same slot, viewers might have some idea of what is being shown.

American programmes are sometimes scheduled in groups of episodes, one episode after another. For example, on 10 November 2004, C4 showed *Sex in the City* at 11.05 p.m. followed by another episode at 11.45 p.m. While few people would be around to watch these programmes at this late time, they might be attracted to tune in to watch the two back-to-back, especially if they were fans, or might set their video recorder to see them later in the week. Also, as these are episodes that C4 has already shown, they have already been amortised and therefore, for the scheduler, are extremely cheap to programme and need not attract a large audience to justify their use. By grouping them together they stand out a little more than if they were not; they can more easily be found. Another example of this kind of scheduling is BBC1's rerun of the first series of *24*, where, as of June 2005, two are being shown, back-to-back, on Friday night at around 11.30 p.m.; this increased in July with the BBC screening three episodes back-to-back – with no breaks between them. This is not the form of scheduling that would have happened much twenty or so years ago. The broadcast day then was shorter, so there were few late-night slots to fill, schedulers, in a less competitive environment, would not be prepared to use programmes in this back-to-back way, with few channels in existence there was no need to group programmes to attract the attention of viewers as most people knew what was showing and when and, with fewer video recorders around, late night showings could not be watched later in the week or the next day.

For most cable and satellite channels, American programmes appear throughout their schedules; on some channels they are used almost all the time, for example Paramount Comedy, for some they are mostly shown in the day and night periods, ITV3. Sometimes they are shown once a day, sometimes many times; sometimes they are shown in blocks or groups. The usual pattern of terrestrial scheduling does not operate on these channels. Indeed, some of these channels are more akin to the second-run channels in America; this is the repeat land of television, of stripped and stranded series, of blocks of the same programmer, this is where one can still find the *X-Files, The Cosby Show, Jerry Springer* and *Chicago Hope*, or where one can find new programmes that have never been able to find themselves on mainstream television, for example *The Wire* on FX.

5.2.3.4   *Quantity: Stripping, stranding and slot dominance*

As scheduling practices have developed over time, American programmes, because of their popularity, low costs and long runs, have come to be used in a number of ways to support and help the schedule. Such uses have included stripping programmes, showing them at the same time everyday each week, or stranding them, when similar programmes are used in the same slot. By stripping programmes it is hoped that they can become part of a viewer's routine; viewers know where to find a particular programme. The BBC has also done this with *The Simpsons*, so successfully that when they recently lost it to C4 its share declined (Deans, 2004b). C4, in a similar way, is now stripping *The Simpsons*, showing it at 6 p.m. on weekdays; Sky has been showing *The Simpsons* for sometime in this fashion, usually showing it in a 7 p.m. slot.

American programmes, because of their long runs, are often able to dominate a time slot longer than domestic programmes. *Friends* could be seen as an example of an American programme that has come to dominate a slot. It has, for C4, been a mainstay of its Friday nights for a number of years. With some 236 episodes being made (Usborne, 2004), C4 has been able to offer the same programme in the same slot for many years. While, the series is no longer being produced, C4 continues to show repeats of *Friends* in the same slot. This presence allows an awareness of the programme to build and be maintained; viewers always know that the programme is there; they know, more or less, what they will get if they tune in; it becomes part of their routine.

Another way American programmes come to dominate a slot is in terms of stranding. Here a slot will be used for a particular type of programme and, when a season of a particular series ends a similar one will replace it (Fanthome, 2003: 139–40). So, for example, C5 currently shows various police series on Monday night. When, *CSI: Crime Scene Investigation* finished on the 19 July 2005 with a Tarantino double bill, it was replaced by a related series *CSI: Miami*. Therefore, when a series ends, and another one replaces it, the viewers' routines are not disrupted; they, hopefully, will continue to watch the similar replacement series in that particular slot. In a slightly different way, C4 often shows its American shows in the 10–11.00 p.m. slot on Wednesday, in what Mark Lawson called 'the cult Americana slot' (Lawson, 2005), for example it has been showing *Desperate Housewives* and is currently showing the new hit series, *Lost*, in the same slot. By using a similar slot viewers get used to the type of programme that will be shown, as well as, over many seasons, remembering where to find a particular programme.

5.2.3.5   Supporting domestic productions: Programme blocks, inheritance factors, pre-echoes and hammocking

American programmes, because of their popularity, low costs and long runs, have come, over time, to be used in a number of ways to support and help domestic programmes. For example, schedulers often work with the idea that the audience attracted to a popular American programme can be passed on to the following domestic programme, what is often called the inheritance factor (Paterson, 1990: 31), or that an audience will tune in early to watch a popular American programme and will therefore watch part of the preceding domestic programme, the pre-echo (ibid.); another way they might be used is for two popular programmes to sit either side of a programme, hammocking (Paterson, 1990: 31; Fiske, 1992: 102). The hope here is that audiences will tune in to watch the popular American programmes and would watch the newer or weaker domestic programme in between.

Another way that American programmes are used is in advertised blocks or zones. The connection between such programmes could be the genre, for example, with comedy or cop shows, or even the country of origin, for example, a block of American programmes. So, for example, C4 has in the past had a comedy zone (block) on Friday nights; something C5 also now does on Sunday with a comedy hour. In such a block, American comedies have often played a vital role, especially as they are often popular and, as they are purchased in large numbers, have a screen presence for long periods of time. The idea is that an audience would tune into the block, not necessarily an individual programme. They would watch the popular programmes they have seen before, but would continue to watch the other ones; that they will keep tuning into the block even when the individual programmes change. Such blocks are also easy to remember and can be marketed as a block, for example C4 marketing of its 'comedy zone' or C5 with its 'comedy hour'. The hope is that they will become part of people's viewing routines. So, for example, C4 was showing, back on 2 October 1992, four comedies in a row, *Cheers* at 9.30 p.m., followed by *Nurses* (comedy set in Miami), then *Terry and Julian* followed by *Paul Merton: The series; Cheers* was a popular American comedy that, for a time, became synonymous with C4. Here it is was being used as part of a block, attracting a large number of people to tune in over many weeks, viewers who would then watch one or more of the other programmes in the block.

5.2.4   The context: The narrative image

I will now turn to my final section, to focus on the way broadcasters enter, in an active way, into a wider discourse that develops around a programme and the channel it is to be shown on; in this way they try to frame, for audiences and critics alike, a way of understanding their channel and its programmes. This discourse appears in a number of places including, the broadcaster's website, official print organs of the channels, such as *Radio Times* and *TV Times*, for the BBC and ITV respectively, television trailers and advertising in magazines, newspapers and on billboards. Through such a discourse, American programmes gain a particular narrative-image or pre-image, a way of understanding such text, a way of framing the programme for the viewer (Ellis, 1982: 24–33; Miller, 2000: 56–60). The broadcasting industry is eager to engage in such a discourse to construct an image beneficial for the programme and their channel. This is not to say that such a pre-image will necessarily be accepted or understood – but it does help us understand how broadcasters, in another way, act as important mediators of American programmes into British television culture.

I will begin by looking at various adverts recently used by Sky in relation to acquired programmes; I will follow this by looking at the attempts, by some broadcasters, to use websites as a way of shaping the viewer's experience of the programme and then, lastly, I will focus on how some broadcasters have promoted their programmes through their own publications and on their own channels.

5.2.4.1   *Advertising*

One space where broadcasters seek to engage with a public debate about television and television programmes is through forms of commercial advertising. It is here they try to frame an understanding of their programmes, to associate their programmes with their channels and to counter any derogatory views. For example, *Sky*, in 2004 undertook a campaign in the national press, including *The Guardian* and *Observer*, to market a number of its American imports. These included *24*, taken off the BBC after the first two series, and *Deadwood*. Sky used a number of adverts, full, half and quarter page in the press, including *The Guardian*, depicting, in colour, one of the main characters of the series, the Sky logo and a limited amount of text. These adverts suggest something of the quality of the programme; they are fairly grainy, with faded colours, like a washed out old-fashioned photograph, usually showing an actor from the series in period dress (The adverts looked at were from *The Guardian*: 20 September 2004, 21 September 2004, 5 October 2004, 2 November 2004, 1 December 2004, 12 December 2004). This is not a glossy series, this is not *Alias Smith and Jones*, a typical 1970s American cowboy series, but one where the grime, dirt and sleaze of the Wild West are foregrounded. This informs the reader that this is an historical series, a series that presents an 'authentic' picture of the past, warts and all. The tag line brings out the nature of the series, '*Deadwood*: A town without law'.

The text of the adverts tells us that this is 'New Drama'; this is not a repeat or a rerun. Sky, seemingly, is the place to see new American programmes, indeed, to see new drama. One of the adverts tells the reader that it is from the makers of *The Sopranos* (HBO), another American programme that people might have already seen on *C4* and *E4*, or at least probably they have heard about. By association, if *The Sopranos* is a 'must see' programme, a critical hit, so too must be *Deadwood*; both are made by a perceived producer of quality programmes, Home Box Office. To give credence to these claims, one advert quotes the renowned TV listings magazine of the BBC, the *Radio Times*, that this is, 'Drama of the week'. This is not just entertainment, this is 'Drama', and all that it implies. Sky, as noted above, while it makes few programmes itself in Britain, is seen here to be showing, what is often viewed as, the prime innovative creative output of television, that which costs the most and has the most kudos, drama (Born, 2004: 15).

Sky, throughout its adverts, uses a number of well-known American programmes to sell its own channels and satellite packages. If the programmes are not well known it informs us about them by associa-tion. These are 'must-see', special American dramas; these are programmes that stand outside of the normal, outside of the flow, this is appointment television (Jancovich and Lyons, 2003: 1–8). These are also programmes exclusive to Sky; these are original, serious, hard-hitting dramas. Sky, through very expensive marketing campaigns, tries its best to frame the programmes for us, to let us know what to expect. They are also letting us know the association of Sky with such programmes, even if produced by someone else. Sky is the home of quality programmes; it is a quality channel.

5.2.4.2   Websites

One new means by which broadcasters can publicise and market their programmes, by which they can try to shape or influence the discourse around their programmes, is via the Web. Unlike the publicity produced for newspapers and magazines, this information is aimed directly at the public, or at least those using the websites, there are no mediators. All broadcasters, including terrestrial channels BBC (<http://www.bbc.co.uk>), C4 (<http://www.channel4.com>), C5 (<http://www.five.tv>) and ITV (<http://www.itv.com>), to the newer channels offered through satellites and cable, such as Living TV (<http://www.livingtv.co.uk>), Bravo (<http://www.bravo.co.uk>), Sky (<http://www.sky.com>) and Paramount Comedy (<http://www.paramountcomedy.co.uk>) now have dedicated websites where they provide various amounts of information about the organisation or company, its channels and programmes. Some of these sites are very extensive; the BBC's online presence offering some 20,000 pages, is one of the largest and most popular sites in Europe (Wells, 2004a). Each site offers information about new programmes, existing popular programmes, schedule information, forum areas, competitions, picture galleries, interviews with the stars of various shows, episode guides, clips and merchandise. Most companies have some corporate pages, but these are often on separate, but linked, websites.

The amount and type of presence given to American programmes depends very much on the amount shown by that channel and their popularity. Therefore, if one compares the BBC's site with that of Sky, one notices very few dedicated Web pages on American programmes on the BBC's website – though it had run a number of cult pages that covered some American programmes – the cult pages ended in July 2005 because of pressure from Ofcom (Gibson, 2004b). SkyOne, on the other hand, relies heavily on American programmes and, while having some Web presence for its own productions, *Dream Team* for example, has many Web pages dedicated to its American shows.

The way the websites present information about such programmes can be divided into two. First, some channels seemingly provide rather sparse pages about their programmes, relying, instead, on providing links to official American websites. For example, C5, which shows a fair number of American programmes, echoes this with nearly half of the programmes mentioned on their home page being American, for example *Charmed, Alias, Law and Order* and *CSI*, and each of these has a linked Web page. However, if you then click through to the respective pages you will find that C5 presents little information about these programmes, instead it directs the Web user on to the official American websites. However, they do, to a degree, try to link the programme with the channel. For example, on the Web page shared by *Law and Order, CSI: Miami, Law and Order: CI, CSI: NY* and *CSI*, we are given times of their next showing and, at the top of the page, the C5 logo. In the background is a picture of bullets and guns, posed in a cityscape outline; these are programmes about law and order, about urban life and decay. The pictures show the various forensic/ law and order teams in various action poses or staring seriously out of the Web page and at the top is the strap line 'America's finest'. In such pictures we see the individual stars of the cast associated with the programme, they are all shown looking fairly moody, there are no smiles, these are serious programmes; the photograph also gives a feel of the style of the programmes, emphasising the high production values. If one clicks through to the official sites it is within a frame which continues to link the programme to C5 by including its logo and links to other parts of the C5 website.

The second form of website tends to be more complex with more information being offered, though still offering links to the American sites. So, for example, C4 has a site for all the American programmes it offers in prime time. On their *Friends website* (<http://www.channel4.com/ entertainment/tv/microsites/F/friends/index.html>), there is a large picture of the six friends looking very attractive and friendly. They are lying down together facing out of the screen, smiling and looking generally relaxed. The picture is set on a colourful background, which reinforces the view that this is a feel-good comedy programme. Much of the rest of the layout style is similar to all the other C4 Web pages. The E4 and C4 logos are at the top, along with the title of the programme, *Friends*, in its usual font, and also, in this case, the Warner Brothers symbol. Linkages are being made here. This is an American programme, but it is being delivered by C4 via its two channels, E4 and C4; it is a surrogate C4 programme. There are the usual links to forums, episode guides, to competitions and the shop. While trying to present a certain view or feeling of the programme, C4 is also keen to involve the Web user, to help create and support a fan base, to attract and target a micro culture, to help these viewers feel it is their show – that they have some ownership (Jones, 2003: 165–8).

The design of Web pages will usually be guided by the existing brand image of the channel, as well as the wider media campaign around certain programmes. It will often use similar graphics on all pages, linked to an overall style of the channel, and will usually use a degree of standardisation; each Web page is laid out in a similar way. While the page informs the Web user, indeed, it shows the user something of the programme, the actors, the story lines and episode guides, it also engages the user with a forum, interactive interviews and competitions. The website does not reach as many people as the newspapers or magazines, but it can be useful in helping to build support for a channel; it often helps create a fan base for the programme which, even on its own, could be a sizeable group of people.

5.2.4.3   Trailers

All broadcasters provide trailers for a number of their upcoming and current programmes. Usually they are shown on their own channels. However, broadcasters can buy time on other medium to trailer their programmes. For example, in 2004 ITV ran adverts in various British cinema chains trailing their new upcoming season, all of which were domestic programmes; while Sky has been buying time to advertise itself, with the use of clips from *24*, on other channels such as C5. Trailers are usually produced as part of a wider advertising-marketing campaign, there to help reinforce our knowledge about a programme and/or the associated channel. The main aim of using trailers is, as Paterson notes, 'to maximise the audience for a channel's programme' (1990: 36). To do this they are played at various points in the schedule, usually at moments when the audience watching might be similar to one the broadcaster hopes to attract.

Trailers come in three main forms: those about new and upcoming programmes; those reminding us about a series that is already showing, perhaps a failing programme that the broadcaster is trying to revitalise; and, lastly, those that tell us that a programme will be starting after this one has finished. This latter form of trailer is often found, on commercial channels at least, in the last advertising break before the end of the current programme or, sometimes, as the cast list is scrolling upwards at the end it is then moved to one side to reveal a clip of the next upcoming show and voice-over telling us to remain tuned, often referred to as End Credit Promotions (ECPs).

Trailers provide a variety of information. There is factual information about the programme, for example the next new episode of *Joey* will be tomorrow night at 8.00 p.m. on C5; it can also provide some information about the types of programmes coming up, often presented by the images and/or voice-over. Hence, with the trailer for *Joey* (broadcast 19 March 2005), it is fairly obvious from the laughter track, the setting, the characters in the clips and the anchor text, the comedy hour, that *Joey* is a sitcom.

Another role is to help provide some framework for understanding the programme, for framing it for the audience; for example, for *Joey*, the trailer includes a conversation between Joey and a girl in a living room. She is talking about what her farther feels about Joey, 'He things you're goofy', 'Why?' Joey replies. 'Well he thinks you're an out of work actor who sits at home in a Jacuzzi playing with toys.' Joey looks a bit perplexed and replies, 'They're not toys, they're heroes.' Cue laughter track. Here we get the idea that this is Joey from *Friends*, that he is, as usual, the butt of the jokes. As in *Friends*, he is still a struggling actor, who is out of work and is a little childish. This series is not a comedy in the style of the more cerebral *Frasier*. His childish nature, and the asso-ciation of the programme with C5, is reinforced as, at the end of the trailer, we see Joey sitting at a kitchen table playing with the C5 logo, part of which he picks up and rolls around. We have a pre-image about what we will get if we tune in; the trailer provides or reinforces our view of the programmes; it also lets us know it is on C5.

5.2.4.4   *Broadcaster's publications:* TV Times *and* Radio Times

Another means by which broadcasters not only inform viewers about what programmes they are showing but also help in the construction of a pre-image of the programme is through their own publications, if they have them. For example, both the BBC and ITV have related listing magazines, *Radio Times* and *TV Times* respectively. While the broadcasters do not have direct control over such magazines, they have some input into what programmes might be publicised and how – indeed, they have in the past helped select the cover story (Patterson, 1990: 37). They might, therefore, use such inputs to publicise the start of a new series; they will also try to construct a pre-image of the programme, and present informa-tion and a way of understanding the series, its characters, actors and relationship to other programmes in the genre and the wider social context (Tunstall, 1993: 13–15). This can be done through pictures and captions, on the front cover or inside, features, interviews and reviews. I now wish to explore an example of how such listing magazines can start to create a pre-image of an American programme, a way of under-standing the programme.

For example, the front cover of the *Radio Times* (22–23 March 1969; Midlands and E. Anglia) is split vertically, with pictures of the two stars of American Western series *The High Chaparral* and *The Virginian*, Leif Erickson and James Drury. At the top of the page we have the *Radio Times* banner and the BBCTV logo. These are two shows that were about to be shown on the BBC. An insert on the pictures tells us that these are 'Two Great Westerns' and that they will be on BBC2 and BBC1. The stress on the importance of these programmes is also carried on inside in the cover story which tells us that 'these are two major Western series running on BBC-tv' (*Radio Times*, 1969: 3). The pictures on the front depict the two main actors in their cowboy gear; Leif looks a little moody while James seems happier, with a grin on his face. We can see the blue sky and a tree in one picture and a horse and fence in the other. This confirms for the reader that these are Westerns in the traditional mode; they seem to be set on a ranch or out in the wilds. Leif, because of his age, and the title of the show, *The High Chaparral*, and the pose, give the impression that he is the wise old patriarch of the *High Chaparral*. James Drury is, we assume, or perhaps know from the picture, the Virginian. He appears to be a cowboy or ranch hand, pictured with his closest friend, as tradition would suggest, his horse. We know the genre and can fill in the missing parts if we have not seen this programme before; or it reconfirms what we already know. The insert is made to look like an old wanted poster, it seems to be confirming that this will be set back in the days of the cowboys, back in the time of the wild west.

Inside, we have a cover story. It tells us little specifically about these two programmes apart for the fact that *The Virginian* is popular, it has in the past pulled in a massive audience, of some 12–13 million. Instead, it questions, Why are Westerns so popular? It notes, it cannot be because these types of shows depict reality, for life then was 'mostly nasty, brutish, and short' (ibid.). Instead, the piece suggests that Westerns are popular because of their moral simplicity and nostalgia. This is a programme form that is similar to any stories of heroes and villains and, because of this, is comprehensible around the world. It is a form that is about a 'vanished, simpler America' (ibid.). Because of this universal form, the Western has little to do with the real American history and therefore belongs to us all. Indeed, that it is 'for all levels of brow' (ibid.), this is a programme that can be enjoyed by all social classes.

In this way the cover and the cover story present a particular image of the programme, indeed of the genre as a whole. These are two great Westerns offered by the BBC. They are not some American mass-spawned product, but part of a noble genre, one that is similar to classical stories; in fact, one day, 'they'll [Hollywood] make *Paradise Lost* starring Leif Erickson' (ibid.). These are programmes that, while dealing with moral issues, are also well made; we can see that for ourselves for the pictures show us that they have been shot outdoors, they are shot on film, they are of a high quality and are in colour (while these are publicity shots, we associate these pictures with the production values of the series). Indeed, this feeling is reinforced when the *Radio Times* notes that *The High Chaparral* will be shown in colour on BBC2.

It can be seen that broadcasters, if they have their own .
zines, will try to use this both to provide information ﹢
upcoming programmes, British and American, and to provide
image or narrative image of the programme – a way of understanᴜ
what the programme is about and how and why it will be relevant tᴏ
the viewer. In the example above we can see how the main cover and
cover story work together to tell the reader about the programme, to
show what the programmes look like and how, in this instant, it frames
the series not just as a Western but a form of morality play; the way
they try to bring out certain aspects of the series that might, they hope,
make it more palatable or attractive to the audience.

5.3 Conclusion

American programmes are constructed and encoded with a certain
system of broadcasting in mind. They have the rhythms required to fit into
American schedules; indeed, they are produced, on one level, as part of
the American flow. The ups and downs of the narrative, the moments
when advert breaks come, the way the programme attracts and attempts
to keep the attention of the viewer, and the way they are segmented are
as much part of the programme as the American supertext (Mattelart
et al., 1983: 93). And while, over time, the US market fragments and the
international market increases in size and importance, and as American
producers will become more aware of the needs of other markets and
might change their productions accordingly (see Osgerby *et al.* [2001:
27–8] for an illustration of how some American producers are tailoring
certain programmes for different overseas markets), for now, the needs
of the American market are still determinant (Balio, 1996: 34; Hoskins
et al., 1997: 50); American programmes are still produced predominantly
for the American supertext.

However, American programmes are taken out of their context of
production and sold on into other markets, including the British
market. The British market is different in many ways to the American
one. It has a different history, ethos, traditions and set of regulations. It
has developed in a different way; its megatext is dissimilar to America's.
Because of this, American programmes have been shown on British
channels in different ways than they are in America. So when an American
programme is inserted into a British supertext (schedule), and interacts
horizontally with the programmes, segments of coherency and narrative rhythms found there, it will tend to work in other ways than it had
within the American supertext. Therefore the experience of the British

audience watching an American programme on British television will be different.

Therefore, to understand the role, meaning and experience of watching American programmes, requires an understanding of how they become part of British television, the way they are used, changed, marketed and assimilated into the flow of programmes. One way of doing this has been to look at the way the text is changed by broadcasters, the way American programmes are used and work within the schedule, within the British supertext, the way their use within the schedules has changed over time, how they work within a new megatext and, lastly, how the discourse around them is shaped by the broadcasters as they frame it for the audience, the contextual view. I will now move on to explore, in Chapter 6, the role of television critics in representing and framing American programmes for the British audience.

6
Discourse of Television Critics

6.1 Introduction

In Chapter 6, I will explore the role of the television critic in helping to shape the public discourse around American programmes. Television critics are important in such a discourse not because they determine the way the public view, understand and value programmes but because they, unlike the public, are able to articulate their views on a regular basis through the media. They are able, through their criticism, or reports, as Jack Gould the American television critic calls them (Gould, 1996), to create a framework for understanding particular programmes; they highlight popular debates surrounding certain programmes, debates they nurture and engage with; they provide pleasure for the public in the reading of the reviews and criticisms, as well as presenting new ways of enjoying and engaging with the programmes themselves. As Fiske notes in relation to the role of secondary texts, such as television criticism, '[they play]...a significant role in influencing which of television's meanings may be activated in any one reading...' (Fiske, 1992: 118).

Fiske suggests that television criticism sits at one end of an axis, working in the viewer's interests against, at the other end, the marketing and publicity material working in the interest of the broadcaster and producer (ibid.: 118–19); at mid-point lie the fan-based magazines and more popular forms of coverage that rely on studios for behind-the-scene information, gossip and access to the stars for interviews. As such, for Fiske, critics help explore, expand and offer different interpretations of programmes than those offered by broadcasters. However, this conceptualisation does little to differentiate the critics and the various strands of television criticism that exist, it offers little insight into the complex and changing nature of television criticism and its role in supporting and resisting certain perceptions of television and culture.

In the first section of this chapter, rather than use Fiske's view of television criticism, I will conceptualise TV criticism and the role of TV critics as operating within a discourse in which there is a struggle over accepted views of the cultural role, nature and importance of television. As I explore this discourse I will seek to identify the dominant, popular, oppositional and subversive positions taken, to analyse their relationships to the wider social and culture context and to understand how such a discourse has and is changing. I will also highlight the symbiotic relationship critics have with media they work for and the television industry they write about. As much as they criticise, review and possibly change television, television and the media in turn shape, limit and constrain their work.

In the second section I will take up these ideas to explore, under five subheadings, different types of television criticism and how they categorise, value and analyse television programmes in general and American programmes in particular. Under the first heading I will look at a form of criticism that started to appear in the broadsheets and quality papers in the early period of television; these tended to borrow from and adapt approaches already apparent within theatre and literature criticism (Poole, 1984: 43). Under the second heading I will look at how as television itself changed and matured, so too did television criticism which, by mixing the serious overtones of existing approaches with some humour and reflectivity, produced impressionistic accounts that, in different ways, allowed some coverage of American programmes, sometimes positive and sometimes negative. This, because of its linkages to the more serious form of criticism, I will call neo-criticism. Under the third heading, I will look at popular criticism, a mixture of reviews, interviews, gossip and soft news, including some coverage not produced by television critics, which has been around since the start of television. Under the fourth heading, I will look at the development of niche or fan forms of criticism, particularly those that present surreal and alternative, if not subversive, understandings and readings of programmes around which the critic and the readers have a special affinity. Under the fifth and last heading, I will look at the development of a new space for criticism, the Internet. Here, members of the public, with access to the Internet, are able, if so inclined, to articulate their views in the public realm in a way once reserved for the media critic.

Throughout I will, for pragmatic reasons of time and resources, focus on criticism that developed in print form, the newspapers (and, at the end, the Internet); this is because it has been one of the most important places to find such work, it is generally reflective of debates appearing elsewhere and, pragmatically, it is easier to access than the other more ephemeral media where criticism appears, for example, on radio or on television itself. Taking up from Mike Poole's work, I will conflate the two activities of reviewing and criticism, partly as the two often merge within the pieces discussed and, also, because little is critical in the sense of 'rigour or scholarship', with most appearing to be more impressionistic (ibid.: 42).

6.2   The discourse of television critics

One television critic has described the role of the critic as 'an interpreter between the medium and the public. A good critic can explain to the layman what the artist is trying to do, and by a reverse process can explain to the artists what, from the public's point of view, he is failing to do' (Worsley, 1970: 11). Such a view suggests that the critic is able to use some inherent knowledge and understanding of culture and television to provide a critical viewpoint of the programme for both the public and the artist. The critic is able both to talk on behalf of the public and to look into the artist's mind. For such a critic, they are there to seek out the best that is shown on television, to applaud this, to hold it up as an example of what is creative and innovative, to be critical of those forms that try but fail and, mostly, to ignore or present little coverage of, those parts of television not deemed worthy. Critics, in this vein, are there to serve the public and broadcasters; to act as an independent arbiter.

However, what I would like to argue here is that they are not independent. To start with, as critics work for the media, if no one reads their copy, they lose their job. They must, therefore, be aware, in some way, of the reader they write for and the needs of their employer; they are also dependent on the television industry for co-operation, access, interviews and the very form about which they write. As Poole notes, 'one would have to say that journalists and critics writing about television operate under the double institutional hegemony of the electronic and print media and this determines what they can and, often more significantly, what they cannot say' (1984: 52). The relationship is dynamic and two way, as Fiske writes, '[i]t is important to talk about their relations with television, and not to describe them as spin-offs from it, for the influence is two-way. Their meanings are read back into television, just as productivity as television determines theirs' (1992: 118). Also, one must question, how can they speak for a public they can never completely know, or to determine what the aims of the artist are, when television works in a way more akin to a factory system than in terms of a lone artist working in a studio or workshop?

Indeed, it could be argued that a critic's critical abilities, their likes and dislikes, are not a gift of nature, they are not tapping into a universal set of values, but are particular cultural dispositions, the result of their education and upbringing and, by dint of this, their class (Storey, 2003: 43–4). They, as critics, are products of a particular social, cultural and political context. As such they come to take on and to utilise particular class values, outlooks and tastes, to provide judgements on television programmes. Critics work within a discursive field that is so structured that, at any given moment, a particular hierarchy of value and taste is in dominance. The hierarchy confers a position of power on those equipped with a corresponding cultural knowledge, or cultural capital; this will usually equate with that held by the dominant class. Such a class will attempt to use its power, 'to impose, by their very existence, a definition of excellence which [is] nothing other than their own way of existing' (Bourdieu cited in Storey, 2003: 45). However, this hierarchy is not stable, other culturally aware groups will struggle for new ways of valuing and understanding culture; ways which will, in the future, increase the value of their cultural capital. A point underlined by Garnham and Williams, who argue that '...all societies are characterised by a struggle between groups and/or classes and class fractions to maximise their interests in order to insure their reproduction' (1980: 215).

Therefore, critics take up positions in the cultural field in relation to their class and associated cultural capital. Those critics with the most cultural capital, usually belonging to the middle and upper classes, will be in a dominant position; they will be accepted as serious critics and will be employed by prestigious media outlets. They will align their views of what constitutes good television and their perceptions of American programmes with the dominant cultural hierarchy and its views on mass culture and American culture.

Others, those from different classes and, perhaps, those refusing to take up allotted positions in the cultural field, will try to subvert the existing cultural hierarchy, to present different views and ways of understanding and valuing television. Those in dominant positions in the field might label these subversives as being inferior in an attempt to discredit their views, as both groups struggle over the meaning and acceptance of television in general and, for the purposes of my interests here, American programmes in particular. The critics engage in a public discourse, through their various media outlets, articulating particular cultural, economic, and political views in relation to television; either providing readings of programmes and understandings of television that reinforce the dominant cultural hierarchy, or offering alternative or subversive views. The public, other cultural actors and the broadcasters themselves, interact with such debates, utilising them in different ways as they watch, evaluate and talk to friends and colleagues about television and, where possible, engaging with these discussions in the public arena. Indeed, broadcasters and producers will try to use marketing and PR to try to influence the critics or the media concerns they work for, to sway the debates and what is reviewed and how; while, in a more limited way, the public might engage in media-run polls, join phone-in shows and write to newspapers and magazines. However, while the industry can react through PR and marketing, the public, without ready access to the media are usually either voiceless or fairly muted; therefore, while not all-powerful, the critics are particularly important in the structuring of the public discourse about television.

6.3   Television criticism and American programmes

In this section, I will explore the discourse of television criticism that has appeared in newspapers in Britain since the 1950s. I will, throughout, focus on a number of different ways critics have reviewed and written about American programmes. The five categories I have divided this section into are not period specific, though some forms of criticism are more associated with, and perhaps more dominant at, certain moments. However, such forms of criticism are not mutually exclusive, some critics and newspapers alike can use and mix different forms of criticism; there are no clear lines of division. One can equally find serious and popular articles and styles within the same paper, if not the same review. As I delineate the different forms of criticism and the views they present of American programmes, I will seek to relate these to the wider discursive field, mapping out how and in what ways their coverage of American programmes relates to dominant and alternative views of popular culture and television. My analysis of these forms of criticism is not undertaken to suggest that American programmes are superior or inferior to British ones, or that the critics know more about judging their worth; it is more that critics are situated at a point in the public discourse where dominant cultural views meet others, popular and alternative. It is a site of struggle between different views of television, popular culture and American programmes. By delineating such a struggle, we can begin to understand the different ways that American programmes have been viewed and valued and from which cultural positions.

6.3.1   Television as art: Fear and loathing the American invasion

Television and its related form of public criticism did not develop within a vacuum in Britain; it developed at a time when the cultural elites felt they were under attack from middlebrow and mass culture (Sinfield, 2004: 44–53). Television, with other forms of the mass media, was seemingly helping to create and to disseminate a new form of popular culture, a mass culture that was eroding the existing cultural hierarchy. Linked or even conflated with worries about this levelling down of culture was the idea of Americanisation (Hebdige, 1986: 194–5). For the elites, the mass media, whether film, music or television, was allowing American culture, directly and indirectly, into Britain. American culture was the epitome of mass culture; a culture created for the lowest common denominator by large corporations seeking profit. It was not there to stimulate people, to create beautiful art. As Strinati suggests, '[f]rom this point of view mass culture is a standardised, formulaic, repetitive and superficial culture, one which celebrates trivial, sentimental, immediate and false pleasures at the expense of serious, intellectual, time-honoured and authentic values' (2003: 12).

Developing out of this context, the criticism that appeared in the 1950s was related to that already employed within literature and theatre; it used a similar approach, framework and set of references. Indeed, a number of the early television critics had past careers as theatre critics, for example, Philip Purser, T. C. Worsley and Peter Black. As Worsley wrote in his 1970 collection of his reviews, 'I came to the medium as an experienced dramatic critic and that is about all, and that bias remains in these articles' (p. 12). In many ways these backgrounds, in theatre and literature, were still predominant for those working in the area in the 1970s and 1980s, such critics include Julian Barnes, Hugo Williams, Martin Amis, Adam Mars-Jones and Peter Ackroyd (Poole, 1984: 53).

Such critics, as they utilised the accepted approaches of theatre criticism, would tend to write about single television plays and playwrights, of actors' performances and the human condition, as illustrated by the following review:

> Many who have delighted in Mr. Clive Exton's brilliantly realistic studies of lower middle class life may have been disturbed by his last play, *Hold My Hand Soldier*. Of course, the grasp of taut, expressive dialogue was as complete as ever, and one could not but applaud the

readiness of the dramatist to try a genre quite different from that in which he had made his name... (*The Times*, 1960c)

They concentrated on the individual text, rather than the workings of television, trying, through their analysis, to expose the inner meanings of a particular work and, by dint of this, the intent of the author (Poole, 1984: 44). By framing their work this way, television critics, tried to help television to gain status, to be accepted as a serious form.

These critics did not feel they were there merely to reflect the popular; they were not there to affirm the views of the public. They felt they were there to scrutinise television, to hold it up to critical analysis, to inform the public, and sometimes the broadcasters, to try to argue for good television. For Philip Purser, television critics, 'might not be able to make you change your mind about the programme you had both seen, but if he was any good he could put his finger on what made it good, or why and where it had failed to rise to its subject' (1992: 130). As Mary Crozier, television critic of *The Guardian* in the 1950s and the 1960s, wrote in a letter to *The Times*, 'Television... throws out a spate of material, good, bad, and indifferent; dramatic, documentary, news, events, and current affairs. The critics try to keep an eye on it; to encourage what is promising and to note what is puerile' (1960a).

While these critics embraced all that television offered, '[o]ne of Peter Black's virtues as a critic was that he embraced the whole span of these offerings' (Purser, 1992: 11), they tended to focus on British productions over American; drama, especially single plays, over other forms; and live over filmed television,

> I called these prefabricated programmes artefacts... artefacts were boring documentaries, situation comedies, nearly all quiz shows, most panel games and an increasing number of entertainments which sounded as if they were live and spontaneous but no longer were. (Ibid.: 134–5)

Behind such views was an accepted hierarchy of what constituted the best or most interesting forms of television, the most creative and innovative, on which the more serious critics concentrated the most. While they did not dismiss the rest on offer, they often thought it inferior. As T. C. Worsley wrote,

> My main interest is in... the so-called... play, the series and serial; and with the last two the problem is really why they need remain so

bad and trivial as they mostly do. Then there is the wide field of documentary to which television has given a home and the chance for much development and experiment. (1970: 12)

Seemingly, apart from documentary, Worsley was less interested in other television genre, for example the sitcom or quiz show. Such a derogatory view can also be discerned in the work of Mary Crozier of *The Guardian*, for example in her review of a new game show that appeared in 1959, ' "Dotto," the "game that turns dots into pictures and pictures into pounds" and television critics into maniacs... "Dotto" defies description for the pen weeps tears of agony'.

American programmes entered into such a critical discourse in several ways: first, by their absence. For many of these serious critics American programmes, though they were popular, were automatically tarred with the brush of mediocrity and required little serious analysis. They were formulaic, glossy, offering little insight into the human condition. Therefore many of the popular programmes of the time were absent from this serious critical discourse; secondly, where they did enter it was often as signifiers of what was or could happen to British television. As Philip Purser indicates in his bibliography where he wrote about how he worried about British television when, in the 1950s,

the promises were forgotten, original programmes fewer, and the ITV companies increasingly dependent on *Gun Law, Superman, I Love Lucy, Medic, Mr District Attorney, The Count of Monte Cristo*, as many as twenty, twenty-five, thirty transatlantic or mid-Atlantic filmlet series winding through the telecine machines every week. (1992: 52)

When the critics might mention American programmes, they were seen as an undemanding form, an easy, less rigorous television. T. C. Worsley even uses the metaphor of drug addiction as a way to describe the attraction of American programmes, 'I was even once a slave, too, to *Perry Mason*, but swore I would break the habit, as the solution in each episode came to bear less and less relation to the exposition, and the formula became more and more ridged' (1970: 14). These were programmes that were not going to stimulate the audience's intellect.

The earliest critics writing on television in Britain set out to provide a type of criticism that would help television to be accepted as a serious cultural form (Poole, 1984: 45). While they argued that they have had to come to terms with television as a new medium, and had to develop new approaches, they were informed by dominant views on culture and associated forms of cultural criticism. This influenced the way they approach television: Programmes were there to be judged, to be criticised; the best had to be highlighted and the worse attacked or forgotten. The interest of the critic was very much on individual programmes and their form, rather than their function and the pleasure they gave. In terms of American programmes, the dominant form, found on British television from the 1950s onwards, were the series and serials which, for these critics, were written to a formula, were standardised and uncreative. These were programmes to be forgotten or, for some, a sign of what could happen if the guard was let down. Of what will happen if television lost its way.

6.3.2 Television as television: Neo-criticism

As television began to develop its own forms and adapted those of other media – the episodic series, television serials, soaps, sitcoms, current affairs, documentaries and variety shows – as it became part of the everyday lives of British people, and those of the critics, a new form of television criticism appeared – what I will call here neo-criticism; the way television was written about changed with the medium. New critics came to prominence, or existing critics changed their style of writing, to embrace a more popular style, one where humour was mixed with some analysis, a mixture that some traditional critics did not like, 'the least good thing about Clive James was the troop of jokers – or wankers, as Dennis Potter classifies them less politely – who followed him' (Purser, 1992: 161). These critics accepted that while they were possibly more knowledgeable about television than the public, they needed to write about it from a similar position as the viewer. As Clive James notes, '[o]ne of the chief functions of a television critic is to stay at home and watch the programmes on an ordinary domestic receiver, just as his readers do' (1981: 16). They had to understand and approach television as a popular medium watched and enjoyed at home; if they failed to do this, their newspapers might look for a critic who could. At one stage Clive James was thought, through his popular style, to add some 10,000 readers to the circulation of the *Observer* (Poole, 1984: 55).

This new form of criticism was more accepting. It was not an attempt to transfer, too literarily, a critical approach from one medium to another, to look at television through the critical eye of the art or theatre critic, nor, however, was it an attempt merely to praise and accept all the programmes produced. It was an attempt to create a form of criticism more in tune with television as a popular medium. Again to quote Clive James, there is not much to choose between the dumb critic who likes everything and the smart one who likes nothing. The first is tube-struck, in the way that some theatre critics are stage-struck. The second is the purist in the way that some neurotic parents try to keep their precious child free of germs, only to see it die of a cut finger. (1983: 20)

Somehow a balance had to be struck between liking and enjoying television while also being discerning, between the critic as critic, and critic as viewer.

These critics, when reviewing American programmes, approached them in a variety of ways. Foremost, however, they treated them as programmes and not some form of cultural invasion. The fact that they were produced in America was no automatic reason to ignore or deni-grate them; though, as Geoffrey Lealand argues, many of the critics lambasted or produced ironic readings of the majority of American soaps and series that were aired in Britain in the 1970s and 1980s (1984: 69–71). The neo-critics accepted that television is a popular domestic medium, a medium to be reviewed in a more reflective way, often mixing their analysis with humour, for example,

> So the final run of *Frasier* began this week, for those who could stay up that late ... Given that so many of *Frasier's* viewers are – like me – thirtysomethings with kids, this was an idiotic way to treat an old and loyal friend. Counting *Frasier* together with its parent, *Cheers*, then the exploits of the baldy shrink have been on Channel 4 throughout most of its existence. Dr Crane would doubtless diagnose something to do with an unhappy childhood or a favourite cuddly bunny among the channel's schedulers. I diagnose stupidity. (Courtauld, 2004a)

In such a review the critic appears to be more interested in his relation-ship to the programme, how it has become part of his life, rather than just dissecting the programmes. For this critic, who has children, *Frasier's* late slot is inconvenient to stay up and watch. He goes on to suggest that this programme is part of his life: it is 'an old friend'. It is a programme that he has followed from the start, and even earlier, by watching the programme from which it was spun off from, *Cheers*. He is not just critically reviewing a text but reflecting on it as a popular cultural form that is part of his life; he writes about it as part of the wider television-watching experience.

American programmes are written about using knowledge that the critic expects the audience to share: knowledge about the main characters and the basic storyline of a programme, knowledge about American television and British programmes in general and the various genre in particular. The critic will bring all these different television references into play as she produces a particular understanding of a programme; American references might be used to explore British programmes, and British references used to explore American ones. Such reviews accept that American programmes, over the last fifty years, are now part and parcel of British culture. This is especially true for certain genre of programme, and for certain age groups of viewers, for whom these programmes are important and are meaningful. As a review from *The Observer* illustrates in relation to *Six Feet Under*,

> Nate Fisher remains under anaesthesia while he has his head examined – a potentially fatal medical drama which, as an end-of-season cliffhanger, saw the normally deliciously dysfunctional Fisher family suddenly morph into the *Waltons*. No matter how dark the show, even an HBO show, you can usually count on US drama delivering a little damp hankie moment just when you don't really need one. (*The Observer*, 2003)

On one level this extract presents a quick synopsis of one episode of *Six Feet Under*. Nate, one of the main characters, has a medical problem and his family are being supportive. On another level it uses a series of reference points to expand this synopsis into a form of analysis. While *Six Feet Under* is usually centred on the 'deliciously dysfunctional Fisher family', it suggests in this episode they have been reduced to *The Waltons*, an American feel-good television show about a family, of the same name, from the 1970s; while it is usually a dark show, and from HBO, the maker of innovative programmes, here it lets the viewer down with 'a little damp hankie moment', as other American programmes seemingly often do. The reviewer is making connections and using references that the viewer will know about, *The Waltons*, HBO's brand and other American shows with their sentimental moments. This critical review tells the reader what the reviewer felt about the programme, why it stands out and highlights its weaknesses. It does this in a way that accepts and frames the programmes in ways that the British reader would understand and make connections with.

This does not mean such criticism just relies on humour and a degree of reflectivity. To establish and keep its status as a form of criticism, to help keep some value to its enterprise, programmes will also be judged using accepted critical frameworks. These frameworks tend to accord with those used by the earlier 'serious' critics in the way they tap into a similar critical concerns and values. For example, on certain occasions, they locate and understand American programmes in terms of the authorial hand behind the show. This is obviously more easily done with genre such as drama, which has a script, narrative and actors, than a talk show. This suggests a falling back onto a traditional notion of culture, one where there is a supposed single creative genius behind the creative form. Though it could be argued that a named person is also a useful device for the viewers in approaching and selecting which programmes to watch, a shorthand for the critic and a useful means for marketing the programme. Indeed, many American producers have, for sometimes, been keen to create and develop recognisable brands by elevating a producer, as an individual, as the main guiding influence; for example, Quinn Martin, Aaron Spelling, Chris Carter, David Kelly and Joss Whedon – some of whom also contribute to the writing of various episodes – are used to identify shows. In a similar way, some corporate bodies, MTM and HBO for example, have managed to also do this with their own names. For example, this highlighting of the creative genius behind a series can be seen with Joanna Coles' piece in *The Times* where she notes, 'David E. Kelly's new prime-time drama series which has transformed Monday nights into Must See TV in America' (Coles, 2000). For the savvy reader, David E. Kelly has also been involved in other notable series such as *Chicago Hope, Ally McBeal* and *L A Law*, series that could be viewed as obtaining a certain level of success and critical acclaim.

Often, in place of the producer, the writer will be specially mentioned, possibly focusing on their skill, or lack of it, in crafting that particular episode. For example, Mark Lawson (2004), writing in *The Guardian* on *Deadwood*, notes how the director and writer work to make a 'western that is slow, vicious and nihilistic in a way that very little cinema – and almost no television outside of HBO – would dare to be. The opening episode begins with a hanging and then gets darker.' And as Marshall writes,

> *The Wire*, a tour de force that dissects America's self-destructive and increasingly asinine war on drugs ... Simon and Burns always set out to write something that would have the subtlety, moral ambiguity and grimly panoramic vision of the modern American novel and they are clearly proud of what they have achieved. *The Wire* is indeed novelistic but it is also chillingly realistic. (2005)

Linked to this, critics will often, also, focus on the quality of the script. They will talk about the verisimilitude of the dialogue, its tightness, rapid delivery and cleverness. For example, some note the quality of the writing on American comedies, including *Friends*, '... some of the one-liners were so taut they might have been botoxed' (*The Observer*, 2004). In a similar vein, a critic at the *Observer* wrote in 1999 about *Sex in the City*, '[then] there is the script which, because it is based on a "Real Life" sparkles even as it reveals the darker underbelly of 90s sexual mores. *Sex*... is smart, intelligent, full of pithy dialogue, arching truism and a major surprise real, dirty language, as spoken by real, dirty girls and boys about real, dirty sex'. This does not mean that all American scripts are or have always been of the same quality, or to the liking of the critics. For example, many of the critics saw the writing in *Angel*, in moments, as 'self-indulgent and dull' (Courtauld, 2004b).

While at times the nationality of the programmes disappears within some reviews, at other moments some critics highlight America's system of production and its different television culture, often focusing on differences between the system that produced the programme and the British context, and stylistic elements, of glossy American programmes compared to more socially realistic British ones. For example, Charlie Courtauld compares how the similar conspiracy spy shows the American *24* and the British one *Spooks* have developed over time,

> A year ago, *24* was the cock of the walk, the programme that everyone wanted to emulate. Split screens, urgent drumbeats and mobile phones popped up almost everywhere in TV drama. Not least in *Spooks*. As such a blatant *24* emulator, *Spooks* was the subject of some derision. But this year the roles are reversed. Now it is *Spooks* which is the superior programme, and *24* stutters rather lamely behind. (Courtauld, 2003)

Initially, it would seem that, for the critic, *24* was ahead of *Spooks*, a programme that was, for some, trying to ape it. However, over time *Spooks* has developed, dropping some of the obvious attempts to emulate *24*, the split screens for example, while *24* has stayed the same. While there is a comparison of different styles, linked back to national culture, this does not mean that the American programme is just being criticised for being American, it is criticised for its lack of development.

Recently a discourse has appeared around the notion of 'must see' television. These are programmes, that, over the last decade, some critics, writers and columnists suggest stand out of the ordinary. For some, these programmes signal the appearance of a new form of quality programmes, a new second golden age, one that harks back to the live television dramas of the 1950s – the first golden age (Thompson, 1997; Wilk, 1999). These are often popular programmes, with audiences and critics alike, many of which are American programmes.

> *Six Feet under, Nip/Tuck, NYPD Blue, CSI, CSI Miami, Law and Order, The Handler, Without a Trace, 24* – the number of superlative American drama series on our screens at the moment is getting ridiculous... It's almost becoming too much; like gorging on caviar. (By way of return British drama at the moment contributes *Shameless*. Just *Shameless*). (*The Mirror*, 2004b)

The reviews and criticisms developing around these must-see programmes follow the impressionistic-literary tradition, often focusing on the acting, scripts and quality of the productions. For example, Pete Clark (2002), writing in the *Evening Standard*, talks about the 'brilliance of *The Sopranos*', the 'deceptive precision of the writing, which frequently appears to freewheel when, in fact, the gears are being engaged with consummate skill'. He notes how '[n]othing in this script is wasted... [where the] verbal efficiency is matched by a mastery of tone...'. He ends by noting that '[t]hought and intelligence is packed into every shot'. For Sarah Vine (2005) writing in *The Times*, '[t]here is, nevertheless, one area in which the Americans succeed without question: *Desperate Housewives*. Last night's episode continued the development of three central characters... Bree showed genuine compassion, Edie was actually nice to someone and Gabrielle learnt to do her laundry – in the spa bath. Brilliant.' A discourse has appeared around American programmes that, using a similar language and values to the older form of more serious criticism, has argued that some American programmes can be viewed as offering quality forms of drama; that while not the same as single plays, they have similar characteristics.

However, not all accept the elevation of such programmes, especially at the expense of British ones. There is a struggle going on in Britain over different values and cultural outlooks, between those that are still critical of American culture and its output and those that, along with other parts of American culture, find it stimulating. As Hadley Freeman (2005) argued in *The Guardian*,

> It is time the belief that American TV is somehow superior to British TV was finally grappled to the ground. Yes, *The Sopranos* is marginally

more appealing than, say, *Gimme Gimme Gimme*. But Britain still clings to the bizarre belief that anything from across the Atlantic has a glamour it can only hope to ape. Nowhere is this more evident than in its blindness to the obvious fault with many US programmes: that they patronise viewers to a degree unreached even by Anne Robinson.

Freeman then goes on to explore moments in *Desperate Housewives* and *Sex in the City*, where she feels the producers have been heavy handed to the point where they, 'prove that American programme-makers have no confidence in viewers' intelligence, somewhat putting paid to the theory that these "witty" shows respect their viewers. British TV? Gimme Gimme Gimme' (Freeman, 2005). Janet Street Porter, a writer and broadcaster, takes up a similar position to American programmes in a piece in *The Independent*; while accepting that *Desperate Housewives* will probably be the next 'must-see' programme of 2005 she feels,

> *Desperate Housewives* certainly looks fantastic, all tracking shots, cranes, super-glossy interiors, loads of lip gloss and soft, warm sun. There is no doubt that the acting is of the highest order and all the production values are exemplary. But it's about as cutting edge as a packet of Symingtons Table Cream.... If nothing else, it proves that Britain and America have very different sensibilities. We are grown-up, sophisticated, knowing and capable of layers of meaning. Sadly, *Desperate Housewives* proves once again American popular culture is one-note – it tells you a story in a childlike, simple way and then clobbers you over the head with it time and time again. Subtle it ain't.' (Porter, 2005)

In this section, I have explored the way a form of neo-criticism has appeared, offering a style of criticism that has mixed humour with serious analysis, which has tried to view the programmes from the position of the viewer, and that has tried to understand television as television. Such an approach has, in varying ways, brought American programmes into a critical dialogue about television. It has managed to do this by first accepting the popular status of television, using references and a language that the television-watching public understand, while, secondly, maintaining critics' credentials by continuing to use existing dominant critical values and approaches, those developed and used by the earlier critics. Hence the critics will often focus on the author behind the programme, the verisimilitude of the script and the performances of the actors. Such a focus has recently, with the appearance of quality American dramas and comedies and changes in the British broadcasting environment, led to critical acclaim by some critics for American programmes. It is less that the critics are seeing more value in American programmes, than that these new forms of programmes are viewed by critics as fitting more with their critical criteria; they offer, seemingly, a cultural distinctiveness often hard to find with many of the popular British programmes.

6.3.3 Popular or 'soft' television criticism

As much as news journalism has developed into, what some label as, hard (serious) and soft (popular) journalism, forms often associated with masculine and feminine values respectively (Allan, 1999: 112–17), so too has television criticism. While a form of analytical television criticism has developed, usually associated with quality newspaper, often written by men, there has, from the start, also been a more popular form of television discourse – What Mary Crozier saw as being ' "news and "gossip", of which, considering the number of "stars" and personalities in the business, there is always plenty' (1958: 200). This has been a form of criticism that has been, at least for certain moments, dominated by female critics and journalists. There seems 'to be a number of assumptions at work here about the "suitability" of women writers to handle television in the kind of gossipy, star-struck fashion that is the hallmark of the tabloid's coverage' (Poole, 1984: 59).

In this section I want to focus on this form of popular television journalism, and related soft news, to explore the way it frames and writes about American programmes – how it makes them part of the reader's live, informs them about what's going on in a programme, future story lines and what is happening behind the scenes. Such popular reviews, criticism or general coverage tend less to argue about the merits of a programme, to offer alternative readings or to explore its form, than to provide a reaffirmation of an already popular programme. What is popular is what is covered. This does not mean that such writers do not write about new up and coming programmes but that when they do this, they rely on their experience of what, they believe, will fit with the popular sentiments of their readers, often influenced by the marketing and publicity that surrounds new programmes and the need of their own media organisations.

This attempt to frame a programme for popular acceptance, to fit it within the way other popular programmes are written about, can be seen with reviews and stories written about *Desperate Housewives* before it was first shown in Britain. As *The Sun* proclaimed,

ONE of the stars of the new TV series *Desperate Housewives* is no stranger to stripping for the cameras – as this snap shows...Marcia Cross, 44, right, is seen baring her boobs in a raunchy 1996 movie called Female Perversions. The exposure clearly helped her telly role in a show dubbed the naughtiest to come out of the U.S. since *Sex and the City*. (*The Sun*, 2005)

Here, *The Sun* starts to frame the programme in terms of a sexual allure, linking it with an already successful programme, *Sex and the City*. The journalists and reviewers will attempt to build up a story, to build up a public debate around the programme, to create a new popular sensation – one that will help sell newspapers, and the programme. They do this not by pointing out the quality of the acting or the script but by focusing, more often than not, on the sexual content of the programme and stories about the actors who play the main roles.

The recent coverage of the popular American shows *Sex and the City, Friends, The Simpsons, ER, Frasier* and *Lost* by this form of journalism or criticism is a mixture of information about the upcoming episodes, previews and reviews, mixed with interviews with the actors, gossip, revelations and fashion tips. It is an attempt to create and nurture a popular discourse about such programmes. Indeed, those programmes that offer more scandal and sexual escapades and that contain good-looking stylish men and women often gain more coverage; they are able to spread out from the more distinct television columns into the surrounding leisure pages and, often, on to the 'news' pages. There is an excess in such programmes that television critics, and television criticism, cannot handle on their own; the discourse is larger than the programme itself. For example, *Sex and the City*, an American comedy, that because of its content matter, a number of independent women living in New York looking for love and sex, was the right kind of programme for this kind of soft journalism to pick up and cover. Hence, fashion reviewers writing for the *Evening Standard* felt at home in covering the fashion aspects of such a show,

ES Fashion Stalker pays homage to Carrie, Samantha, Miranda and Charlotte and their wardrobes.

CARRIE How to sum up Carrie Bradshaw's dress sense?

Eclectic. The New York clotheshorse has pioneered more styles over the past six series than Coco Chanel.

Carrie has singlehandedly brought us such classics as the corsage, the name necklace and the flat cap, plus dangerously high heels and a cornucopia of designer dresses. We've laughed, we've cooed, we've copied; and all the while we've admired Carrie for having such continual fashion fun.

Favourite designers: Matthew Williamson, Christian Dior, Donna Karan, Marni, Anna Molinari, Vivienne Westwood, Manolo Blahnik, Jimmy Choo and vintage.

(*Evening Standard*, 2000)

Likewise, much of the coverage also highlights, and in some ways creates, gossip and stories about what is going on behind the scenes, for example the story that the actors on *Desperate Housewives* had fallen out and were bitching about each other received many column inches; as Lorraine Kelly wrote in *The Sun*,

[a]lthough they are all mature women, it appears the stars of C4's Desperate Housewives are a bunch of spoiled brats. It seems they can barely stand the sight of each other. And while producers have been trying to keep their bitching under wraps, it all kicked off when they posed in swimsuits for Vanity Fare. (Kelly, 2005)

Often the journalist will mix the fictional world, the 'reel' (fictional) world, with the 'real' world, the worlds of the character and actor, adding to the pleasure and enjoyment of the viewers as they start to imagine what was happening between the actors when the programme was filmed; the degree to which the different lives collide (Fiske, 1992: 124–6). For example, Jenny Eden writing in *The Sun* on 9 April 2005 explores the developing relationship between James Denton, who plays Mike Delfino, and Terri Hatcher, who plays Susan. A relationship that is strained when he is implicated in a murder: 'The game could be up for *Desperate Housewives'* mystery man Mike Delfino. His true identity is at risk of being revealed when Mike is arrested for Mrs Hubber's murder...Ironically, Susan...ends up being Mike's alibi. The night of Mrs Huber's death was the first time they had sex'. James comments that 'snogging co-star Terri is one of the perks of the job' (ibid.). Such coverage allows the world of the *Desperate Housewives* to take on new dimension, where the lives of actors and characters merge, and where the viewer/reader can follow both aspects and how they interact.

Within the television previews and reviews, where the focus is more on the programme rather than on the surrounding elements, the language and references used is populist, similar in tone to what is found elsewhere is the paper. For example, as Fiona Morrow wrote in *The Sun* about the start of a new series of the medical drama *ER*, 'Hospital drama *ER* is famous for its dramatic scenes, and you won't be disappointed when the new series starts. It kicks off with two episodes back-to-back, during which everyone is thrown into the fray as a multiple car crash has Chicago County General's ER overflowing with serious casualties.' The article goes little further than telling the reader they will not be let down and provides a basic outline of what happens – there is a car crash with casualties. Interspersed throughout the piece, is an interview with one of the actors, Abby, who is asked why she thinks *ER* succeeds: 'She believes ER is such a success because it mixes personal stories with heart-stopping action' (Murrow, 2004). It would seem that the little analysis or reflection that appears in this review is, in the end, left to one of the actors. It is not up to the writer to say what they think.

Where this form of 'criticism' covers American programmes, it is as popular culture, as a leisure activity. The writers associated with this form, and the papers in which it is found, are less interested in taking a standpoint on issues of quality or supporting domestic over American productions, than in reflecting what they think the public wants to read about. The American programmes covered stand side by side with reviews of British programmes, soaps such as *East Enders* and *Coronation Street*, documentaries such as *Jamie Oliver's School Dinners*, reality programmes like *Big Brother*, and comedies such as *The Office*. They are spoken about in an easy-going, non-analytical manner. While some of the work focuses on the programmes, much ties the programme into the lives of the reader: What was that dress or make-up that so and so was wearing? What is the latest fashion in New York? The coverage also provides background information, gossip from the show and interviews with the stars. American programmes, in this way, are covered as British programmes but, perhaps, with a hint of the supposed excitement of America, that 'other' culture across the Atlantic; the nation that gave us Hollywood, New York, LA, expensive fashion, beautiful people and fast cars.

This form of popular discourse, this 'soft' criticism, found within the media, and here I have concentrated on the newspapers, does not overtly subvert or undermine the existing dominant cultural hierarchy. It does, however, open up a popular discourse around television and particular television programmes for its readers. It opens them up for the viewer to actively engage with the text in a way they understand,

and it helps them find new forms of pleasure and enjoyment. However, this is a form of television writing that reaffirms, by constituting itself as the polar opposite, the hierarchical relationships of elite and mass, of high and low culture. The critics, newspapers and readers are aware that this is non-serious criticism; if you want the serious criticism, buy another kind of paper.

6.3.4   Surreal and ironic television criticism: The carnivalesque

However, some of the writing found within British newspapers subverts the accepted hierarchy of the popular and serious overtly. On one hand it is often comic, surreal, if not tinged with a hint of black humour, on the other, it is fastidious and knowledgeable. Often, because of its humour and the style of writing, it attracts youngish readers who have come to share the same views; in many ways the writer is a fan of television, like those that read these columns. As Jim Shelley wrote, under the pseudonym Tapehead, about his early enthusiasm for television: 'At the start, Tapehead was positively evangelical, unlike even the most successful TV critics who, to this day, seem to write as if writing about television is a drag and something that stops them enjoying the fresh air or writing books. Tapehead couldn't watch enough of it' (Shelley, 2001).

Such work appears across different types of British newspapers, often in small hidden-away columns. It is a form of cult criticism that is not aiming to be, or to reflect, the popular, indeed it thrives on and likes its exclusiveness; nor is it offering a form of detached critical analysis, this is left to the more serious critics. This form of criticism is there to look at programmes in new, less reverential ways, without the framework often employed by other critics.

For example, Charlie Brooker of *The Guardian* has, for a number of years, been writing a column called 'Screen Burn' for the 'Saturday Guide'. In his somewhat surreal exposition of programmes shown in the week, he occasionally picks on an American programme. For example, in 2002, *24* was reviewed in a series of weekly articles. Rather than outlining the story, writing about behind-the-scenes gossip, or undertaking some form of critical analysis of the programme, week by week he explored the flaws, mistakes, indeed the illogic of the programme, often helped by readers who would send in their comments. He offers another way of understanding the programme, another way of enjoying it. For example, on 30 March 2002 he wrote,

Anyway, back to the insanely addictive *24*... For some reason, the Noble Senator seems to think he'll be able to function on the most important day of his political career without enjoying a moment's shut-eye the night before. Didn't he see *Touch the Truck*? Assassination will be the least of his worries once sleep deprivation kicks in and he starts swatting invisible demons in the middle of a pre-election press conference.

While this is a programme that he likes watching, this does not stop him being critical of it. However, this criticism has an ironic edge to it. He is not just criticising the programme in the usual way, to discover the intent of the author or the programme as a text but, instead, he helps the reader/viewer to look at the inconsistencies, to laugh at them, to enjoy the programme, to gain new and different pleasures from the programme. The quote above points out that the Senator, on the eve of his election for the position of President, is staying up without any sleep, why? The next day, the most important in his political life, he would not be able, in a normal world, to fully function. To extend this point further, Brooker then links this observation to an earlier satirical piece he wrote on the British programme, *Touch the Truck*, where contestants must keep touching a truck, without sleep, until only one is left. For Brooker, both programmes are as ludicrous and entertaining, this is the excess that some television provides; its meaning cannot be understood, or contained, through normal critical analysis. New pleasures are found in this excess. In a similar way, he tackles other American programmes, sometimes pronouncing them worth watching but always providing a surreal and unusual way of thinking about and enjoying them. In this vein, he writes about an American reality television programme *Manhunter*:

> *Manhunter* is hosted by a terrifying thing called Jaaaahrn Walsh. Jaaaahrn's delivery lurks halfway between John Wayne and an animatronic theme-park dummy employed to entertain queuefuls of impatient visitors wailing outside the ghost train... He shouts, over-emphasises every other word, and punctuates his speech with so many ridiculous hand gestures he'll have his own eye out if he's not careful. (Brooker, 2000)

After reading this, it is hard to watch *Manhunter* in the way the producers meant; however serious the presenter tries to be, the more earnest he looks, the more peculiar his presentation style appears. Indeed, it is hard to view similar programmes in the way one has done before. Brooker has opened up the excess of the programme, of the genre, to new pleasures.

In a similar way, Jim Shelly, who used to write for *The Guardian* under the nom-de-plume Tapehead, offers, in a column for *The Mirror* entitled 'Shellyision', a similar manic and strange way of viewing and enjoying television programmes, including some American programmes. Here the writer offers ludicrous interpretations of programmes, raising insane view points, problems with the inner logic of the programmes and comparing them to other programmes, films and everyday life. Shelly does not just present straight reviews of the programme but uses a mixture of irony, satire and blunt critical attacks to present a different way of thinking about the programme, its supposed popularity and its viewers,

> THE last episode of Friends was a big event chez Shelleyvision. Like so many people (girls) around the country last Friday night, I had a party to mark the occasion.
>
> I wanted to make sure they really were finishing and weren't coming back. Not so much a Farewell Friends party as a F*** Right Off Friends party. I still can't understand how so many supposedly sussed British people (girls) liked Friends, let alone aspired to the values the six beefcakes and bimbos symbolised (coffee-house lifestyle, inane friend-ships, lovely hair). Fifty one million Americans can be wrong, right?
>
> (*The Mirror*, 2004a)

Rather than sing the praises of *Friends*, on the eve of its last every episode, or to attempt some form of critical analysis, he lampoons the programme and those that watch it. He, seemingly, cannot wait for it to finish.

Therefore, in terms of a discourse about American programmes, of how they should or might be understood, such a form of criticism, while only aimed at and only read by a minority, presents new ways of understanding American programmes – indeed, all television. Any accepted way of critically analysing a programme is ignored. This is 'carnivalesque' criticism, for a moment turning the dominant stan-dards, values and hierarchy on its head; it opens up the television text so that different pleasures can be accessed and explored (Fiske, 1992: 94–5). However, such a criticism, with its tendency to incorporate and target niche groups, means that it only tends to engage with a minority, usually the knowing, knowledgeable viewer or fan. It is also open to a question that, while it might ignore more popular or critical approaches, those that enjoy this form of criticism and writing also, at the same time, accept and read other forms of television criticism and reviews – that viewers might hold on to a number of different ways of understanding and valuing programmes, including American programmes, accepting some form of critical hierarchy, dependent on context.

6.3.5 The Internet: The public as critic

While the public has traditionally been limited in how they can enter the debates about television, apart from writing into newspapers or phoning up radio shows, and while they are generally positioned as non-experts in most debates, this exclusion, technological and cultural, is changing with the rise of the Web and sites dedicated to television criticism and reviewing. A new form of public criticism is appearing: one that mixes the public's and the critic's role; that allows anyone with Web access and wishes to be part of a pubic debate about television to do so (though it has to be noted that fanzines and some magazines have also provided an avenue of output for the public for some time). These sites, and closely related ones, provide detailed information about the television industry, what is being produced and what has been produced, space for discussions, often including interactive chat pages, and the ability to allow easily accessible and often extensive television reviews to be posted and read. Some sites offer all these elements, while some focus on a mixture of these functions. These sites while usually focused on the broadcasting system of particular nations often, partly because of the global flows and knowledge of programmes, are still open to input from people from many nations. For example, TVTome (<http://www.tvtome.com>), an American site, includes some reviews of British programmes written by British correspondents. Likewise, British Web users can use these sites to see what is being written about American programmes.

Such sites provide space for a more open, horizontal form of discussion about television programmes (discussion between individuals rather than the more vertical, up–down, discussions from critic to readers and viewers). No longer do you have to be a professional critic to reach thousands or millions of people; now any one can review a programme, post it on a website and become active in the wider public discourse about television. Therefore, sites such as *Off Telly* (<http://www.offthetelly.co.uk>), tvtome (<http://www.tvtome.com>), (<http://www.thefutoncritic.com>) and the student zone (<http://www.thestudentzone.com>) offer a variety of space for would-be television reviewers or critics. Looking at the reviews on such sites, which cover a wide range of American programmes, one is struck by the similarity and differences of reviewing styles. While some primarily focus on critically analysing the form and content of programmes, others tend to present a more general overview that is often culturally, politically or socially contextualised. For example, in a review on *South Park* located on a British student site we can see the way they emphasise and highlight a sequence in *South Park* within the wider context of American's attitude to war,

> Full of the usual close to the knuckle humour look out for the anti-war banners held by the boys and listen closely to the episode's musical contribution for some contemporary fun poking at America's attitudes to war. (<http://www.thestudentzone.com/articles/tv-southpark.html>, accessed 12 May 2005)

Such a review highlights an aspect of a programme that might not have been picked up by other critics or reviewers. It allows groups or individuals to provide a more political focus to a review, opening the text up to new or different readings. This is not to suggest that the *South Park* creator's intentions were not in the first place to comment on the war, but the Web provides a space where this can be highlighted.

Some of the reviews appear to present serious analysis of programmes, while others are written with more humour. It is evident that both these types of reviewing styles are similar to those found in the newspaper medium, it is as if the conventions of criticism are still being followed even on the Web. For example, in a review of *Six Feet Under*, one reviewer provides not only an overview of what happens in the episode, but also explores the characters' motives, the development of the storyline and, ultimately, what the reviewer felt about the series:

> The viewer feels their pain, too, and this is the point of *Six Feet Under*. Despite being a programme that draws heavily on fantasy sequences, it feels real. It maybe a savage reality but it is still a reality. You believe that they are a family and that they are experiencing the problems we observe on screen. The characters as individuals are not especially likeable but put together you come to realise how they depend and rely on one another. In short, you care what happens to them. (<http://www.offthetelly.co.uk/reviews/2003/sixfeetunder.htm>, accessed 12 May 2005)

This type of review, with its focus on the text presented in an impressionistic style, is similar to the more analytical serious reviews covered under the neo-criticism section.

Most of the reviews on the Web seem, possibly for obvious reasons, to be written by fans. It would seem that many of these 'public' reviews are using their new-found voice to articulate their views about programmes which are or were their favourites, '[t]he *West Wing*'s cast and crew don't seem able to take things seriously anymore, the programme's not worth sticking with even . . . let alone respect' (<http://www.offthetelly.co.uk/reviews/2004/westwing.htm>, accessed 12 May 2005). This is especially true with some of the more cult-styled American shows that, while not always on mainstream television, and often receiving little coverage in the mainstream press, are watched religiously by a small fan base; for example, *Seinfeld*, *FireFly*, *Arrested Development* and *Millennium*.

American programmes enter this space in a number of ways. They are popular programmes on British television that people wish to express their views on; they are niche programmes that adoring fans wish to write about, often showing off their knowledge of such programmes; they are programmes to ridicule, to criticise; and they are programmes to hold up as the best examples of the genre. The main point to make is that, for most of these sites, American programmes are covered, winning both praise and criticism; they are written about by those that view them as part of their television culture and not some form of alien import.

The Web-based form of criticism is a mixture of all that is found in the media: serious, comic, popular and surreal. The difference is that it is overwhelmingly written by the public, not full-time critics. These are those wishing to be critics, those who just want to be part of a public debate about television, those who just like to note how much they like a programme, those that are attacking accepted ways of thinking and talking about television and culture, and fans who view particular programmes as their own – a form of textual poaching, as Henry Jenkins calls it (1991). While some do this in a way that upholds accepted values and styles of how to critically appraise television programmes, others use the space to attempt new ways of writing about programmes; see, for example, Charlie Brooker's website, TVGoHome (<http://www.TVGoHOme.com>) – now closed, but archived, still allowing public access. It was here that he was able to experiment with his style that later fed into his *Guardian* column.

6.4 Conclusion

In this chapter, I have explored the way American programmes have been reviewed and critically assessed by British television critics. Such criticism, while not all powerful, it does not decide which programmes will be popular, it is indicative of a wider public discourse – a discourse where the broadcasting industry, the viewers, the media for which the critic works and various cultural elites and groupings are in contention as they seek to determine how television programmes, including American ones, are to be judged, valued, understood and written about. Critics, with access to the media and their accepted role as television experts, occupy a powerful location in these debates. However, the position taken by a critic, siding with dominant cultural views or trying to present a popular or alternative reading and understanding, depends on their social background, the cultural capital they wield and the media they work for.

The earlier, more serious forms of television critics tended to align themselves with dominant cultural values, and therefore sought to use accepted forms of critical analysis, such as those offered by literature and theatre criticism. They have therefore tended to view American culture and its television programmes as being crass and inferior; they were the product of a factory system producing formulaic standardised filmed product, rather than a serious cultural form seeking to explore the human condition or to stimulate thought. The second group of critics, the neo-critics as I have called them, mixed the popular and comic with a form of critical analysis. Such critics, more accepting of television as a form of popular culture, were more prepared to cover and review all programmes, American included, though they tended to criticise and lampoon many of the American shows in the 1970s and 1980s (Lealand, 1984: 69). This form of criticism was less an attempt to overturn and challenge all aspects of the older serious form of criticism, than to update it in line with changes in television programmes and the wider acceptance of television by society. In this way, while they enjoyed all forms of television, they tended to acclaim those where the authorial hand and good performances were evident.

The more 'populist' form of television writing, which has been around since the start of television, has few critical pretensions; critics working in this form write about gossip, scandals and the behind-the-scenes antics of the stars of popular programmes. American programmes, in this way, are mostly seen no differently than British productions. If it is popular, or is presented as such, if it can help sell newspapers, it is covered. This is a form of criticism that knows its place; it is not a form of criticism that is trying to overturn the cultural hierarchy. Another form identified were the more surreal forms of criticism that, I argued, are subversive in intent; this form presented new, informed and different ways of experiencing and viewing programmes, including American programmes. These critics often turned the meanings of programmes on their heads; they sought new pleasures from television. This was a criticism of the carnivalesque. However, such coverage is aimed at and read by a minority group of readers, and in some ways is as elitist as some of the more serious television criticism. With the development of the Web, it would seem that the public now has a chance of engaging more actively in the critical discourse around television programmes. This does not, however, necessarily mean that new ways of understanding and valuing American programmes will appear, for many that publish on the Web are informed by and take on similar values and styles of criticism as that found in the media.

While, in the early days of criticism, it was hard to find critical work or reviews about American programmes, over time, they have come to be written about in a range of ways, from various cultural positions. Indeed, the derogatory and critical remarks found in the early television criticism of American programmes have, in terms of certain programmes, now turned to acclaim. However, it would seem that this has been due to changes less in criticism than in the programmes themselves. American producers, as they shape their programmes to attract niche groups, including the affluent middle-class viewers, are producing programmes that equate, in various ways, to the cultural values of the critics. At a time when the British mainstream channels, BBC1 and ITV1, are increasingly producing more popular programmes, many now view American programmes as offering a cultural distinctiveness not found in many British programmes; a discourse which the channels showing such programmes both support and use to their own benefit. I will now, in Chapter 7, look at the future role of American programmes on British screens.

7
The Next Generation?

7.1 Introduction

As television enters what for Ellis (2002) and others is its third age, it would seem that its very nature, as a broadcast medium, is changing. Indeed, for Ellis, the seeds of change were evident in the second age with the coming of analogue satellite and cable. Such new forms of distribution have hurried the end of the old broadcasting regimes dominated by a handful of broadcast channels. The emerging multi-channel television environment is one where there is a complex mix of local, national, regional and global channels, offering broadcast, narrowcast and themed channels, with a number of channels being owned and operated by a small number of global media firms, many of which are American. Television as a medium is also changing from a one-way form of transmission, one where viewers are generally perceived as being passive, to a form where a limit degree of interactivity is encouraged, but mostly in the benefit of the media organisation; at the end of the day they are there to sell a restricted range of commodities for a profit.

While some of the changes are linked to technological developments, we must be wary of falling into a technological determinist position. These technological developments are funded and shaped by the needs of large corporations, some of which are linked, in various ways, to the American media industry. For example, Toshiba and Sony, seemingly with little public demand, have now developed two rival advanced DVD formats – HD-DVD and Blu-ray. To help the successful diffusion of this technology, they both require the Hollywood studios to take up and use their systems (Busfield, 2004; Schofield, 2005). Both groups are prepared to shape the technology to placate the concerns of the studios, to get them on board, so to speak, such that the new DVD standards will 'contain stronger anti-piracy protection' than earlier systems (Gentile, 2004). However, alongside this important technological–industrial axis of development there have been other social, cultural, economic and political changes that have, in their way, come to transform television.

Indeed, looking at how broadcasting has changed in Europe since the 1980s it would seem as if some form of revolution has occurred. Increasingly, most European national television systems now have commercial sectors, often operating under a weak set of regulations, in which a multitude of new services are on offer, some of which are offered by a number of high profile global branded channels; no longer are all the channels seeking to serve, or are regulated to serve, the national audience; each, taking different strategies, caters to an array of different cultural, social and ethnic groups. It would now seem that the old public service broadcasters in Europe, under increased political and economic pressure, are in crisis (Tracey, 1998). The notion of television being solely a national concern, broadcasting a diverse schedule over a few channels for a national audience, has long gone.

In the light of these developments I will, in this chapter, bring my exploration of the role of American programmes on British screens up to date and, indeed, to look a little way into the future. Under the first two headings I will explore how the broadcasting environments in America and Britain, are changing, and how this is affecting the relationship between the two markets. I will then focus on two specific strategies being taken by American media firms as they seek to exploit their programmes and channels in the overseas markets, including Britain; firstly, by the creation of branded global channels, a route by which American distributors can circumnavigate and supplement their sales of programmes to British broadcasters; and, secondly, by a strategy of creating, marketing and exploiting a new form of high profile 'quality' form of programme; a programme that has been marketed as 'must-see' which, in some cases, has become a sub-brand in its own right. Under the last heading, I will look at the on-coming technological changes in more detail to explore how television is changing and how this will affect the role and experience of watching American programmes on television in Britain; indeed, to suggest that the dialogue that has happened between the different cultures, mediated through national broadcasters, might now be entering a new phase, one where the viewer will, in the end, be able to select what they want to watch, when and from whichever source.

7.2   Changes in the US broadcasting environment: The supply side

Up until the 1980s three main networks, ABC, NBC and CBS, had dominated the American broadcasting environment. They commissioned most of the expensive peak time programmes; they attracted most of the advertising revenue and were the most watched (Comstock, 1991: 27–33). As Comstock notes, the networks had, in the 1960s and 1970s, a combined share of 90 per cent in the prime-time hours of 8.00–11.00 p.m. (ibid.: 29). Over time, to stop the networks abusing their powerful position in the broadcasting market, the Federal Communication Commission (FCC) bought in various important regulations. One particular regulation being the Financial Interest and Syndication Rule (FinSyn), passed in 1971, which was to limit any exploitation of their position as the main access points to the American national airwaves; this meant that the networks were restricted to being allowed to commission and then screen most programmes two times only, after which the rights would revert back to the producer (Holt, 2003: 14–15; Mittell, 2003: 47); though this regulation was fought through the courts until 1979. So while the networks determine what was to be made, it was the producers and distributors who could exploit these in the domestic syndication and overseas markets.

Such developments began to help the creation of competition to the networks. On one front it helped entrench the already powerful position of the production sector, made up of the major studios and large and small independent companies (Anderson, 1994; Alvey, 2000: 34–51). Throughout the 1970s, this group of producers and distributors, as they exploited their programme libraries through the domestic and overseas markets, grew in size into large global media firms; interestingly one member of this group was Viacom, a distribution company spun off by CBS because of the FinSyn rules (Holt, 2003: 21). On another front new television channels were appearing which, by using satellite and cable forms of distribution, were able to provide new national television channels; two early channels were Home Box Office and WTBS (now Turner Broadcasting System) (Head *et al.*, 1998: 60–1). It would seem that regulation, such as the passing of the FinSyn rules, helped in the 1970s to encourage the break up of the 'the most heavily centralised, vertically integrated, standardised and homogenised period of US network television' (Hilmes, 2003b: 62)

In the early 1980s the Federal Communication Commission (FCC), under Mark Fowler, with developments in technology and a shift in thinking, conversely started to deregulate broadcasting, but the aim of encouraging more competition (Holt, 2003). This was not just for the sake of American audiences, to provide more choice, but also to stimulate the new high-tech hardware and software industries; industries which were increasingly viewed as vital for America's economy (Schiller, 1996: 52–4). Mark Fowler argued that with the new means of delivering television, cable and satellite, the old argument for the regulation of the scarce airwaves no longer applied (Holt, 2003: 12–13). Now there could be true competition; the market would be able to fully respond to the demands of the audience. Following this strategy, the FCC, throughout the eighties and into the nineties, repealed most of its regulations allowing a more market driven industry to develop. For example, the FinSyn regulation was withdrawn in 1995, allowing networks to again own their own programmes; the Prime Time Access Rule was ended, a rule that had limited the number of hours of networked material that could be offered in prime time (Head *et al.*, 1998: 220–1); and the formula limiting the number of broadcast licences any media owner could own was relaxed and its formula changed – changed from a limit on the number of stations that could be owned and operated, the O' and O's, to a limit on market reach – initially 25 per cent; the 1996 Telecommunications Act increased the maximum allowed market reach of all the broadcast stations owned by a single owner from 25 to 35 per cent, though steps to increase this further have, so far, been halted (Helmore, 2003; Holt, 2003: 16, 22; Shin, 2005). To increase competition and to encourage the development of new networks, the FCC also began to issue an increasing number of broadcast licences. While many of the new stations were initially independent, they soon began to sign up with emerging networks (Holt, 2003: 18). The FCC's hopes were soon rewarded by the appearance of the Fox network (Balio, 1996: 27–8).

In the mid-1980s Rupert Murdoch signalled his intent to create a fourth network, Fox, which would utilise programmes from his new production base Twentieth Century Fox (Tunstall and Palmer, 1991: 125–6; Head *et al.*, 1998: 75–6). Much to the annoyance of the big three networks, Fox was able to escape the still existing FinSyn regulations, initially as it had too small a coverage to be considered by the FCC as a network and, later, by an exception made by the FCC (Head *et al.*, 1998: 220). Slowly, other terrestrial networks appeared utilising some of the newly enfranchised independent stations as affiliates; the Warner Brothers Network (WB) and United Paramount Network (UPN) were launched by Warner Brothers and Paramount, respectively, in 1995, while other cable and satellite networks appeared or continued to grow in size, for example

HBO, TBS, ShowTime, CNN and MTV. By 2001 the number of channels that an average household could receive was up from 39 to 55 since 1993 (Hilmes, 2003b: 64).

Increasingly, throughout this time the old networks found their market share being eroded. While in 1980 they attracted some 90 per cent of the audience share, this was down by the 1990s to 60 per cent for the networks, Fox included (Hoskins *et al.*, 1997: 48). However, they were still the main means by which advertisers could reach the mass audience (Head *et al.*, 1998: 240). Other channels could only offer niche audiences or a small audience share. Interestingly, recently they seemed to have reversed this decline in viewing figures:

> The big four US networks, CBS, NBC, ABC and Fox, collectively finished 2004–5 with audiences up on the previous year, against an average decline of 3 per cent per year for the past 10 years. Of the four, only NBC lost share (down 16 per cent), while CBS and Fox both showed modest increases (4 and 2 per cent respectively) and ABC delivered a remarkable 17 per cent improvement. (Goldsmith, 2005)

Incomes were also up considerably for this year, 'ABC was duly rewarded with revenues up by almost 30 per cent to $2.6bn. CBS followed with a steady performance, achieving price increases of 3–5 per cent and revenue gains of 10 per cent for a final tally of $2.1bn' (ibid.). The networks, while facing new forms of competition, were also helped by the FCC when it finally ended the FinSyn rule in the late 1990s; this meant they again could own and exploit the programmes they commissioned, in both domestic and overseas markets; a point which is important as they spend billions of dollars per year on prime-time programmes. These moves have led to an increase in the number of programmes owned by the networks. In 1995 the networks only owned on average 40 per cent of their schedules, by 2000, CBS, for example, owned some 68 per cent (Holt, 2003: 16–17).

While the networks had since the introduction of the FinSyn rules fought for their ending, and while they were relieved when they finally went, others have been more apprehensive about such developments. The large media or communication firms involved in film and television production and distribution, such as Disney, Time Warner, Liberty Media Corporation or Viacom, were worried that with the ending of FinSyn, the amount of programmes commissioned by networks which they were able to own would decrease. These programmes, in many ways paid for by the networks, were an important reason for the growth and success of these media companies. They responded by starting a merger spree (Holt, 2003: 15–23). A limited number of these companies were able to buy one of the major networks, for example Disney bought ABC in 1995 and Viacom CBS in 1999 (ibid.: 19), while others started up their own channels or bought into other existing ones, for example, Time Warner set up WB (The Warner Brothers Network) (Head *et al.*, 1998: 49). Also, behind such mergers was a driving belief in the benefits of horizontal and vertical integration (Balio, 1996: 34–6). Synergy was the order of the day as companies sought to exploit their assets through every stage of production, distribution/sales and transmission. Such firms, with their huge turnover were not just looking at expansion in the US markets. Indeed, with existing limits on media ownership and the maturity of the US market many saw the new developing markets abroad, especially in Europe, as key targets. As one media analyst noted, 'the long-term growth opportunities overseas dwarf what we think is likely to occur in the United States' (Cook cited in Herman and McChesney, 1997: 42). With such developments the large American media firms, such as Viacom, Time Warner, Liberty Media and Disney, began to develop strategies to exploit their brands, channels and programmes, further afield.

7.3 Changes in the British broadcasting environment: The demand side

While the American broadcasting environment, its industrial structures, channels and programmes it produces, has changed, so equally has the British television environment and its demands for and use of American programmes – the pull factors spoken of in Chapter 3. Behind these developments four forces can be identified: ideological-political, economic-commercial, social and cultural and technological (a similar breakdown of factors is suggested by Weymouth and Lamizet, 1996: 13–26).

First, with the election of the Conservative government in 1979, there was a move towards a market-driven philosophy or ideology in which the catchwords were 'consumer choice'. No longer was public service broadcasting seen as the only way to deliver broadcasting services; indeed, those of the right, such as Veljanovski and Bishop, criticised the existing system as stifling consumer choice and the workings of the market (1983: Chapter 3). The Conservative government, influenced by such work and various reports, such as the study of cable produced by the Information Technology Panel (1982) and the Hunt Report (1982), accepted the need to develop a technologically advanced infrastructure to help the economy of the nation. While, initially, the Conservative government sought to support the development of a satellite service within the existing regime, for example the BBC was encouraged to develop satellite television, the policy that developed around cable was more market orientated from the start. However, by the end of their time in office commercial private companies were at the forefront of cable and satellite developments (Goodwin, 1998: 38–68). The government saw this as a way of developing a national resource with private investment rather than public money. However, while such investors were attracted by the possibility of offering entertainment services over such networks, they were worried about operating in a too heavily regulated system. They therefore lobbied vigorously for a weakening of the regulatory regime. The market driven approach that the Conservative government came to advocate could be viewed, as Tracey notes, as similar to American policy implemented by the FCC (1998: 47–8). A dual system developed in Britain, on one side being the public service broadcasters and on the other the new private commercial broadcasters working within a weaker regime; these were similar to developments happening in many other European nations (Wieten *et al.*, 2000: xi).

Secondly, technological developments meant that there was an end to airwave scarcity. In the early eighties it was apparent that cable and a form of Direct to Home (DTH) satellite broadcasting could be the backbone of a new high-tech superhighway linking the home, media companies and businesses. Initially the development of such an infrastructure could be encouraged and supported through the provision of entertainment services, including television, which could then, later, be expanded to deliver new interactive services (Steemers and Wise, 2000: 101–2). With the spread of interactive digital technologies from the computer industries into telecommunications and the media sectors, it was evident that digital terrestrial, cable and satellite forms of distribution would soon be able to offer many more channels and interactive services than delivered by the existing analogue systems. Indeed, by 2005 Sky was offering hundreds of digital channels and a number of interactive services through its own decoding box (<http://www.sky.co.uk>).

Thirdly, for Eric Hobsbawm (1994), since the 1960s European nations had been going through huge social and cultural changes or, as he suggests, a revolution. On the social level, class was on a decline, family ties weakening, sexual freedoms were increasing and a transnational youth culture was developing; increasingly, it would seem a more individual-focused culture was triumphing over a more collective form of society (Weymouth and Lamizet, 1996: 13–17). Broadcasters were slowly waking up to these seismic changes; the mass national audience, for which services were produced and aimed, was in fact segmented. Demands from different social and cultural groups could no longer be adequately met through the existing form of broadcasting based around a limited number of channels offering mainstream programming. The UK had a heterogeneous culture; it was made up of different ethnic groups, family groups, nationals, age groups and classes all of which wanted to be served. For Michael Tracey, public service broadcasting was in crisis for 'if "the nation" and "the public" are dissolved – assuming they ever existed – then what is there left to serve?' (1998: 279).

Fourthly, the economic importance of the media sector was recognised by all governments, which were keen to encourage developments in the media. With the huge amounts of investment required, and the size of the encroaching competition, there was an accepted need for mergers in the media and communication's sector to allow the creation of larger national companies; companies that could then act as flag wavers abroad (Steemers, 2004: 61–4). Therefore, over time, the regulations limiting mergers of media and television companies in Britain have slowly been weakened. Indeed, with the 2003 Communication Act the way was open for the merger of the English ITV franchises into one company, which was finalised in February 2004 (<http://www.itvplc.com/itv/merger>, accessed 10 April 2005). However, such developments have left open the possibility that one of the main terrestrial channels might 'fall' into the hands of a foreign owner; the fear, as usual, was that it would be an American firm (Steemers, 2004: 63–4). However, in July 2005, RTL, a European-based company, was the first foreign company to gain full control of a British terrestrial channel, C5, which attracted little criticism, though an earlier possibility of an American company taking over C5 had caused some consternation (Milmo, 2005b).

However, at the same time, government and the regulators accepted the need for some consolidation in the industry, other policies were fragmenting the sector (Steemers, 2004: 64–70). Increasingly regulation was brought in to encourage the creation of a strong production sector, initially with the creation of C4 and then by a requirement on the BBC and ITV to use 25 per cent of independent productions. This growing sector has pressured to be allowed to have ownership of the programmes it produces; they hoped to limited broadcasters to being allowed to only being able to screen a programme a limited number of times before its ownership reverted back to the producer. For example, C4 has recently moved to assigning more of the overseas rights to participating independents (Milmo, 2005a). By such development, the British market has began to see the creation of a new set of powerful media companies.

Some of these have been called the 'super-indies', though small in comparison to American global media firms. Increasingly these companies are stretching their muscles, developing formats and programme brands to be sold on within the national market and internationally. For example, RDF has taken and developed its successful British programmes *Housewife Swap* and *Scrap Heap Challenge* in America (Steemers, 2004: 99–101; Saini, 2005). These companies, as they build up their programme libraries, might also be able, in time, to compete with American distributors in selling domestic productions to channels in Britain; this could equally be to American channels operating in Britain, hoping to increase their popularity by mixing domestic products with American products, and to other cable and satellite channels.

Such developments have led to an increase in the number of channels being offered to British audiences. In the early eighties there had only been four analogue national terrestrial channels, BBC1, BBC2, ITV and C4 (and its Welsh equivalent S4C), with a few fledgling cable channels. By the late 1990s these had been joined by C5 and around 40–50 cable and satellite channels. With the coming of digital television the number of channels on offer have increased three- or fourfold. For example, the current Sky and NTL digital packages now include some 250 channels, as well as offering Near Video On Demand and an array of radio stations; terrestrial digital channels, initially provided under the Ondigital and ITVdigital banners, but now operated by Freeview, while more limited in number, offer around thirty channels along with an additional pay top-up option of some 10 extra channels. These digital services not only offer television services but also interactive services, including games, shopping, email and internet browsing. By 2004, some 12 million homes had some form of multi-channel access, nearly half the homes in Britain (<http://www.barb.co.uk/tvfacts>, accessed 10 April 2005). The whole British broadcasting landscape, once one of scarcity, public service commitments and the comfortable duopoly of the BBC and ITV, is truly no more.

Operating in this new environment, developing new branded channels, have been a number of global companies: News Corp, RTL, Viacom, Flextech, Liberty Media, Disney and Time Warner. Each own and operate a number of different television channels, singularly or in partnerships, usually supplied by their own extensive programme and film libraries and/or linked production companies. However, in terms of audience share, turnover and investment into domestic production, there is still a divide between the older existing broadcasters and newer ones. The BBC, ITV, C4 and C5, the existing terrestrial networks, still attract the majority of viewers, dominate the turnover in the sector (with the exception of Sky) and are the largest investors in domestic production; while imports play various roles for such channels they do not dominate their output. For example, according to BARB, the average overall share in February 2005 of the terrestrial channels was 71 per cent compared to 28 per cent for other channels. Though it must be noted that the terrestrial's share has been decreasing over time, for example, in February 1999 it was standing at 86 per cent to 13 per cent respectively (<http://www.barb.co.uk/viewing summary/monthreports>, accessed 10 April 2005).

While the production of programmes in Britain is still important for British broadcasters, audiences and the economy, in many ways their use, at least in terms of a first run, is very much restricted to the existing terrestrial channels. Much of what is transmitted across the range of the new channels, beyond sport and films, are American programmes, British repeats or cheaper British productions, for example, while Sky One has commissioned a few programmes like *Dream Team*, a sort of *Footballers' Wives*, and *Hex*, a *Buffy*-like programme made by Sony Pictures, most are American programmes; and while Living TV does show some domestic production between American programmes, these tend to be cheaply made – for example, their reality styled programme, *Most Haunted*.

It would seem that the British market has been going through similar developments as America, but with some different outcomes. While, for example, the main networks in America have now regained control over their programmes, British broadcasters are losing some control over theirs. Such changes are leading to new types of relationships developing between the channels operating in Britain and the American programme suppliers. No longer are the large terrestrial channels the only market, that is, the only buyers, there are other smaller terrestrial channels, new cable and satellite channels and, for some American media firms, their own channels; likewise a new supply of British-made programmes is appearing, one which might replace some of the bought-in American programmes. American global companies are also facing competition as British-European regulatory changes have started to create new European television-focused media companies, for example Canal Plus and RTL (Chalaby, 2005a: 5; 2005b: 48). Once American programmes were shown within a mixed schedule, now they are equally likely to be foregrounded on themed entertainment, sport, documentary, film or children's channels. While American media firms have been in the past restricted in what they could own and operate in Britain, the possibility of buying into a large national terrestrial channel has increased. Indeed, there are currently rumours that there will be an American backed bid for ITV.

It would seem that as the British market has changed so too have relationships between the markets, the role of American programmes and the way the public experiences them. I now wish to look, in more detail, at how American companies have repositioned themselves to take advantage of the changing broadcasting regimes in Europe and Britain. To begin with, I will focus on the development of American-branded global channels; and then, secondly, I will look at their development of different types of high profile programmes, some of which have taken on a sub-brand status, often being marketed as 'must-see' programmes.

7.4 Branding: Global channels of the future

Until the 1980s American firms operating in Europe had generally been limited to selling programmes to the few national broadcasters and the occasional co-production or pre-sale, with any direct ownership of channels prohibited or at least limited. However, many American media firms had felt that the monopoly nature of most European markets, where there were often only one or two buyers of programmes, had meant prices were kept low for their programmes; indeed, they were often shown in less desirable slots, with an increasing tendency for domestic productions to be shown in peak hours. While world television programme production was estimated to be $70 billion in 1989, the international market, which American firms dominated, accounted for only $2.4 billion. Some analysts felt that unless American distributors pressured for change and pushed Europe to open up, this situation would continue (Segrave, 1998: 224–5, 238).

As new technologies came on stream, such as cable and satellite, and as European governments embraced or accepted an opening of their hitherto closed markets, American firms sought to own and operate channels there. They hoped that while competition would push programme prices up, by owning their own channels they could side step European buyers completely. By 1992 there were some 150 channels (50 of which were satellite based) in operation in Europe compared to 40 in 1980 (Segrave, 1998: 213); and, linked to this, the number of hours of programmes required increased many times over. For example, while the British market required some 20,000–30,000 hours per year in the early 1980s, this had risen by 2003 to 740,000 hours (The Communications Market, 2004: 8).

American media companies believed they were well placed to benefit from these developments. They were of enormous size with potential synergies to be had from operating on a global basis. Indeed, to develop and survive as a major player such companies had to 'mobilise a vast array of global brands to command both content and distribution' (Bart cited in Holt, 2003: 11). These companies had the expertise, programme libraries and the financial and global muscle not only to market their programmes for sale to new and existing channels abroad, but also to launch and nurture their own channels over a period of time. As Bob Ross, vice president of Turner, noted,

> The company's conscious strategy is simply to exploit what we've already paid for: CNN already had [international] bureaus; we owned the MGM and Hanna-Barbera libraries... We could either let these assets sit in the vault or take them into new markets as full services. Our incremental costs are lower than someone without such cross-elasticity. In the short run, syndication revenues will be higher than [establishing international] networks, but in time, that will switch. (cited in Segrave, 1998: 234)

However, these companies soon realised that to have success in these new markets required a balance between the use of American programmes and local needs, though control would ultimately stay in the US. For example, when MTV rolled out its form of music television it soon found that it had to localise its output, taking some account of the cultural and linguistic differences (Roe and Meyer, 2000: 143, 147–50); for Hallmark, some '70–80 per cent of total programming came from the Hallmark library, with the balance consisting of locally acquired programmes' (McMurria, 2003: 81). They also accepted that, to make the most of their assets, of attracting audiences to their channels, they would need to do so using a well-known brand. While some companies were able to enter the international market with a pre-existing recognisable worldwide brand, such as Disney, others often had to follow strategies to develop or raise the recognition of their brand outside of America, for example, Hallmark who, 'hired Lubin Lawrence, a research firm in New York which specialises in developing international corporate brands' (ibid.). Once a brand name is developed a package of channels can be created to exploit this or, vice versa, a portfolio of channels can be created around which a brand is established. For example, Discovery now offers a portfolio of channels in Britain – Discovery Channel, Discovery Wings, Discovery Science, Discovery Home and Leisure, Discovery Civilisation and Discovery Travel (and Living TV). With more channels on offer, the profile of the brand increases, with audiences, advertisers and platform providers (cable and satellite) (ibid.: 72).

However, as Holt notes, the picture is not quite as straightforward as firms using only their own material on their channels. Many different decisions are made as firms seek to maximise turnover, profits, exposure and control of their brand. For example, in pursuit of profits or particular content, a corporation might sell a programme to or produce programmes for a competitor or, alternatively, buy or commission them from a competitor. For example, in the American market NBC has been paying Warner Bros. some $13 million per episode to produce *ER* (ibid.: 25). From such a deal NBC gains a programme vital for its Thursday night line-up, while Warner Bros. is able to make more money than it would by showing *ER* itself. Likewise, Fox initially sold *24* to the BBC, rather than to its sister company Sky, as it could get more exposure and income from such a sale.

Through such branded channels American media firms have been able to circumnavigate the traditional gatekeepers to directly access British audiences. For Nick Lovegrove, '[t]here's a real prospect of American companies being the gatekeepers of entertainment distribution in large parts of Europe and indeed around the world' (cited in Segrave, 1998: 236). However, apart from the movie and sports channels, most of these channels do not yet attract huge audiences. For example, in Britain, Discovery's portfolio of 8 channels attracted only a 1.5 per cent share of total viewing in February 2005 (24 minutes of average weekly viewing per person) according to BARB (<http://www.barb.co.uk>, accessed June 2005). This is partly due to the limited number of homes subscribed to cable and satellite packages, though this is increasing, and also, as many argue, the preference of viewers for British domestic productions, few of which are found on these channels. It could also be put down to the tendency of viewers to focus on a limited range of channels, five to ten seems to be the optimum number even when hundreds are on offer – which are usually, at the moment, dominated by the terrestrial channels (McMurria, 2003: 72). However, with the cost of the material already mostly covered in the US market, and with the cheapness of distributing such material through a series of worldwide branded channels, the running costs for such channels are, relatively speaking, small – though the launch costs are huge. These American firms, with their deep pockets, are here for the long haul. That is not to say that these large media firms are happy with the situation and are not adapting their market model or programming strategies over time to try to increase their audience share or to cut cost. For example, SkyOne has moved away from a staple of cheaper American imports, to a strategy of acquiring some of the more expensive 'must see' American imports and commissioning a limited number of British productions in an attempt to take it upmarket.

> It made sense for us to use Sky One as a shop window for existing Sky subscribers and non-subscribers,' explains Baker. His brief over the past six months has been to take the channel upmarket, playing to its strengths in quality US acquisitions while also commissioning more homegrown product, majoring on popular factual shows such as last week's Julie Burchill documentary on chavs. (Interview with Richard Baker by Owen Gibson, 2005c)

7.5 Programmes as sub-brands

As American media firms have sought to develop a global strategy around branded channels, they have benefited from the changing profile of some of the programmes being made by the American system – some of which they have created, nurtured and promoted as 'must see' programmes. The time when American firms have sought to take advantage of the opening-up of many broadcasting regimes, has also been a time when American television is going through, for some, another golden age – mostly in terms of drama and comedy programmes (Thompson, 1997).

As the American market became more competitive, as it fragmented, all broadcasters began to develop particular programme strategies to survive; while the networks, with their large turnover and investment in programmes, tended to produce programmes still able to attract a mass audience, though some attempts are made to target a more upmarket profile viewer, some of the smaller channels, unable or unwilling to compete head-to-head with these still powerful networks, have developed strategies of aiming at more specific niche audiences. WB, for example, started by aiming its output at the 18–34 age group, and UPN at men between the ages of 18 and 49 (Levy, 1996: 51). Another example is Home Box Office (HBO), which, since the early seventies, has come to offer films and, more recently, original high quality programmes, without advertising, for those willing and able to pay for such a service (Hilmes, 2003: 64).

Some attempts have also been made to create new forms, programmes that 'play on differences between people in different micro cultures'; programmes that, rather than just appeal to a small niche group can, instead, attract a diverse range of viewers by accepting their heterogeneous nature (Nelson, 1997: 96). Such developments have meant that the types of fictional programmes on offer to British broadcasters have been supplemented by a new range of upmarket and 'must-see' programmes; programmes that, if they are marketed correctly, can obtain a decent return for the American producers. Indeed, some of these programmes have been developed and nurtured as sub-brands.

One genre of programmes that have become popular in British channels, have been the teen drama series (for a discussion about how to define such a genre, see Davis and Dickinson, 2004: 1–13). These include the rather sassy and knowing *Buffy the Vampire Slayer* as well as other programmes such as *Angel, Dawson's Creek, OC, Charmed, Dead Like Me* and *Popular* that explore teenage angst against and in an array of different contexts (ibid.). These programmes have managed to cater to the desires of both teenagers and the ageing 'youth' viewer, those who still wish to live out their teenage fantasies. Other, more adult-orientated drama, attracting an upmarket and older ABC1 grouping, have included programmes such as *Homicide, NYPD Blue, West Wing, ER* and *The Sopranos*, following on very much in the earlier tradition of *Hill Street Blues* and *St Elsewhere*. These follow a now stable pattern of using a large ensemble cast in a well-crafted multi-layered flexi-narrative form that 'better responds to and reveals the complexity, ambiguity and lack of closure that typifies the contemporary world' (Nelson, 1997: 38). These series explore a side of American society missing from the early formulaic action series like *Starsky and Hutch, A-Team, Six Million Dollar Man* and *Kojak*. One American channel closely associated with these 'quality' programmes, with its 'Original Series', is Home Box Office. HBO have sold themselves to the American public, and indeed, to international audiences, as a producer of 'high quality' programmes; in America this is a subscription channel that has aimed at affluent viewers wishing to see programmes undisturbed by adverts (Creeber, 2004: 157–8).

Helping this sense of quality, of a new form of 'must-see' high-profile programmes has been the well-publicised work of a number of auteurs and performers, many of whom work in film; increasingly, American television is, again, the place to work. For examples, the cult director Quentin Tarantino has helped direct an episode of *ER* ('*Motherhood*'), a TV series based around an idea from John Grisham as well as, more recently, the finale of the latest *CSI: Crime Scene Investigation* series ('Grave Danger') shown on C5 at 9–11.00 p.m. 19 July 2005. Steve Buscemi, a well-known actor, has directed episodes of *Homicide: Life on the Streets* ('Finnegan's Wake'), *OZ* ('US Male' and 'Cuts like a knife') as well as *The Sopranos* ('Everybody Hurts', 'In Camelot' and 'Pine barren'), which he then later joined as a member of the cast for a number of episodes until killed by Tony Soprano. Some of the programmes have allowed the writer and director to experiment with, to push the boundaries of, television drama; for example, the live broadcast, in America, of an episode of *ER*, surreal dream sequences in *The Sopranos* and a purely dialogue-based episode of *Homicide*. For these reasons, writers, directors and actors are able to explore creative freedoms now found in television series that in many ways are not found so much in mainstream Hollywood (Creeber, 2004: 100–8).

Other programme genre, like sci-fi, have also changed, becoming not only both more refined and specialised for fans but also, as they have utilised modern CGI, more attractive to larger audiences. These are series with production values akin to Hollywood films they are often spun off from, for example *Star Trek: The Next Generation, Star Gate* and *Star Trek: Enterprise*. Adult cartoon series like *The Simpsons, South Park* and *King of the Hill* have also appeared that, in various ways, critique American culture and society in a way alien to the earlier cartoons more specifically aimed at children, for example *Scooby Doo* and *Tom and Jerry*. There have also been programmes harder to pigeonhole, such as *Ally McBeal*, which, following on from the reflexive eighties series *Moonlighting*, presents a rather surreal view of life in America, often with dream-like sequences which seem more appropriate for a David Lynch film; a director who has also found work on American television with *Twin Peaks*. There have also been a number of series that have opened up the once taboo area of sex on American television; this has partly been because subscription channels, on which some of these programmes appear, have more leeway than the networks. Such programmes as *Sex in the City* and *The L Word* have touched on a variety of subjects, and portrayals, that would have once been left on the cutting-room floor. As Holden suggests, '[n]ever in an American film or TV series has sophisticated girl talk been more explicit, with every kink and sexual twitch of the urban mating game noted and wittily dissected' (cited in Akass and McCabe, 2004: 3).

A few of these programmes, helped by associated publicity, PR, marketing and merchandise, have become recognisable sub-brands (Ellis, 2002: 166–7). Indeed, in some instances, they have become as recognisable as the channel they are shown on. For example, because of the raised profile of such programmes as *Friends, The Simpsons* and *Buffy the Vampire Slayer*, they are able to move from channel to channel taking their audiences with them. People tune in to see the programme, not to necessarily to watch the channel. These programmes are very attractive for channels operating in Britain; they draw audiences, kudos and add to the profile of the channel. Hence C5 is now showing *Buffy the Vampire Slayer*, picking up on this existing sub-brand in a hope to attract young audiences; Living TV is showing *The L Word*, helped by the hype that accompanied the programme from America; and, C4 has benefited from popular coverage of *Desperate Housewives*, for example the cover story of *Vanity Fare* that suggested that the main actors are not getting along. American firms have been keen to develop strategies to protect and promote the brand image of such programmes, not only for further exploitation in the broadcast market but also in the growing DVD market and associated merchandising markets (BBC News, 2002).

7.6   New technologies: The end of the broadcaster?

Generally the underlying technological and organisational form of television has altered little over some fifty years. Broadcast schedules are planned, constructed and transmitted centrally, being watched, mostly, in domestic settings on smallish television sets. While audiences could be active, they could write or phone in to the broadcaster, they were somewhat limited in how they could interact with a programme or programmer. Acting as gatekeepers to these channels were national broadcasters; it was they who commissioned, produced and acquired programmes and then, using their intuition or audience research, constructed a schedule for the imagined audience; broadcasters decided what American programmes were bought and were available to the British public.

However, more recently, new developments in television technology have meant that the supposed 'tyranny' of the scheduler, the limited amount of channels available and the way viewers can interact with the programme providers have changed dramatically. One of the first developments was that of the video cassette player (VCR) in the 1970s (Winston, 1998: 128–9). This was a technology that seemed to extend the power of the viewer which, initially, worried the media industry. In particular, some of the Hollywood studios were concerned about piracy, of the illegal copying of their films and programmes (ibid.: 127). However, even Hollywood was to realise that here was a new market, a new means by which they could sell their films and television programmes; it was just that they wanted to control it. Though, it was obvious that, for the viewers, the video machine was not just a way of watching Hollywood films but also offered the possibility for time shifting, watching broadcast programmes when they wanted, rather than when scheduled – an early form of what some have called Me-TV (ibid.; Hoskins *et al.*, 1997: 133).

Within twenty years, the pre-recorded video/DVD market has grown tremendously, such that now, for film, it rivals cinema exhibition in terms of turnover (Briggs and Burke, 2002: 303–4). Initially much of the growth was in the rented sector, an area American media firms were quick to move into, for example with the spread of the American-owned Blockbuster franchise (Segrave, 1998: 218). However, as the price of video cassettes, and then later DVDs, dropped, the number of programmes and films sold directly to the public has grown (BBC News, 2002). Increasingly, television series, such as *Buffy*, are sold in large numbers on DVD and video, often packaged in boxed sets; these are 'must' buy for fans. For example, some 200,000 UK *Buffy* fans have purchased seasons one, two and three (Hill and Calcutt, 2001). These sets are often sold with added extras, such as interviews, outtakes, quizzes and the like, which help add value to these sub-brands, helping to cultivate and support a fan base or microculture (Jones, 2003: 165–8). This is a new way, relatively speaking, by which American distributors have been able to exploit their products in the British market.

Another development that has increased the amount of choice available to the viewer has been with the development of satellite and cable channels. Initially using analogue technologies but now switching over to digital technologies, these new platforms are able to offer hundreds of different types of channels: this is truly the end of scarcity (Ellis, 2002: 61–73). The sheer number of channels, however, creates a problem of knowing what is on and when. In response, platform owners have created electronic programme guides (EPGs) to provide a way of navigating around the multitude of programmes and channels; broadcasters quickly accepted the importance of dominating such a guide, as it essentially shaped the way the audiences navigated and accessed television; in a way it helped guide their choices.

Alongside EPGs, a new form of advanced 'video' recorder has also been developed. This is an 'intelligent' recorder, often using a hard disk measured in gigabytes; this development marries computing technologies with the needs of the television industry. Such machines, one of the most famous being the TiVo, are marketed as personal video recorders (PVRs); these are able to seek out and record programmes according to a user's personal profile. As the TiVo website notes, 'TiVo makes it easy for discriminating entertainment enthusiasts to get exactly what they want form the world of television. And not only what they want, but when they want it' (<http://www.tivo.com>, accessed 12 April 2005). They are helped in this by an EPG which, beyond just storing channels numbers and programme times, also categorises programmes. In some ways this brings the idea of Me-TV, the construction of personal television schedule, one step nearer (Hoskins *et al.*, 1997: 133). It would seem that this technology, as it takes off, might signal the end of the broadcaster as the dominant gatekeeper. That the viewer, or the PVR guided by the profile of the viewer, could find, select and record an array of programmes that could then be watched when desired.

The media industry has responded in a number of ways. First, media companies have sought control over PVR systems, or a tie-up with PVR firms, so that they can gain access to and shape how it collects data about a person's viewing habits and related profile; this information can increase the broadcaster's knowledge of their potential audience. For example, Sky has developed its own PVR, Sky+, while others, such as Discovery, Universal, Showtime and NBC, use TiVo to advertise their channels and films (<http://www.tivo.com/5.4.asp>, accessed 12 April 2005). Secondly, firms are struggling for control over the EPGs, which inform users what programmes are on and when (Gibson, 2005d). Most firms wish to have their channel assigned the lowest number possible on an EPG, as viewers often only access regularly those channels numbered in the low teens. In Britain, regulators have come to be involved as they try to stop owners of such guides from abusing what often is monopoly control over a decoding box and linked EPG system. Thirdly, firms have attempted to push their programmes, to market their programmes, to make them become 'must see' events through PVRs. For example, in 2002 the BBC paid TiVo for its PVRs to record for users the second episode of a BBC comedy, *Dossa and Joe* (<http://www.theregister.co.uk/202/05/24/bbc_hijacks_tivo_recorders>, accessed 12 April 2005; Wells, 2002).

While television firms digest these developments and seek to bolster their schedules, other technologies are appearing that might be harder to control. For example, some broadband and cable operators now offer pay-per-view services over their systems. Customers, with such a service, can through their television set/decoder select any programme or film on offer that can then be delivered to their homes via their cable or broadband connection. Operators like Homechoice (<http://www.homechoice.co.uk>) and NTL (<http://www.ntlworld.com>) already operate such a service – though neither is yet offered nationwide. While such services, so far, only offer a limited range of programmes and films, a system operating over the Internet could potentially offer a huge selection of programmes from all over the world. While the Internet is better known for music swapping services between individual users, the peer-to-peer software made famous by Napster, television programmes and films are also beginning to be swapped and sold via the Internet through such software as ZaZaa, Morpheus and Bitorrent (Naughton, 2004). As broadband is rolled out across Britain and other nations, the possibility of using such software to offer and find programmes available anywhere in the globe has increased. Such technology is now moving to using software that will allow users to download a programme or film from multiple sources, helping to speed up downloading times. The media industry, yet again worried about copyright, has tried to stifle the development of peer-to-peer software, often taking those illegally offering or downloading programmes or films, or those offering the software used, to court (Norton, 2005). However, in the long run, the media industry might find this as another means, another market, by which to exploit their material. Indeed, Bertelsmann is already experimenting with a new peer-to-peer service resource that seeks payment for protected programmes (Blau, 2005) and the BBC is looking at such technologies that share multiple sites to distribute content as a means of opening up its own programme archive (BBC, 2003; Gibson, 2005h).

American distributors or producers could, in years to come, put all their wares online, allowing consumers to pay to watch particular programmes or films when they want. This, in some ways, could spell the end of the gatekeeping role of broadcasters; it would be the end of scheduled services. It would open libraries of millions of hours of programmes and films on a worldwide scale. However, it would be unlikely that such developments would signal the end of broadcasting and narrowcasting as people still, seemingly, like to watch a schedule of programmes; indeed, some people enjoy sitting down and surfing the multitude of channels, dipping into short segments of programmes; people like to watch live events and share the experience of watching together with a wider community, for example, look at the continued audiences for sport events and reality television programmes like *Big Brother* and soaps, many of which gain audiences in their millions; in homes with videos, the forerunning of these forms of Me-TV, scheduled programmes are still watched. However, as was shown with *24* recently, when thousands of people downloaded new episodes of it from American sites before it was shown in Britain, there are times when new technologies are useful in getting to see programmes outside of the constraints of scheduled services (BBC News, 2005). As these new forms of technology appear, which provide a type of ME-TV, they will do so alongside existing forms of television, as much as radio and film continued to exist alongside broadcast television.

7.7   Conclusion

Once, British viewers could watch, what British broadcasters would describe as, the best of American television, encased and infused within a national schedule; these programmes were bought and selected by British broadcasters acting as gatekeepers of the airwaves. However, increasingly it is now possible to experience American programmes and American-styled television channels in a more unmediated fashion, warts and all. Many American media firms now offer their own branded channels that tend to provide a similar diet to that offered in America, though usually interspersed with some local content. This development would suggest not the end of gatekeeping but the creation of new forms. Those working for these new channels will still have to select and filter what programmes are shown and when.

However, with the development of video, DVD, PVR and now peer-to-peer communities on the Internet, the possibility that the viewer might be able to choose what they want to watch has also increased. Though this selection can only be from what has been produced and is on offer, whether legally or illegally, what the viewer knows about and what the viewer can afford to access. Media firms have responded to these technologies by trying to push their products over these new media, paying for trailers and adverts to be uploaded onto PVRs and, occasionally, for their programmes to be recorded – to be involved in categorising programmes, the way users' profiles are created and then used by broadcasters to shape their programmes for particular audience groups. They will also make sure that they are well positioned to control the new conditional access technologies, the decoding boxes, and associated EPGs as they seek to control the way viewers navigate their way around the new television world. Indeed, the importance of creating high-profile programme brands will become increasingly important; producers will have to inculcate knowledge about their programme so that viewers will then seek it out among the array of others on offer. However, as most audiences still seemingly prefer national products, and as many audiences still watch, for some of their time, scheduled channels, we might have to think of such developments more in terms of additional or supplementary ways to experience television – another window of opportunity.

While it might seem that we will be able to see more and more American programmes, often in a similar way to how they are watched in America, we might find that we, the viewers, will operate as a kind of 'gate-keeper'; viewers will be as selective as current broadcasters. For some, American programmes will be an important part of their week's viewing, for others not. For some, such programmes should be experienced as part of a blend of programmes, and for some, they should be viewed within a particular themed context. For some, American programmes will be viewed outside of the broadcast context, as stand-alone programmes. Whatever happens, American programmes will be as much part of British television's future as it was in the past.

Conclusion

Aims

As outlined in the introduction, now, a time when American programmes can be watched in Britain 24/7, is a good moment to reflect on and to re-evaluate the past, current and future role of American programmes on British screens. As I explored in Chapter 1, for many years the dominant view has been to dismiss, malign or downplay the role of American programmes; the raison d'être of British broadcasting was to produce domestic programmes. Much of the writing and research that had focus on American programmes had been at either the macro level, studying the programme flows between nations, or the micro level, analysing American programmes and their reception and consumption. For example, the work of Katz and Liebes (1986) on the way different social groups read *Dallas*.

In this work, however, I have sought to develop a more middle- or meso-level approach, similar to that taken by Cunningham and Jacka (1996: 22); an approach that focuses on how and why programmes are bought, and how they are used and become part of the British television. Therefore, rather than viewing American culture as imposed on British culture, or open to multiple readings, I have conceptualised the interaction of American programmes with British television as a form of dynamic assimilation; one where the programme is changed and helps change the culture it is consumed within. To help guide this work I have adapted and, sometimes loosely, utilised work by Nancy Morris (2002), Jeffery Miller (2000), John Ellis (2002) and Nick Browne (1984), among others. Utilising their ideas, I focus on those moments in the broadcasting process when programmes are selected and acquired by broadcasters and then shaped, changed, assimilated and used by and within a schedule; moments where imported programmes interact with an existing culture; moments where American programmes become part of British television.

Changing context, changing relationships

American programmes are not produced, bought or sold in a vacuum; they are bought by British broadcasters working for organisations which operate within a particular broadcasting regime, a regime with its own histories and conventions, which exists within a particular economic, political and cultural situation. Likewise, American programmes are produced for specific organisations within a particular regime, with their own histories and conventions; they are created within and for a particular economic, political and cultural context. Therefore to understand the trade in programmes – what is produced, what is on offer, how it is sold, what is bought, how it is used and how it is assimilated – requires, in the first instance, an understanding of the relationship between the two markets; there is a need to understand how the different British and American broadcasting regimes develop requirements and needs to both sell and buy programmes.

As I explored in Chapter 3, the American and British markets both developed push and pull factors, reasons for selling and buying programmes, ideas and personnel. As the American market developed, it has, for economic, cultural and political reasons, been dominated by push factors, push factors that have encouraged American firms to distribute and sell their programmes abroad (Hoskins *et al.*, 1997: 75–6). The success of American firms in finding, developing and exploiting overseas markets has been helped by their comparative advantage; an advantage which has meant that American programmes, covering their costs in the large home market, could then be sold at very low prices abroad; any return was profit. They have also been helped by a low cultural discount because of the wide acceptance of the English language and American culture (Hoskins and Mirus, 1988: 32–3; Collins, 1990: 52–73).

In Britain, pull factors have been evident from the start, though push factors have also existed, leading to the development of a successful export business (Steemers, 2004). British broadcasters, at different moments and times, realised they needed to buy in American programmes, and could benefit from such purchases. This could be because of the low cost and the high production values of American programmes, combined with the demand of their audiences and the needs of the schedule. The amount purchased, however, was generally kept in check; they were bought, mostly, to support the schedule, to support British productions. Most British broadcasters saw their domestic productions as the mainstay of their output, and have always invested heavily in it.

Therefore, to understand why particular types of American programmes were and are bought, the way they are used in the schedules and how they become part of British television culture requires an understanding of the underlying economics of the system, and the relationships between different national markets. While attempts have been made to create a broadcasting system that would rely mostly on domestic programmes, the needs of competition, innovation, cost and demands from audiences have always meant that some trade has always been required, though its nature and scale have changed over time. However, while an economic discourse provides one important view of the reasons for buying American programmes, there is also a need to understand how, culturally, such programmes are bought and used, indeed, how they become part of British television culture.

Active Assimilation

American programmes do not appear just willy-nilly on British television, nor do economic forces completely determine their selection or use. While an economic view, as outlined above, starts to delineate the complex processes, forces and relationships at work, there is also a need to understand what happens from the point of view of those that make the actual decisions, the broadcasters – how they view the context within which they work, the array of forces that impinge upon them, and how they balance these with the needs of the channel, what is on offer, what other channels are doing and so on. At the end of the day it is broadcasters that buy and use programmes, not forces.

In Chapter 4, I explored how broadcasters buy and use programmes; broadcasters do not just purchase any programme, there are many on offer, and most channels, especially the terrestrial ones, have finite needs. Broadcasters therefore, watch, understand and value programmes as professionals situated within particular organisations and broadcasting contexts; they also interpret programmes from within the shared national culture; they share, in this way, what Morris calls a deep cultural structure (2002). Broadcasters view actively, thinking and weighing up the various needs of their channels, what the programme controller or director of television might think, the needs of the channel as a brand, the possible time slot for the programme, the cost of the programme in relation to the existing budget and the target audience; consciously and unconsciously they culturally decode the programmes, thinking about the needs of the audience, will it make sense to them and will it work within the British cultural context. As they buy programmes they do so actively, re-imagining the programme as being part of British television.

Likewise, American programmes are not just thrown unaltered in some higgledy-piggledy way into the schedule in any slot. As I explore in Chapter 5, they are actively assimilated; they are changed, adapted and carefully positioned with the schedule (supertext) and, in differing ways, interact with the programmes, channels and the wider environment around them (the metatext). The purchased programme or series is often changed to help it fit with the perceived requirements of the channel, the limits imposed by regulations and the needs of the wider British culture. It might be edited, as *Buffy the Vampire Slayer* was when shown in an early slot, or if a series, might be shown in a different way to the way it was in America, for example some of the episodes of *Angel* were not shown because of their content (Hill and Calcutt, 2001).

American programmes do not appear unannounced, broadcasters will, in an active way, create a narrative image, a way for the public to understand such programmes (Ellis, 1982: 24–5). They do this through adverts, trailers, websites and listing magazines. Through these they try to shape the image of a programme to align it to particular audiences the broadcaster is targeting. For example, *The Sopranos* is sold, or marketed by C4, not as a crime programme, but as a quality American television drama; one that they hope will hit a cord with the affluent ABC1 audience; *24* is marketed to audiences with a sense of irony, accepting some of the criticism of the fantastical nature of the programme. Through advertising, publicity and PR broadcasters engage in a public discourse as they seek to create a narrative image (Ellis, 1982: 24–5; Miller, 2000: 38–9), a way to frame the programme for the audience; a way of helping in the acceptance of such programmes by the public.

Public discourses: Television criticism

In Chapter 6, I explored the role of critics in the public discourse that exists around television and its programmes. This is a discourse, as noted above, which broadcasters through marketing, PR and advertising engage with, trying to direct and shape the coverage of their channel and its programmes in a beneficial way. The critics, in some ways, have an equally, if not more influential voice. They are influential in two ways: first, they have access to the media so their views can be heard or read on a weekly or daily basis, often by millions of readers; secondly, they are positioned in such a discourse as experts, they are independent professionals who make their living watching, engaging with and writing about television. However, while they have an important role in such debates, they are not all powerful. Indeed, with the ubiquitous nature of television, everyone, in various ways, feels able to pontificate on the latest series or serial; everyone is, in a way, a television critic.

Television critics and their resulting criticism and reviews can be viewed as systematic of larger and wider cultural debates about taste and value in society. Initially, serious television critics tried to gain acceptance of television as a serious cultural form, and they did so by aligning themselves with dominant cultural views, views often associated with the cultural elites (Poole, 1984: 44). They would often look at television through the frameworks of theatre and literary criticism, viewing American programmes in a derogatory fashion, as a standardised, formulaic, repetitive form. However, over time, other forms of criticism have appeared: some have attempted to understand television as television, rather than as an art form, to study and analyse all forms; others have presented more popular coverage, often focusing more on the behind-the-scene gossip rather than on the programmes; others have presented alternative or even subversive understandings of American programmes. It would seem that, increasingly, with the plethora of media outlets, and the different forms of criticism that have appeared, depending on the media consumed, different types of coverage of American programmes can be gained. Indeed, with the Internet, the budding member of the public who wishes their views to be read, can now do so – though still in a restricted form.

Future relationships and uses

In Chapter 7, I explored how television is undergoing changes that some argue would see the end of broadcasting as the dominant form. These are developments that are leading towards the appearance of hundreds of channels, delivered off-air, through cable and satellite; indeed, such developments see the end of television as a broadcast form, one free at the point of use, towards forms of pay-TV, narrowcasting, themed channels and pay per view. It would seem, for some, that this is a new age, what, for Ellis, is an age of plenty (2002).

Such developments have led to dramatic changes in both the American and British markets. Indeed, the old relationship dominated by American distributors selling programmes to British broadcasters is metamorphosing. New global firms, many of which are American or have major operations there, have appeared that are seeking to exploit their competitive advantages at a time when European markets are opening to more competition. The American-based media are using their muscle to supplement increased sales to the plethora of new channels with their own branded channels; no longer will they have to rely on British broadcasters buying their product. As the bottleneck of broadcasting disappears, and as the market is flooded by hundreds of channels, many media firms have started to concentrate on developing and marketing sub-brands of programmes – the key attraction. Seemingly, as the cry has been before, content is king, or at least more of a force than it was.

While the American developments have led to the creation of huge media companies, British ones are still fairly small; indeed some policy moves might well fragment the market further. If anything, the commercial terrestrial channels might well find themselves coming under foreign ownerships. With the appearance of hundreds of channels, operating under a weaker regime, the main terrestrial channels have come to depend more on their distinctive domestic programmes, while the smaller terrestrial channels and some cable and satellite channels are still relying on using high-profile American programmes as an important strategy for attracting upmarket audiences.

Some have argued that technological developments are actually leading to the end of television as we have known it (Gilder, 1994). Where television has been, for along time, associated with making a diverse range of programmes which are then transmitted in a planned schedule, new ways of buying and watching programmes are developing. One popular concept that seeks to explain such developments has been Me-TV (Hoskins *et al.*, 1997: 133; Winston, 1998: 127). This, its proponents argue, is a future where the viewer can, using such technologies, escape the tyranny of the schedulers. Through devices such as Personal Video Recorders (PVR), Internet software like Bitorrent (Naughton, 2004) and pay-per-view systems like Homechoice, the viewer can watch what they like whenever they want, though usually at a cost. While the firms offering such technology are selling them in terms of offering increased autonomy for the viewer, the existing broadcasters and rights holders of programmes and films are more wary. There is an ongoing struggle, as there often is on new technologies, over how these technologies will develop and who will control them.

Conclusion

American television programmes have been part and parcel of British television for many years. However, for many years there has been little serious coverage of their important economic or cultural role. Often they have been maligned, forgotten or criticised by a dominant discourse that has viewed American culture as crass, formulaic and standardised; a mass culture that was eroding and destroying the British indigenous culture. Some, who have tried to study this developing relationship, have adhered to a media and cultural imperialism type of approach, which in some ways has taken a similar line; American culture and media were dominating and affecting other nations' culture, including Britain's. While from the 1980s, some work has appeared that has touched on popular American programmes shown on British screens, this has usually been done by focusing either on their development in the American market (Osgerby and Gough-Yates, 2001; Akass and McCabe, 2004; Creeber, 2004) or by studying the way audiences read and consume American text; this latter work has come to suggest that texts are polysemic and open, which allows many different readings and interpretations. Few explore how American programmes are assimilated into the British television culture.

In this work I have sought to complement those works that have tended to focus on the middle level, Segrave (1998), Ellis (2002), Browne (1984) and Steemers (2004), the point where British and American markets meet, where broadcasters buy and use programmes, where American programmes are sold or framed for the British viewers. I have looked at how the relationships between the British and American markets have developed, the possible reasons for buying American programmes, the way they are selected and used by broadcasters, the way they are assimilated and interact with the schedule and the way they are framed by a wider public discourse. At the end, I have looked at some of the more recent developments to gauge how things might develop in the future. Through such work I have attempted to understand the changing role and use of American programmes as an active dynamic process, where the process of assimilation is two way: American programmes are changed, framed and adapted by broadcasters and also, at the same time, they interact with it, they become part of and, eventually, integrated into the cultural deep structures. American programmes in this way must not be viewed as something external to British television, but, as they come into the British context, they must be viewed as a vital and integral part of British television culture.

Bibliography

Adorno, T. W. (with E. Frenkel-Brunswik *et al.*) (1950) *The Authoritarian Personality* (New York: Norton, 1969).

——. (2002) *The Culture Industry: Selected Essays on Mass Culture*, ed. J. M. Bernstein (London: Routledge).

Akass, K. and J. McCabe (eds) (2004) *Reading Sex and the City* (London: I. B. Tauris).

Allan, S. (1999) *News Culture* (Buckingham: Open University Press).

Alvarado, M. (1996) 'Selling television', in A. Moran (ed.) *Film Policy: International, National and Regional Perspective* (London: Routledge), pp. 62–71.

Alvey, M. (2000) 'The Independents: Rethinking the television studio system', in H. Newcomb (ed.) *Television: The Critical View*, 6th edition (Oxford: Oxford University Press), pp. 34–51.

Anderson, C. (1994) *Hollywood TV: The Studio System in the Fifties* (Austin, USA: University of Texas Press).

Ang, I. (1985) *Watching Dallas: Soap Opera and the Melodramatic Imagination* (London: Methuen).

——. (1991) *Desperately Seeking the Audience* (London: Routledge).

Arlidge, J. (2001) 'Why this is now the golden age of TV', *The Observer*, 9 September.

Arnold, M. (1969) *Culture and Anarchy*, ed. J. D. Wilson (London: Cambridge University Press).

Aron, R. (1983) *Main Currents in Sociological Thought* (London: Pelican).

Aspinall, A. (2005) 'Why American TV is thinking out of the box', *The Birmingham Post*, 15 April.

Balio, T. (1996) 'Adjusting to the new global economy: Hollywood in the 1990s', in A. Moran (ed.) *Film Policy: International, National and Regional Perspectives* (London: Routledge), pp. 23–38.

Baxter, B. (1992) (Buyer, Feature Films BBC1 & BBC2), Interview, London.

BBC (2002) *Annual Report and Accounts: 2001/2* (London: BBC).

——. (2003) *Annual Report and Accounts: 2002/3* (London: BBC).

——. (2004) *Annual Report and Accounts: 2003/4* (London: BBC).

BBC News (2001) 'Survivor goes once a week', <http://news.bbc.co.uk/1/hi/entertainment/tv_and_radio/1373940.stm>, 6 June. Accessed 27 June 2005.

——. (2002) 'Next generation DVD born', <http://news.bbc.co.uk/1/hi/entertainment/new_media/1829241.stm>, 21 February. Accessed 25 July 2005.

——. (2003) 'Dyke to open up BBC archive', <http://news.bbc.co.uk/1/hi/entertainment/tv_and_radio/3177479.stm>, 24 August. Accessed 25 July 2005.

——. (2005) 'UK net users leading TV downloads', <http://news.bbc.co.uk/2/hi/technology/4276255.stm>, 19 February. Accessed 1 March 2005.

Beadle, G. (1957) 'British and American Film in BBC Television Programmes', *T16/599/1* (Caversham: BBC).

Beadle, G. (1963) *Television: A Critical Review* (London: George Allen & Unwin).

Beaumont, I. (2002) <http://www.xtv.com/tv/understandingtv/choices.htm>. Accessed 22 June 2005.

Beavis, S. and K. Ahmen (1998) 'ITV Stations hit out at Channel 4's "populism" ', *The Guardian*, 30 January.

Bennett, T. and J. Woollacott (1987) *Bond and Beyond: The Political Career of a Popular Hero* (London: Methuen).

Bignell, J. (2004) *An Introduction to Television Studies* (London: Routledge).

Black, P. (1972) *The Biggest Aspidistra in the World: A Personal Celebration of 50 Years of the BBC* (London: BBC).

——. (1973) *The Mirror in the Corner: People's Television* (London: Hutchinson).

Blau, J. (2005) 'Bertelsmann Launches New Peer-to-Peer Service', <http://www.pcworld>. Accessed 1 April.

Blumber, J. G. (ed.) (1992) 'Part I: Western European television in transition', in *Television and the Public Interest: Vulnerable Values in West European Broadcasting* (London: Sage), pp. 7–42.

Boddy, W. (1993) *Fifties Television: The Industry and Its Critics* (Urbana: University of Illinois Press).

Bonner, P. and L. Aston (1998) *Independent Television in Britain*, Vol. 5 (London: Macmillan).

——. (2003) *Independent Television in Britain*, Vol. 6 (London: Macmillan).

Born, G. (2003) 'Strategy, positioning and projection in digital television: Channel Four and the commercialisation of public service broadcasting in the UK', *Media, Culture and Society*, 25, pp. 773–99.

——. (2004) *Uncertain Vision: Birt, Dyke and the Reinvention of the BBC* (London: Secker & Warburg).

Born, M. (2002) 'BSkyB poaches Airey from Channel 5 for £1 m a year', <http://www.telegraph.co.uk/news/main.jhtml?xml=/news/2002/09/23/nairey23.xml>, 3 September. Accessed 16 June 2005.

Boulton, J. (1992) (Acquisitioner BSkyB), Interview, London.

Boyd-Barrett, O. (1979) 'Media imperialism: Towards as international framework for the Analysis of Media Systems', in J. Curran, M. Gurevitch and J. Woollacott (eds) *Mass Communication and Society* (London: Edward Arnold), pp. 116–35.

——. (1995) 'Approaches to "new audience research" ' in O. Boyd-Barrett and C. Newbold (eds) *Approaches to Media: A Reader* (London: Arnold), pp. 498–504.

——. (1998) 'Media imperialism reformulated', in D. K. Thussu (ed.) *Electronic Empires: Global Media and Local Resistance* (London: Arnold), pp. 157–76.

Brants, K. and E. D. Bens (2000) 'The status of TV broadcasting in Europe', in J. Wieten, G. Murdoch and P. Dahlgren (eds) *Television Across Europe: A Comparative Introduction* (London: Sage), pp. 7–22.

Briggs, A. (1961) *The History of Broadcasting in the United Kingdom: The Birth of Broadcasting*, Vol. I (Oxford: Oxford University Press).

——. (1965) *The History of Broadcasting in the United Kingdom: The Golden Age of Wireless*, Vol. II (Oxford: Oxford University Press).

——. (1970) *The History of Broadcasting in the United Kingdom: The War of Words*, Vol. III (Oxford: Oxford University Press).

——. (1979) *The History of Broadcasting in the United Kingdom: Sound and Vision*, Vol. IV (Oxford: Oxford University Press).

——. (1995) *The History of Broadcasting in the United Kingdom: Competition 1955–1974*, Vol. V (Oxford: Oxford University Press).

Briggs, A. and P. Burke (2002) *A Social History of the Media: From Gutenberg to the Internet* (Cambridge: Polity).

Brookeman, C. (1984) *American Culture and Society Since the 1930s* (London: Schocken Books).

Brooker, C. (2000) 'The Justice League of America', *The Guardian*, 2 September.

——. (2002) 'The "What the Fuck?" Factor', *The Guardian*, 30 March.

——. (2005) *Screen Burn: Television with Its Face Torn Off* (Faber & Faber, *The Guardian*: London).

Brown, M. (2000) 'With Friends like these . . .', *The Guardian*, 6 November.

——. (2002) 'Second to none', *The Guardian*, 15 April.

——. (2004) 'Calling the slots', *The Guardian*, 20 September.

Browne, N. (1984) 'The political economy of the television (super) text', *Quarterly Review of Film Studies*, 9(3), pp. 174–82.

Burns, T. (1977) *The BBC, Public Institutions and Private World* (London: Macmillan).

Burr, V. (2005) *Buffy vs the BBC: Moral Questions and How to Avoid Them*, <http://slayage.tv/essays/slayage8/Burr.htm>. Accessed 1 May 2005.

Busfield, S. (2004) 'Titanic battle over new DVD format: It could be VHS v Betamax all over again in the next technology clash', *The Guardian*, 23 November.

Cantor, M. G. (1971) *The Hollywood TV Producer: His Work and His Audience* (New York: Basic Books).

Cantor, M. G. and J. M. Cantor (1986) 'American television in the international marketplace', *Communication Research*, 13(3), pp. 509–20.

——. (1992) *Prime-Time Television: Content and Control*, 2nd edition (Newbury Park: Sage).

Carey, J. (1992) *The Intellectuals and the Masses: Pride and Prejudice among the Literary Intelligentsia 1880–1939* (London: Faber & Faber).

Carter, M. (2004) 'Why the US loves British reality', *The Guardian*, 1 March.

Carter, S. (2004) 'I'll make the BBC raise its game', *The Guardian*, 10 October.

Caughie, J. (1991) 'Before the Golden Age', in J. Corner (ed.) *Popular Television in Britain: Studies in Cultural History* (London: BFI), pp. 22–41.

Chadha, K. and A. Kavoori (2000) 'Media imperialism revisited: Some findings from the Asian case', *Media, Culture and Society*, 22, pp. 415–32.

Chalaby, J. K. (ed.) (2005a) 'Towards an understanding of media transnationalism', *Transnational Television Worldwide: Towards a New Media Order* (London: I. B. Tauris), pp. 1–13.

——. (ed.) (2005b) 'The quiet invention of a new medium: Twenty years of transnational television in Europe', *Transnational Television Worldwide: Towards a New Media Order* (London: I. B. Tauris), pp. 43–65.

Channel Four (2003) *C4 Annual accounts 2002* (London: Channel Four).

Childs, T. (1992) (Drama producer at Central Television broadcaster), Interview, London.

Clark, P. (2002) 'The Anatomy of a hit', *Evening Standard*, 20 December.

——. (2005) 'First-class lesson in homicide', *Evening Standard*, 14 April.

Coles, J. (2000) 'Nine Lives of the Ally Cat', *The Times*, 9 October.

Collins, A. (2000) 'TV duel: May the best family win', *The Guardian*, 15 October.

——. (2001) 'Can you tell your E4 from your C4?', *The Guardian*, 7 January.

Collins, J. (1992) 'Television and PostModernism', in R. C. Allen (ed.) *Channels of Discourse, reassembled: Contemporary criticism*, 2nd edition (London: The University of North Carolina Press), pp. 327–53.

Collins, R. (1990) *Television: Policy and Culture* (London: Unwin Hyman).

Comstock, G. (1991) *Television in America*, 2nd edition (London: Sage).

Cornell, P., M. Day and K. Topping (1993) *The Guinness Book of Classic TV*, (London: Guinness).

Corner, J. (ed.) (1991) *Popular Television in Britain: Studies in Cultural History* (London: BFI).

——. (1999) *Critical Ideas in Television Studies* (Oxford: Clarendon Press).

Courtauld, C. (2003) 'What a load of rubble', *Independent on Sunday*, 10 August.

——. (2004a) 'And now back to the jungle for some serious analysis...', *Independent on Sunday*, 1 February.

——. (2004b) 'And lo, the angel of the thesps came down', *Independent on Sunday*, 15 February.

Cox, E. (2005) 'What to watch tonight', *The Sun*, 6 April.

Creeber, G. (2004) *Serial Television: Big Drama on the Small Screen* (London: BFI).

Crisell, A. (1997) *An Introductory History of British Broadcasting* (London: Routledge).

Crozier, M. (1958) *Broadcasting: Sound and Television* (London: Oxford University Press).

——. (1959) 'Dotto, Dottier, Dottiest', *The Bedside 'Guardian' 8: A Selection from the Manchester Guardian 1958–1959* (London: Collins), pp. 59–60.

Cunningham, S. and E. Jacka (1996) *Australian Television and International Mediascapes* (Cambridge: Cambridge University Press).

Cunningham, S., E. Jacka and J. Sinclair (1998) 'Global and regional dynamics of international television flows', in D. Thussu (ed.) *Electronic Empires: Global Media and Local Resistance* (London: Arnold), pp. 175–92.

Curran, C. (1979) *A Seamless Robe: Broadcasting Philosophy and Practice* (London: Collins).

Curran, J. and J. Seaton (1997) *Power without Responsibility: The Press and Broadcasting in Britain* (London: Routledge).

Davis, G. and K. Dickinson (eds) (2004) *Teen TV: Genre, Consumption and Identity* (London: BFI).

DCMS (2005) *Review of the BBC's Royal Charter Green Paper – A Strong BBC, Independent of Government* (London: HMSO).

Deans, J. (2003) 'BBC talks to buy 24 collapse', *The Guardian*, 5 December.

——. (2004a) '... while its ratings hit all-time low', *The Guardian*, 14 December.

——. (2004b) 'Channel 4 pins Friday hopes on Homer and Bart', *The Guardian*, 7 May.

——. (2005) 'The last laugh', *The Guardian*, 17 January.

Dienst, M. (1994) *Still Life in Real Time* (Durham, NC: Duke University Press).

Dromgoole, J. (2004) 'The cost of buying in bulk', *The Guardian*, 5 October.

Dunkley, C. (1985) *Television Today and Tomorrow: Wall-to-Wall Dallas?* (London: Penguin).

Dyer, G. (1973) *Light Entertainment* (London: BFI).

Eden, J. (2005) 'Rumbled?', *The Sun*, 9 April.

Elliot, T. S. (1939) *The Idea of a Christian Intellectual Movement in America* (New York: Basic Books).

——. (1976 – first published 1932) *Selected Essays* (London: Faber & Faber).

Ellis, J. (1982) *Visible Fictions: Cinema; Television; Video* (London: Routledge & Kegan and Paul).

——. (2000) 'Scheduling: The last creative act in television?', *Media, Culture and Society*, 22, pp. 25–38.

——. (2002) *Seeing Things: Television in the Age of Uncertainty* (London: I. B. Tauris).

——. (2003) 'Channel Four: Innovation in form and content?', in M. Hilmes (ed.) *The Television History Book* (London: BFI), pp. 95–8.

Estall, M. (2002) *Fantasy Film League*, <http://fantasyfilmleague.com> Filed 10 February. Accessed 3 March 2005

Evening Standard (2000) 'Sex and the city', 19 March.

Fanthome, C. (2003) *Channel 5: The Early Years* (Luton: University of Luton Press).

Fejes, F. (1981) 'Media imperialism: An assessment', *Media, Culture and Society*, 3(3), pp. 281–9.

Feuer, J. (2003) 'Quality drama in the US: The new "Golden Age"?', in M. Hilmes (ed.) *The Television History Book* (London: BFI), pp. 98–102.

Fiske, J. (1987) *Television Culture* (London: Methuen).

——. (1992) *Television Culture* (London: Routledge).

Fiske, J. and J. Hartley (1978) *Reading Television* (London: Methuen).

Franklin, B. (ed.) (2001) *British Television Policy: A Reader* (London: Routledge).

Freedom party (2003) <http://www.freedomparty.org/issupapr/ca_03.htm>. Accessed July 4 2005.

Freeman, H. (2005) 'Channel surfing: Patronised by the dead', *The Guardian*, 12 April.

Garnham, N. and G. Locksley (1991) 'The economics of broadcasting', in J. G. Blumler and T. J. Nossiter (eds) *Broadcasting Finance in Transition: A Comparative Handbook* (Oxford: Oxford University Press), pp. 8–22.

Garnham, N. and R. Williams (1980) 'Pierre Bourdieu and the sociology of culture: An introduction', *Media, Culture and Society*, 2(3), pp. 209–23.

Garnham, N., G. Locksley and R. Collins (1987) *The Economics of Television: The UK Case* (London: Sage).

Gentile, G. (2004) 'Film Studios take sides over new DVDs', *The Guardian*, 30 November.

Gibson, J. (2004) 'The smiling cavalier', *The Guardian*, 23 February.

Gibson, O. (2004) 'BBC Shuts websites to assist charter renewal pitch', *The Guardian*, 12 December.

Gibson, O. (2005a) 'Lost finds record audience', *The Guardian*, 12 August.

——. (2005b) 'Laurie's bedside manner wins over the US', *The Guardian*, 23 May.

——. (2005c) 'Looking after number one: James Baker is back in charge at Sky's flagship channel, and he has a radical makeover in mind', *The Guardian*, 28 February.

——. (2005d) 'Sky faces inquiry after ITV complaint', *The Guardian*, 7 January.

——. (2005e) 'BBC Licence fee safe – at least until 2016', *The Guardian*, 3 March.

——. (2005f) 'BBC under fire for £1.5 m deal to buy US series', *The Guardian*, 4 March.

——. (2005g) 'Five sets sights of drama and comedy', *The Guardian*, 26 August.

——. (2005h) 'BBC puts shows on net and mobiles', *The Guardian*, 26 August.

Gilder, G. (1994) *Life After Television: The Coming Transformation of Media and American Life* (New York: Norton).

Gitlin, T. (1985) *Inside Prime Time* (New York: Pantheon).

Goddard, P. (1991) ' "Hancock's Half Hour": A Watershed in British Television Comedy', in J. Corner (ed.) *Popular Television in Britain* (London: BFI), pp. 75–89.

Goldsmith, J. (2005) 'Lessons from America', *The Guardian*, 11 July.

Goodwin, P. (1998) *Television under the Tories: Broadcasting Policy 1979–1997* (London: BFI).

Gould, J. (1996) 'Early criticism, like early television, grappled with the same problems as today', *Quill*, 84(10), <http://web33.epnet.com>. Accessed 20 May 2005.

Graham, A. (1999) 'Broadcasting policy in the multimedia age', in A. Graham C. Koboldt, S. Hogg, B. Robinson, D. Currie, M. Siner, G. Mather, J. Le Grand, B. New and I. Corfield (eds) *Public Purposes in Broadcasting: Funding the BBC* (Luton: University of Luton Press), pp. 17–46.

Graham, A. and G. Davies (1992) 'The public funding of broadcasting', in T. Congdon, B. Sturgess, NERA, W. B. Shew, A. Graham and G. Davies (eds) *Paying for Broadcasting: The Handbook* (London: Routledge), pp. 167–221.

Graham, A., C. Koboldt, S. Hogg, B. Robinson, D. Currie, M. Siner, G. Mather, J. Le Grand, B. New and I. Corfield (1999) *Public Purposes in Broadcasting: Funding the BBC* (Luton: University of Luton Press).

Gripsrud, J. (1995) *The Dynasty Years: Hollywood Television and Critical Media Studies* (London: Routledge).

Gripsrud, J. (1997) 'Television, broadcasting, flow: Key metaphors in TV theory', in D. Lusted and C. Geraghty (eds) *The Television Studies Book* (London: Arnold), pp. 17–32.

Hall, S. (1996) 'Encoding/decoding', in P. Marris and S. Thornham (eds) *Media Studies: A Reader* (Edinburgh: Edinburgh University Press), pp. 51–61.

Halliwell, L. and P. Purser (1985) *Halliwell's Television Companion* (London: Paladin).

Harbord, J. and J. Wright (1992) *40 Years of British Television* (London: Boxtree).

Hartley, J. (1977) 'Encouraging signs: Television and the power of dirt, speech, and scandalous categories', in W. Rowland and B. Watkins (eds) (1983) *Interpreting Television: Current Research Perspectives* (Beverly Hills: Sage), pp. 119–41.

Hartley, J. (1978) 'Invisible fictions', *Textual Practice*, 1(2), pp. 121–38.

Harvey, S. (1994) 'Channel 4 Television: From Anna to Grade', in S. Hood (ed.) *Behind the Screens: The Structure of British Television in the Nineties* (London: Lawrence and Wishart), pp. 102–32.

Havens, T. (2000) ' "The biggest show in the world" race and the global popularity of *The Cosby Show*', *Media, Culture and Society*, 22, pp. 371–91.

Head, S., C. Sterling, L. Schofield, T. Spann and M. McGregor (1998) *Broadcasting in American: A Survey of Electronic Media*, 8th edition (Boston: Houghton Mifflin Company).

Hearst, S. (1992) 'Broadcasting regulation in Britain', in J. G. Blumler (ed.) *Television and the Public Interest: Vulnerable Values in West European Broadcasting* (London: Sage), pp. 61–78.

Heath, S. (1990) 'Representing television', in P. Mellencamp (ed.) *Logics of Television* (Bloomington, Ind.: Indiana University Press), pp. 267–302.

Heath, S. and G. Skirrow (1977) 'Television: A world in action', *Screen*, 18(2), pp. 7–59.

Hebdige, D. (1986) 'Towards a cartography of taste', in B. Waites, T. Bennett and G. Martin (eds) *Popular Culture: Past and Present* (London: Croom Helm/Open University Press), pp. 194–218.

Helmore, E. (2003) 'Who sets the TV control?', *The Observer*, 8 June.

Herman, E. S. and R. W. McChesney (1997) *The Global Media: The New Missionaries of Corporate Capitalism* (London: Cassell).

Hesmondhalgh, D. (2002) *The Cultural Industries* (London: Sage).

Higgins, J. M. (2004) 'Although NBC remains No. 1, CBS is close behind', *Broadcasting and Cable*, 13 December (B & C Research).

Hills, A. (1992) (C4 Head of Presentations and Promotions), Interview, London.

Hill, A. and I. Calcutt (2001) 'Vampire Hunters: The scheduling and reception of Buffy the Vampire Slayer and Angel in the UK', *Intensities: The Journal of Cult Media*, 1, <http://www.cult-media/issue1/Ahill.htm>. Accessed 1 May 2005.

Hilmes, M. (ed.) (2003a) *The Television History Book* (London: BFI).

——. (2003b) 'US television in the multichannel age', in M. Hilmes (ed.) *The Television History Book* (London: BFI), pp. 62–7.

Hobsbawn, E. (1984) *Industry and Empire, Volume 3: The Pelican Economic History of Britain* (London: Pelican).

——. (1994) *Age of Extremes: The Short Twentieth Century 1914–1991* (London: Michael Joseph).

Hoggart, R. (1957) *The Uses of Literacy* (London: Pelican).

Holden, S. (1999) 'Tickets to Fantasies of Urban Desire', *New York Times: E1, E2*, 20 July.

Holt, J. (2003) 'Vertical vision: Deregulation, industrial economy and prime-time design', in M. Jancovich and J. Lyon (eds) *Quality Popular Television* (London: BFI), pp. 11–31.

Home Office (1988) *Broadcasting in the '90s: Competition, Choice and Quality*. Cmnd 517 (London: HMSO).

Horsman, M. (1998) *Sky High: The Amazing Story of BSkyB – and the egos, deals and ambitions that revolutionised TV broadcasting* (London: Orion Business Books).

Hoskins, C. and R. Mirus (1988) 'Reason for the US domination of the international trade in television programmes', *Media, Culture and Society*, 10, pp. 499–515.

Hoskins, C., S. McFadyen and A. Finn (1997) *Global Television and Film: An Introduction to the Economics of the Business* (Oxford: Oxford University Press).

Houston, B. (1984) 'Viewing television: The metapsychology of endless consumption', *Quarterly Review of Film Studies*, 1(3), Summer, pp. 183–95.

Howdon, A. (1992) (Head of Acquisition Group BBC Television), Interview, London.

Hunt Report (1982) *Report of the Inquiry into Cable Expansion and Broadcasting Policy* (London: Home Office).

ITAP (Cabinet Office Information Technology Advisory Panel) (1982) *Cable Systems* (London: Cabinet Office).

James, C. (1981) *Visions Before Midnight* (London: Picador).

——. (1982) *The Crystal Bucket* (London: Picador).

——. (1983) *Glued to the Box* (London: Picador).

Jancovich, M. and J. Lyons (eds) (2003) *Quality Popular Television* (London: BFI).

Jenkins, C. (1961) *Power Behind the Screen: Ownership, Control and Motivation in British Commercial Television* (London: MacGibbon).

Jenkins, H. (1991) *Textual Poachers: Television Fans and Participatory Culture* (London: Routledge).

Jennings, R. (2003) 'Satellites and cable programmes in the UK', in M. Hilmes (ed.) *The Television History Book* (London: BFI), pp. 112–14.

Jensen, K. B. (1995) *The Social Semiotics of Mass Communication* (London: Sage).

Johnson, L. (1979) *The Cultural Critics* (London: Routledge and Kegan Paul).

Johnson, R. (1996) 'What is cultural studies anyway?', in J. Storey (ed.) *What is Cultural Studies? A Reader* (London: Edward Arnold), pp. 75–114.

Jones, S. G. (2003) 'Web wars: Resistance, online fandom and studio censorship', in M. Jancovich and J. Lyons (eds) *Quality Popular Television* (London: BFI), pp. 163–80.

Joseph, J. (2002) 'Why can't we do a British West Wing?', *The Times*, 29 May.

Kaplan, E. A. (ed.) (1983) *Regarding Television: Critical Approaches* (Frederick, MD: University Publications of America).

Katz, E. and T. Liebes (1986) 'Mutual aid in the decoding of Dallas: Preliminary notes from a cross-cultural study', in P. Drummond and R. Paterson (eds) *Television in Transition: Papers from the First International Television Studies Conference* (London: BFI), pp. 187–98.

Kelly, L. (2005) 'Terrible-Opinion', *The Sun*, 9 April.

Kelner, M. (2000) 'King of New York', *The Guardian*, 10 October.

Kivikuru, U. (1988) 'From Import to Modelling: Finland – An Example of old Periphery Dependency', *European Journal of Communication*, 3, pp. 9–34.

Knowledge Research (1991) *TV, UK Special Report* (Peterborough: Knowledge Research).

Koboldt, C., S. Hogg and B. Robinson (1999) 'The implications of funding for broadcasting output', in A. Graham, C. Koboldt, S. Hogg, B. Robinson, D. Currie, M. Siner, G. Mather, J. Le Grand, B. New and I. Cornfield (eds) *Public Purposes in Broadcasting: Funding the BBC* (Luton: University of Luton Press).

Kumar, K. (1983) *Prophecy and Progress* (London: Pelican).

Laing, S. (1991) 'Banging In Some Reality: The Original "Z Cars" ', in J. Corner (ed.) *Popular Television in Britain: Studies in Cultural History* (London: BFI), pp. 125–44.

Lawson, M. (2000) 'Cold comfort', *The Guardian*, 6 November.

——. (2004) 'The West has never been wilder', *The Guardian*, 20 September.

——. (2005) 'After the crash . . .', *The Guardian*, 5 August.

Lealand, G. (1984) *American Television Programmes on British Screens* (London: Broadcasting Research Unit Working Paper).

Lee, C-C. (1979) *Media Imperialism Reconsidered: The Homogenizing Television* (Beverly Hills, CA: Sage).

LeMahieu, D. (1988) *A Culture for Democracy: Mass Communication and the Cultivated Mind in Britain* (Oxford: Clarendon).

Lenventhal, C. (1991) (Director of acquisitions at C4), Interview, London.

Levy, J. D. (1996) 'Evolution and competition in the American video market', in A. Moran (ed.) *Film Policy: International, National and Regional Perspectives* (London: Routledge), pp. 39–61.

Liebes, T. and Katz, E. (1990) *The Export and Meaning: Cross Cultural Readings of 'Dallas'* (New York: Oxford University Press).

Lowenthal, L. (1957) 'Historical perspectives of popular culture', in B. Rosenberg and G. Mackenzie (eds) *Mass Culture* (Glencoe, IL: Free Press).

MacDonald, G. (1992) (Ex-Controller BBC2/Managing Director Anglia Films), Interview, London.

Macdonald, M. (1991) (Chief Film Buyer Channel Four), Interview, London.

Macshire, I. (1993) (BBC buyer series. Editor series programme acquisitions), Interview, London.

Markwick, A. (1987) *The Pelican Social History of Britain: British Society Since 1945* (London: Penguin).

Marshall, B. (2005) 'Good Cop, Better Cop', *The Guardian*, 16 April.

Martin, P. (2005) 'Mr Show Biz', *The Daily Mirror*, 14 April.

Mattelart, A., X. Delcourt and M. Mattelart (1983) *International Image Markets: In Search of an Alternative Perspective* (London: Comedia publishing).

Mazzoleni, G. and M. Palmer (1992) 'The Building of Media Empires', in K. Siune and W. Truetzschler (eds) *Dynamics of Media Politics: Broadcast and Electronic Media in Western Europe* (London: Sage), pp. 26–41.

McChesney, R. W. (1994) *Telecommunications, Mass Media, & Democracy: The Battle for the Control of US Broadcasting, 1928–1935* (Oxford: Oxford University Press).

McMurria, J. (2003) 'Long-format TV: Globalisation and Network Branding in a Multi-Channel Era', in M. Jancovich and J. Lyons (eds) *Quality Popular Television* (London: BFI), pp. 65–87.

Miège, B., P. Pajon and J. M. Salün (1986) *L'industrialisation de l'audiovisuel* (Paris: Aubier).

Miège, B. (1989) 'The cultural commodity', *Media, Culture and Society*, 1, pp. 38–59.

Miller, J. (2000) *Something Completely Different: British Television and American Culture* (London: University of Minnesota Press).

Miller, T. (1996) 'The Crime of Monsieur Lang: GATT, the screen, and the new international division of cultural labour', in A. Moran (ed.) *Film Policy: International, National and Regional Perspectives* (London: Routledge), pp. 72–84.

Miller, T. and G. Yúdice (2002) *Cultural Policy* (London: Sage).

Miller, T., D. Rowe, J. McKay and G. Lawrence (2003) 'The over-production of US sports and the new international division of cultural labor', *International Review for the Sociology of Sport*, 38(4), pp. 427–40.

Milmo, D. (2005a) 'Channel 4 suffers for Big Brothers success', *The Guardian*, 7 January.

——. (2005b) 'RTL takes full control of Channel Five', *The Guardian*, 21 July.

Mittell, J. (2003) 'The "classic Network System" in the US', in M. Hilmes (ed.) *The Television History Book* (London: BFI), pp. 44–9.

Modleski, T. (1983) 'The Rhythms of Reception: Daytime Television and Women's Work', in A. E. Kaplan (ed.) *Regarding Television: Critical Approaches* (Frederick, MD: University Publications of America), pp. 67–75.

Moran, A. (2003) 'The global television format trade', in M. Hilmes (ed.) *The Television History Book* (London: BFI), pp. 118–21.

Morely, D. and K. Robins (1997) *Spaces of Identity: Global Media, Electronic Landscapes and Cultural Boundaries* (London: Routledge).

Morris, N. (2002) 'The myth of unadulterated culture meets the threat of imported media', *Media, Culture and Society*, 24, pp. 278–89.

Mosco, V. (1996) *The Political Economy of Communication* (London: Sage).

Moss, T. (1992) (Deputy head of Youth and entertainment features department), Interview, London.

Murdoch, G. (1994) 'Money talks: Broadcasting, finance and public culture', in S. Hood (ed.) *Behind the Screens: The Structure of British Television in the Nineties* (London: Lawrence & Wishart), pp. 155–83.

Murphy, M. (1992) (Senior Vice President for Serial Drama for Grundy in Europe), Interview, London.

Murrow, F. (2004) 'Abby ever after?', *The Sun*, 17 January.

Naughton, J. (2004) 'Hollywood's nightmare has arrived', *The Observer: Business Section*, 7 March.

Negrine, R. (1994) *Politics and the Mass Media in Britain* (London: Routledge).

Negus, K. (1992) *Producing Pop* (London: Edward Arnold).

Nelson, R. (1997) *TV Drama in Transition: Forms, Values and Cultural Change* (London: Macmillan).

NERA (1992) 'Subscription', in T. Congdon, B. Sturgess, NERA, W. B. Shew, A. Graham and G. Davies (eds) *Paying for Broadcasting: The Handbook* (London: Routledge), pp. 92–164.

Nordenstreng, K. and T. Varis (1974) *Television Traffic: One-Way Street? A Survey and Analysis of the International Flow of Television Material. Reports and Papers on Mass Communication, No.70* (Paris: UNESCO).

Norton, Q. (2005) 'May the source be with you', *The Guardian*, 2 February.

Nossiter, T. J. (1991) 'British television: A mixed economy', in J. G. Blumler and T. J. Nossiter (eds) *Broadcasting Finance in Transition: A Comparative Handbook* (Oxford: Oxford University Press), pp. 95–143.

OFCOM (2004) *The Communication Market, 2004* (London: OFCOM).

O'Malley, T. (1994) *Closedown? The BBC and Government Broadcasting Policy, 1979–92* (London: Pluto).

——. (2003a) 'Satellite, cable and new channels in the UK (Rupert Murdoch)', in M. Hilmes (ed.) *The Television History Book* (London: BFI) pp. 59–62.

——. (2003b) 'The BBC adapts to competition', in M. Hilmes (ed.) *The Television History Book* (London: BFI), pp. 86–9.

Osgerby, B. and A. Gough-Yates (eds) (2001) *Action TV: Tough Guys, Smooth Operators and Foxy Chicks* (London: Routledge).

Osgerby, B., A. Gough-Yates and M. Wells (2001) 'The business of action: Television history and the development of the action TV series', in B. Osgerby and A. Gough-Yates (eds) *Action TV: Tough Guys, Smooth Operators and Foxy Chicks* (London: Routledge), pp. 13–31.

PACT (2005) 'UK Dominates Global Formats Market', <http://www.pact.co.uk/news/art_dtl.asp?art_id=2331>. Accessed 22 June 2005.

Parks, L. (2003) 'US television abroad: Exporting culture', in M. Hilmes (ed.) *The Television History Book* (London: BFI), pp. 115–18.

Paterson, P. (2002) 'Yanks win the pace race', *Daily Mail*, 24 June.

Paterson, R. (1990) 'A suitable schedule for the family', in A. Goodwin and G. Whannel (eds) *Understanding Television* (London: Routledge), pp. 30–41.

——. (1998) 'Drama and entertainment', in A. Smith with R. Paterson (eds) *Television: An International History* (Oxford: Oxford University Press), pp. 57–68.

Peacock Committee (1986) *Report of the Committee on Financing the BBC*. Cmnd 9824 (London: HMSO).

Peacock, M. (1965) 'BBC-1 Winter Pattern 1965/6', T16/149/4 (Cavisham: BBC), 7 April.

Pennant-Rea, R. and C. Crook (1986) *The Economist Economics* (London: Pelican).

Perren, A. (2003) 'New US networks in the 1990s', in M. Hilmes (ed.) *The Television History Book* (London: BFI), pp. 107–12.

Phillips, W. (1997) 'Bored with the USA?', *Broadcast*, 10 January, p. 30.

Pilkington (1962) *Report*. Cmnd. 1753 (London: HMSO).

Plantin, M. (1991) (Director of Programmes LWT), Interview, London.

Pool, I. de S. (1977) 'The changing flow of television', *Journal of Communication*, 27(2), pp. 139–49.

Poole, M. (1984) 'The cult of the generalist: British television criticism 1936–83', *Screen*, 25(2), pp. 41–61.

Porter, J. (2005) 'The banality of American popular culture', *The Independent*, 6 January.

Potter, J. (1989) *Independent Television in Britain*, Vol. 3 (London: Macmillan).

——. (1990) *Independent Television in Britain*, Vol. 4 (London: Macmillan).

Purser, P. (1992) *Done Viewing: A Personal Account of the Best Years of Our Television* (London: Quarter Books).

Quinn, A. (1991) 'Scheduling for a new era in ITV', *The Leader: Granada Television*, 3, March, p. 2.

Radio Times (1956) 20–26 December (London).

——. (1968) 26 October to 1 November (Midlands and E. Anglia).

——. (1969) 22–28 March (Midlands and E. Anglia).

Reith, J. C. W. (1949) *Into the Wind* (London: Hodder and Stoughton).

Ridell, S. (1996) 'Resistance Through Routines', *European Journal of Communication*, 11(4), pp. 557–82.

Robertson, R. (1995) 'Mapping and the global condition', in A. Sreberny-Mohammadi, D. Winseck, J. McKenna and O, Boyd-Barrett (ed.) *Media in Global Context* (London: Arnold), pp. 2–10.

Robinson, J. (2004) 'Pap – or "porn with a purpose"?', *The Guardian*, 18 July.

Roe, K. and G. Meyer (2000) 'Music television: MTV-Europe', in J. Wieten, G. Murdoch and P. Dahlgren (eds) *Television Across Europe: A Comparative Introduction* (London: Sage), pp. 141–57.

Rowland, W. and B. Watkin (eds) (1983) *Interpreting Television: Current Research Perspectives* (Beverly Hills: Sage).

Ryan, B. (1992) *Making Capital from Culture* (Berlin and New York: Walter de Gruyter).

Saini, A. (2005) 'TV's big indies aim for a growth spurt', *The Observer*, 12 June.

Sartori, C. (1996) 'The media in Italy', in T. Weymouth and B. Lamizet (eds) *Markets and Myths: Forces for Change in the European Media* (London: Longman), pp. 134–72.

Scannell, P. (1990) 'Public service: The history of a concept', in A. Goodwin and G. Whannel (eds) *Understanding Television* (London: Routledge), pp. 11–29.

Scannell, P. and D. Cardiff (1991) *A Social History of British Broadcasting. Vol I, 1922–1939: Serving the Nation* (London: Blackwell).

Schiller, H. (1969) *Mass Communications and American Empire* (New York: A. M. Kelley).

——. (1996) *Information Inequality: The Deepening Social Crisis of America* (London: Routledge).

Schlesinger, P. (1991) *Media, State and Nation: Political Violence and Collective Identities* (London: Sage).

Segrave, K. (1998) *American Television Abroad: Hollywood's Attempt to Dominate World Television* (North Carolina, US: McFarland).

Seldon, A. and F. G. Pennance (1965) *Everyman's Dictionary of Economics* (London: J. M. Dent).

Sendall, B. (1982) *Independent Television in Britain*, Vol. 1 (London: Macmillan).

——. (1983) *Independent Television in Britain*, Vol. 2 (London: Macmillan).

Sepstrup, P. (1990) *Transnationalisation of Television in Western Europe* (London: John Libbey).

Seymour-Ure, C. (1993) *The British Press and Broadcasting since 1945* (Oxford: Blackwell).

Shelley, J. (2001) *Interference: Tapehead versus Television* (London: Atlantic Books).

——. (2005) 'Jim Shelley call the cops', *The Guardian: The Guide*, 2 April.

Sherwin, A. (2002) 'BBC's latest passion is for political drama', *The Times*, 29 May.

Shew, W. (1992) 'Trends in the organisation of programme production', in T. Congdon, B. Sturgess, NERA, W. Shew, A. Graham and G. Davies (eds) *Paying for Broadcasting: The Handbook* (London: Routledge), pp. 64–91.

Shin, A. (2005) 'Limits on media ownership stand', *Washington Post*, 14 June.

Shivas, M. (1992) (Head of Drama and Films Department BBC), Interview, London.

Shoemaker, P. J. and S. D. Reese (1991) *Mediating the Message: Theories of Influences on Mass Media Content* (London: Longman).

Sinfield, A. (2004) *Literature, Politics and Culture in Post War Britain* (London: Continuum).

Slater, C. (1992) (Regional scheduler and buyer for Central), Interview, Birmingham.

Smith, A. (1937; orig. 1776) *An Inquiry into the Nature and causes of The Wealth of Nations* (New York: Modern Library).

Schofield, J. (2005) 'Inside IT', *The Guardian*, 1 September.

Sreberny–Mohammadi, A. (1996) 'The global and the local in international communication', in J. Curran and M. Gurevitch (eds) *Mass Media and Society* (London: Arnold), pp. 178–203.

Steemers, J. (2004) *Selling Television: British Television in the Global Marketplace* (London: BFI).

Steemers, J. and R. Wise (2000) 'Old media, new media and the state', in R. Wise (ed.) *Multimedia: A Critical Introduction* (London: Routledge), pp. 59–114.

Stevenson, N. (2002) *Understanding Media Cultures* (London: Sage).

Storey, J. (1999) *Cultural Consumption and Everyday Life* (London: Arnold).

——. (2001) *Cultural Theory and Popular Culture: An Introduction* (Harlow: Pearson, Prentice Hall).

——. (2003) *Inventing Popular Culture* (Oxford: Blackwell).

Straubhaar, J. D. (1996) 'Distinguishing the global, regional and national levels of world television', in A. Screberny-Mohammadi, D. Winseck, J. McKenna and O. Boyd-Barrett (eds) (1997) *Media in a Global Context: A Reader* (London: Arnold), pp. 284–98.

Strinati, D. (2001) *An Introduction to Theories of Popular Culture* (London: Routledge).

——. (2003) *An Introduction to Theories of Popular Culture*, 2nd edition (London: Routledge).

Strinati, D. and S. Wagg (eds) (1992) *Come on Down? Popular Media Culture in Post-war Britain* (London: Routledge).

Television Business International Yearbook 1996 (1997) (London: Media and Telecoms).

The Communications Market (2004) <http://www.ofcom.org.uk/research/cm/cmpdf/>. Accessed 2 June 2005.

The Guardian (2004) 'Why US shows will be cheaper', 27 September.

The Mirror (2004a) 'Overpaid, overly thick and over at last', 1 June.

——. (2004b) 'Shelly on the telly: Another case of great drama', 13 February.

——. (2004c) 'Shelly vision: Sponsor of the week', 27 January.

The Observer (1960) 'The use of television', 25 September.

——. (1962) 'Going the whole Hoggart', 1 July.

——. (1999) 'Sex and the city: Tell your friends', 10 January.

——. (2003) 'And don't spare the hearses: The finale of Six Feet Under offered a damp hankie moment, but in south London they do think differently', 24 August.

——. (2004) 'Farewell, Famous Five', 23 May.

The Register website (2002) 'The BBC hijacks TiVo recorders', <www.theregister. co.uk/202/05/24/bbc_hijacks_tivo_recorders/> Filed 24 May. Accessed 12 April 2005.

The student zone <http://www.thestudentzone.com/articles/tv-southpark.html>. Accessed 12 May 2005.

The Sun (2005) 'Porn past of TV wife', 4 January.

The Times (1950) 'Television listings', 15 July.

——. (1950) 'Television listings', 21 July.

——. (1960a) 'Letters to the editor: Television criticism', 8 November.

——. (1960b) 'A play about violence', 7 October.

——. (1960c) 'Television play of force and power', 24 October.

——. (1974) 'Television listings', 10–16 October.

——. (1992) 'Television listings', 7 October.

——. (1995) 'Home is best', 1 November.

Thomas, H. (1977) *With an Independent Air: Encounters during a Lifetime of Broadcasting* (London: Weidenfeld and Nicolson).

Thompson, E. P. (1982) *The Making of the English Working Class* (London: Penguin).

Thompson, G. (1984) ' "Rolling Back" the State? Economic intervention 1975–82', in G. McLennan, D. Held and S. Hall (eds) *State and Society in Contemporary Britain: A Critical Introduction* (London: Polity), pp. 274–98.

Thompson, R. J. (1997) *Television's Second Golden Age: From Hill Street Blues to ER* (USA: Syracuse University Press).

Thumin, J. (ed.) (2002) *Small Screens, Big Ideas: Television in the 1950s* (London: I. B. Tauris).

Tocqueville, A. de (1961) *Democracy in America*, 2 vols (New York: Schocken Books).

Tomlinson, J. (1991) *Cultural Imperialism* (London: Pinter).

Tracey, M. (1985) 'The Poisoned chalice? International television and the idea of dominance', *Daedalus*, 114, pp. 17–54.

——. (1988) 'Popular culture and the economics of global television', *Intermedia*, 19(2), pp. 9–25.

——. (1998) *The Decline and fall of Public Service Broadcasting* (Oxford University Press).

Tunstall, J. (1977) *The Media are American* (London: Constable).

——. (1986) *The Media in Britain* (London: Constable).

——. (1993) *Television Producers* (London: Routledge).

Tunstall, J. and M. Palmer (1991) *Media Moguls* (London: Routledge).

Turner, G. (1996) *British Cultural Studies: An Introduction*, 2nd edition (London: Routledge).

USAtoday website (2005)< www.usatoday.com/news/opinion/2005–03–29> Filed 29 May. Accessed 12 June 2005.

Usborne, D. (2004) 'Farewell to "Friends": after 236 episodes, 50 m wave goodbye', *The Independent*, 8 May.

Varis, T. (1985) *International Flow of Television Programmes* (Paris: UNESCO).

Veljanovski, C. G. and W. D. Bishop (1983) *Choice by Cable: The Economics of a New Era in Television*, Hobart Paper 96 (London: Institute of Economic Affairs).

Vine, S. (2005) 'Momentous event speaks for itself – Last Night's TV', *The Times*, 21 April.

Waller, G. (1988) 'Flow, genre, and the television text', in G. R. Edgerton, M. Marsden and J. Nachbar (eds) *In the Eye of the Beholder: Critical Perspectives in Popular Film and Television* (Bowling Green, US: Bowling Green State University Press), pp. 55–66.

Waterman, D. (1988) 'World Television Trade: The Economic Effects of Privatisation and New Technology', *Telecommunication Policy*, June, pp. 141–51.

Webster, D. (1984) 'Direct broadcast satellites: Proximity, sovereignty and national identity', *Foreign Affairs* 62, summer, pp. 1169–74.

Wells, M. (2002) 'Subscriber fury at TV "junk mail" ', *The Guardian*, 30 May.

——. (2003) 'Where the Writer is King', *The Guardian*, 27 January.

——. (2004a) 'BBC "did not have know-how for web" ', *The Guardian*, 6 July.

——. (2004b) 'BBC inquiry as viewers attack drop in quality', *The Guardian*, 14 July.

Weymouth, T. and B. Lamizet (eds) (1996) *Markets and Myths: Forces for Change in the European Media* (London: Longman).

Wheatley, H. (2003) 'ITV 1955–89: Populism and Experimentation', in M. Hilmes (ed.) *The Television History Book* (London: BFI), pp. 76–81.

Wieten, J., G. Murdock and P. Dahlgren (eds) (2000) *Television Across Europe: A Comparative Introduction* (London: Sage).

Wiggins, M. (1962) 'Going the Whole Hoggart', *The Observer*, 1 July.

Wilk, M. (1999) *The Golden Age of Television: Notes from Survivors* (Chicago: Silver Spring Press).

Williams, K. (1998) *Get Me a Murder a Day! A History of Mass Communication in Britain* (London: Arnold).

Williams, R. (1979) *Television: Technology and Cultural Form* (Glasgow: Fontana/ Collins).

Williams, S. and Jones, I. (2005) 'That is so 1991!', <http://www.offthetelly.co.uk/ pdf/month.pdf>. Accessed 26 March 2005.

Winston, B. (1998) *Media Technology and Society. A History: From the Telegraph to the Internet* (London: Routledge).

Worsley, T. C. (1970) *Television: The Ephemeral Art* (Alan Ross: London).

Files consulted at the BBC Written Archives at Caversham

When referring, in the text of the book, to material from the BBC Written Archives at Caversham (WAC), I use their file index notation (for example, T16/29S).

Files accessed – Television

T16/29S, TV Policy artists: Radio and Television. Safeguards Comm. 1956–65.

T16/438/2, TV Policy Programme Management board Papers 1964.

T16/48, TV Policy Commercial TV 1953–60.

T16/599/1, US Films on BBC TV.

T41/303/1, Purchase of Programmes – General.

T41/9/1, Timing and Programmes – General.
T47/32/1, Timing and Scheduling Policy.
T6/144/1, TV Films memo's File 1A.
T66/6/1, TV Press office Star Trek 1969–1994.

Specific references
T6/144/1, BBC memo (1949) Tel Film Booking Manager to H Tel F 'Evening Films: Monday', 26 September 1949.
T16/599/1, 'British and American Film in BBC Television Programmes', 11 June 1957.
T16/599/1, Joanna Spicer Head of Programme Planning to C.P. Tel 'Hired Films and Co-production Films', 16 January 1959.
T16/29S, Note of a Meeting with the Radio and Television Safeguards committee at Broadcasting House on 15 January 1965.
T66/6/1, Memo *Star Trek* BBC TV Press Office, 9 October 1976.

Websites used (specific articles found online and referred to in the text will appear in the main body of the bibliography).

Barb, http://www.barb.co.uk.
BBC, http://www.bbc.co.uk.
Bravo, http://www.bravo.co.uk.
C4, http://www.channel4.com.
C5, http://www.five.tv.
Daily Telegraph, http://www.telegraph.co.uk.
Fantasy Film League, http://fantasyfilmleague.com.
Firefly, http://www.scifispace.com/html/firefly.php.
Freedom Party, http://www.freedomparty.org.
Friends, http://www.channel4.com/entertainment/tv/microsites/F/friends/index.html.
Futon Critic, http://www.futoncritic.com.
Homechoice, http://www.homechoice.co.uk.
Intensities: The Journal of Cult Media, http://www.cult-media.com.
ITV, http://www.itv.com.
ITV plc, http://www.itvplc.com/itv/merger.
Living TV, http://www.livingtv.co.uk.
National Statistics 2002–3, http://www.statistics.gov.uk.
Ofcom, http://www.ofcom.org.uk.
Off the telly, http://www.offthetelly.co.uk/reviews.
Paramount Comedy, http://www.paramountcomedy.co.uk.
Sky, http://www.sky.com.
Television fan, http://www.tv.com.
The futon critic, http://www.thefutoncritic.com.
The Guardian, http://www.guardian.co.uk.
The Register, http://www.theregister.co.uk.
The student zone, http://www.thestudentzone.com.
Tivo, http://www.tivo.com.
TVGoHome, http://ntk.net/tvgohome.
Tvtome, http://www.tvtome.com.
USAtoday, http://www.usatoday.com.

Index